Advance Praise for

REDISCOVERING THE SOUL OF BUSINESS

"*Rediscovering the Soul of Business* is a splendid book, so good in fact that I feel honored to be asked for my comments. Not only does it contain work by the most profound and insightful thinkers in the field, but it is presented in a way that brings this thoughtful and provocative material out of the realm of theory and into the world of business and management.

Surely the most prevalent critique we—all of us who concern ourselves with the human spirit at work—hear is that, 'This is all very well and good, but things don't work that way in the 'real world'.' In my case, I hear, 'Well, that stuff might be okay in your business but not in my business.'

Rediscovering the Soul of Business should go a long way in dispelling the notions that these concerns, these philosophies, these observations are mere intellectual exercises—and should convince the most ardent skeptic that if the 'real world' is not involved with the soul of business, then it's high time to change our definition of the 'real world.'"

— Jim Autry, author
Life and Work and *Love & Profit*

"Yes. Yes. Yes! Stories and reflections on what matters most in business. *Rediscovering the Soul in Business* has it all, on each and every page. Teach this in business school; craft CEO courses around this material; recommend it for all students of business; then, possibly, you will see the light at the end of the tunnel."
— Anita Roddick, founder and CEO
The Body Shop
author, *Body and Soul*

More praise...

"As corporate structures become more open, allowing people to express themselves more fully, we will deal more and more with the whole person. And we'll rediscover the soul of the individual and maybe even the corporation. This book will stand as a key reference work on the soul in the business arena.
— Perry Pascarella, vice president-editorial
Penton Publishing

"*Rediscovering the Soul of Business* is an incredibly rich, deep, and diverse resource on the emerging values of business. Once again, Mr. Renesch attracts and orchestrates the most brilliant and articulate minds on the subject. Three thumbs up!"
— Richard Bliss Brooke, president and CEO
Oxyfresh, USA, Inc.

"*Rediscovering the Soul of Business* takes transformational thinking to the next level. It provides a deep and significant framework for anyone looking to create meaningful and sustainable change."
— Darrell J. Brown, president and executive director
Leaders magazine

"This book addresses in a careful and interesting way what may be the most important issue organizations will face over the next several years: how to make the work people do every day meaningful in their lives."
— Lawrence Perlman, chairman and CEO
Ceridian Corporation

More praise...

"The beauty of this anthology is that it offers a stereoscopic view of a most sensitive and far reaching topic. A book that is both intellectual and respectful of the subject matter and useful in the workaday world is a real treat."

— John R. O'Neil, author
The Paradox of Success

"The authors put words to the feelings so many accept or deny as part of the price of working in Corporate America. Very provocative and unsettling reading!"

— Lindy Ashmore, director
Corporate Service Quality
Charles Schwab & Co.

"READ THIS! If it does nothing more than help your organization produce extraordinary results, it's worth it. If it helps *you* discover what you are uniquely called to do, it's golden."

— Rick Dexter, director
AT&T Network Systems

"An important anthology: It looks beneath the socioquakes that currently rattle every institution and individual. The authors, by looking deeper, explore evolution's shifting tectonic plates. This richer, happier view puts surface turbulence into perspective by showing the affirmative trends that are shaping the future."

— Robert L. Schwartz
The Tarrytown Group

More praise...

"A stimulating potpourri. Confirms, clarifies, and guides us toward much of what we aspire to be. Challenges us to explore possibilities that hadn't been on our radar screen."
— Jack Lowe, CEO
TDIndustries

"A vast frontier is opening beyond the Information Age that should be even more revolutionary—call it the 'Spiritual Age.' This book explores how that unseen but everpresent world of the soul will electrify our organizations with both excitement and peace, hope and foreboding, joy and sadness, and all the other rich realities of the human spirit."
—William E. Halal, author
The New Management
professor, The George Washington University

"Honest, personal stories...Stories about the heart and soul of business in the throes of transformation."
— Bob Rosen, president
Healthy Companies

"The depth, breadth, and humanness of this book are amazing. It makes you laugh and cry and know yourself—just like the soul itself. This is the one book to read on soul in business because it captures the heart of business and how it can be manifested so that we not only survive but also prosper in the most profound way. I was taken by the book. It's a treasure chest of the soul.
— Michael Ray, co-author
Creativity in Business, The Path of the Everyday Hero,
The Creative Spirit
co-editor, *The New Paradigm in Business,*
The New Entrepreneurs

Rediscovering the

SOUL

OF

BUSINESS

A RENAISSANCE OF VALUES

"The universe is holding its breath, waiting for you to take your place."

—David Whyte, poet
author, *The Heart Aroused*
plenary address to 1995 annual conference of
Institute of Noetic Sciences

Rediscovering the
SOUL
OF
BUSINESS

A RENAISSANCE OF VALUES

Featuring essays by:

Gary Zukav • Ron Kertzner and Susan Jordan Kertzner
Bill DeFoore • Barbara Shipka
Peter B. Vaill • Elaine Gagné
Richard J. Biederstedt • Magaly d. Rodriguez
Michele Bleskan • Colleen Burke and Lois Hogan
Matthew Fox • Mark Youngblood • Dorothy E. Fischer
Kathleen M. Redmond and Juli Ann Reynolds
Joel Levey • Charles Handy • Jayme Rolls
Jacqueline Haessly • Robert Leaver • Marie Morgan
Michael Frye • Evangeline Caridas • Alex N. Pattakos
Mark Leavitt and Marie Morgan • Thomas Moore

EDITORS: BILL DEFOORE AND JOHN RENESCH

NewLeadersPress

STERLING &
STONE, INC.
San Francisco

New Leaders Press
Sterling & Stone, Inc.
1668 Lombard St.
San Francisco, CA 94123
415/928-1473
415/928-3346 (fax)

To purchase additional copies or inquire about bulk discounts for multiple orders, contact any of the distributors listed in the rear of this book (see Page 378).

Permissions and Credits

The editors and publisher wish to acknowledge the following sources:

"The Rediscovery of Anguish" by Peter Vaill was first published by the Association for Creative Change in its publication *Creative Change*, Vol. 10 No. 3, 1990 and is published with permission.

"Reflections on a Spirituality at Work" by Matthew Fox was first published by *Creation Spirituality* magazine, May/June 1992, Vol. 8, No. 3, and is published with permission.

"Guidelines for Dialogue," the sidebar in "Letters to Andre" by Marie Morgan, is published with permission; copyright 1994, Marie Morgan and Peter and Trudy Johnson-Lenz.

Photo Credits: Photo of Evangeline Caridas by Gittings; photo of Charles Handy by Elizabeth Handy; Ron and Susan Kertzner photo by Koby-Antupit Studio; photo of Thomas Moore by Fred Stimson.

 ⁊cled paper.

Table of Contents

Preface

This phenomenal collection of writings is the result of a rare collaboration of an exceptional group of people—men and women who share a common interest and are willing to cooperate in a collective endeavor to create value for you, the reader.

As the world of commercial enterprise continues to grope for new and better ways to be more effective, increase individual productivity, and maintain or grow marketshares, a vacuum is left in the wake of all this eager pursuit. Part of this residual vacuum is the loss of some part of the human experience—what many call the soul. This loss has resulted in a general dissatisfaction or "lack of meaning" in work.

As a result, the worlds of business and philosophy have been drawing together over the past several years. We have chief executives writing poetry (James Autry) and poets working with corporate executives (David Whyte). We have the natural sciences overlapping leadership styles (Margaret Wheatley) and business founders writing about soul (Tom Chappell and Anita Roddick). A priest writes about "re-inventing" work (Matthew Fox) and an internationally renowned business consultant writes about "doing what's right" (Charles Handy).

The authors of this anthology come together to blend the worlds of commerce and human consciousness, reuniting us with our souls—the very essence of our humanness. This unique combination of visionary authors, consultants, and executives offers a piece of the bridge between these two worlds—worlds that have become separate over the past couple of centuries.

Selecting a sequence for this magnificent collection was an interesting experience, since a variety of positions could be assumed in order to begin the process. The editors chose to cluster these writings around five key areas—perspective on the human experience at work, engaging the process of being human, the reuniting or rediscovering of our souls, the organizational perspective and, finally, applying all the learnings.

In Part One, bestselling author Gary Zukav leads off with a perspective of business from the point of view of human evolution and spirituality. Ken and Susan Kertzner share their personal journeys, both individually and as a husband and wife professional team. Bill DeFoore examines the darker side of work life, including the shadow. Barbara Shipka uses anecdotal and metaphorical approaches to revealing soulful work, while Peter Vaill asks the reader to examine anguish and the habitual suppression of emotion that occurs in our society. Elaine Gagné shares a very personal experience to emphasize another often suppressed emotion—fear.

Four original manuscripts comprise Part Two. Leading off is a metaphorical comparison to the Tin Man and the heart of business by Richard Biederstedt. Using a fairy tale to demonstrate her point, Magaly d. Rodriquez shares her own learnings in her quest for spirit. Michele Bleskan reflects upon dreams as a vehicle for soul transformation while Colleen Burke and Lois Hogan team up with a fairy tale focused on the hallowed Kingdom of "busyness."

Part Three starts off with Matthew Fox examining work as a meaningful activity. Soulful business is the focus of Mark Youngblood's essay and Dorothy Fischer looks at the challenge of the soul in the system in which it operates. Kathleen Redmond and Juli Ann Reynolds describe the benefits of a process they developed to reveal the soul. In conclusion of this part, Joel Levey examines the role of heart in discovering soul by sharing a story of a corporate retreat.

For an organizational perspective, four authors offer original essays in Part Four, starting with London's Charles Handy's description of a new sense of purpose for business. Jayme Rolls examines organizational transformations as a return to soul. Jacqueline Haessly points to soul work as the ultimate challenge for the modern corporation, while Robert Leaver proposes the commonwealth as a model for organizational healing.

Applications of soulful work are clustered together in Part Five. Marie Morgan shares her letters to a client, coaching him as a new leader. Michael Frye explores the relationship between personal growth and organizational performance while Evangeline Caridas looks at the same relationship from a different perspective. Alex Pattakos focuses on a government's search for its soul and Mark Leavitt and Marie Morgan's essay examines the health care industry's soulful search. In our final essay, Thomas Moore explores caring for the soul of business.

Acknowledgments

This book has been a collaboration involving many people, including some who are not otherwise acknowledged as an author, editor, or publisher.

Several authors wish to express their appreciation for people who were inspiring and helpful in their creative process.

Barbara Shipka gratefully and humbly acknowledges the members of the diversity task force for so magnificently demonstrating the power of vulnerability, authenticity, and self-responsibility. Thank you! And thank you to Linda White Greve for the title "Beadwork"—an art that crosses culture, gender, race, class.

Elaine Gagné wishes to acknowledge Don, her greatest teacher; Terry and Luke who are always with her; Zack, for his spunk and determination to heal; and all people who have the courage to see through fear.

Richard Biederstedt thanks Donna for supporting him in his quest for the truth. To Bill DeFoore for allowing him into this wonderful project. To his parents and family for their understanding. To Lynda for helping him see what's important. To Bo for teaching him about unconditional love. To all the Tin Men and Women who are still looking for their hearts and to New Leaders Press for "giving this Tin Man a way to express what's in his heart."

Magaly d. Rodriguez thanks her colleagues Carol Ann Cappuzzo and Karen Lundquist and her son Rene for their unconditional love and support. It means more to her than she can express. She also thanks Mark, whose enormous heart, genius in business and wisdom with people makes him such an inspiring leader. To Evans, Kathy and their creative teams, she offers many thanks for proving again that business life can be more fun and successful without the game board. And finally, she thanks Kevin Todeschi for his excellent ideas and editing assistance with her essay.

Michele Bleskan wishes to thank Debra Rabe, Margaret Purcell and Pamela Ostrum for their encouragement and inspiration in writing her essay. She sends much love and gratitude to her dear friend Lynn Hunter for her continuous support to her growth and all her creative endeavors. To her daughter Christina, she says, "you are always in my heart."

Colleen Burke and Lois Hogan acknowledge ideas, quotes, poems and direct inspirations form the following sources: Tao Te

Ching, Novalis, Rumi, Angeles Arrien, Robert Bly, Robert Bosnak, Deepak Chopra, Joe Dominguez, Clarissa Pinkola Estés, James Hillman, Sam Keen, and Marion Woodman.

Dorothy Fischer offers her biggest thank you to Sarah Beaty who midwifed her essay every step of the way—"A friend in need is a friend indeed!" She offers additional thanks to Catherine Morris Adelstein, for maintaining the soul of their business at InnerAwareness and for constant friendship, support, and vision; Bill DeFoore, for faith, trust, encouragement and patience; LaRue Eppler, for role modeling a soulful business, and mentoring her; Jan Smith, Barksdale McNider and Jeannette Siegel, for ideas, insights, and validation; her parents R.W. and Noreen Fischer, her sister Barbara Fischer, her sister and brother-in-law Richard and Martha Fischer Denton, for unceasing love and understanding. "Mom and Dad, thank you for teaching me about soul, and how to never give up," she writes. To Josef Patik, "God Bless You." She also thanks her many friends and clients who continue to be a source for inspiration and learning. She also acknowledges you, the reader, for "being willing to look for ways to enhance the quality of soul in our world."

Joel Levey offers his heartfelt thanks to his beloved wife Michelle for her fierce wisdom, loving support. His gratitude extends to many other sources of inspiration in writing his essay including: Bill Veltrop; the late Jon Dunnington; George Pór; Chris Thorsen; and the teams at Hewlett-Packard, Travelers Insurance, AT&T, Shell, Gulf, Petro Canada, Imperial Oil, TransAltra Utilites, Kellogg Construction, Group Health Cooperative HMO, the U.S. Army Green Berets, and International Center for Organization Design. He also offers special thanks to Bill DeFoore and John Renesch for their extraordinary support in writing his essay.

Marie Morgan thanks Andre Carothers for the privilege of helping him to help save the planet while they both learn more about leadership. Dr. Charles Johnston and his one year intensive at the Institute for Creative Development in Seattle, Washington have greatly shaped her own leadership teaching. Peter Senge's work, and its outgrowth, the Dialogue Project at M.I.T., have also been formative. The leaders and willing learners in her Formative Leadership course have made possible the synthesizing of these mentors with her own work in spiritual coaching.

Evangeline Caridas' chapter is a collection of knowledge

and wisdom of innumerable individuals. She wants to express heartfelt appreciation to everyone of them. Some of the people that deserve a special thanks are Nancy Sammis, Frank Heckman, Mihalyi Csikszentmihalyi, Robert Karasek, Merrelyn Emery and Ann Wheeler. In a addition she wants to acknowledge her beloved grandmother, Evangeline Ioannidis, whose spiritual guidance assisted her on this project.

Mark Leavitt and Marie Morgan are grateful for the generous cooperation of the Dialogue Project facilitators from the Grand Junction project for agreeing to be interviewed while their own write-up was in process: Mitch Saunders, Bernadette Prinster and Barbara Sowada.

Co-editor Bill DeFoore is deeply grateful to the community of authors who have made this book a reality. He also wants to acknowledge the many "unsung heroes" who silently and powerfully maintain soulfulness in their daily lives and businesses— not because they learned to do it, but because that is who they are. He also offers personal thanks to Jan Smith, Donna Monroe, and Vanessa Pratt for their assistance and support.

Co-editor, John Renesch wishes to acknowledge all the authors for their incredible contribution of wisdom, particularly those who have previously published books on this subject, like Thomas Moore, Gary Zukav, Peter Vaill, and Matthew Fox. These writers have paved the way for a business book like this, focused on the human spirit. He also thanks Charles Handy for contributing a part of his forthcoming book. All of these writers are mentors and elders for many of us who are venturing into new territory. He also offers a special thanks to Robert Rabbin for his special counsel and friendship and Bill and Caryn Sechrest for their hospitality in Dallas. Finally, he thanks Bill DeFoore, his collaborator on this project, who was a great ally, even in the face of great difficulty.

New Leaders Press, the book's publisher, thanks everyone connected with the design and production of this book. This includes production editor Neal Vahle, the composition team of Cathleen Moore, Carolynn Crandall and Chuck Karp, New Leaders Press staff members John Renesch, Amy Kahn, Cathleen Moore, and Claudette Allison. For her creative cover design, we thank Sue Malikowski of Autographix; we also thank Marsh McDonald for her artwork used on the cover. As the final stage of the book's production, our printer deserves special thanks: Lyle

Mumford and his colleagues at Publishers Press have been terrific allies over the last several years and we are grateful for their support.

The advisory board of New Leaders Press/Sterling & Stone, Inc. has been invaluable as a continuing resource and we wish to acknowledge each of them: Pat Barrentine, David Berenson, William Halal, Willis Harman, Paul Hwoschinsky, Jim Liebig, William Miller, Shirley Nelson, Christine Oster, Steven Piersanti, Catherine Pyke, James O'Toole, Michael Ray, Stephen Roulac, Jeremy Tarcher, Peggy Umanzio, and Dennis White.

For those generous people who agreed to preview this collection in advance of its publication, the editors and authors are profoundly grateful. These people are: Lindy Ashmore, James Autry, Richard Brooke, Darrell Brown, Rick Dexter, William Halal, Jack Lowe, John O'Neil, Perry Pascarella, Lawrence Perlman, Michael Ray, Anita Roddick, Bob Rosen, and Robert Schwartz.

Finally, this book exists because of the talent, experience, and active participation of the authors. This collection has been a true collaboration—a partnership in a very real sense among the authors, editors, and publisher who worked together in creating this unique offering. We thank you one and all.

"There's a new spirit abroad in the land. The old days of grab and greed are on their way out. We're beginning to think of what we owe the other fellow—not just what we're compelled to give him. The time's coming, Watson, when we shan't be able to fill our bellies in comfort while other folk go hungry. Or sleep in warm beds, while others shiver in the cold. We shan't be able to kneel and thank God for blessings before our shining altars while men anywhere are kneeling to either physical or spiritual subjection...God willing, we'll live to see that day..."

—Basil Rathbone as Sherlock Holmes
talking to Dr. Watson (Nigel Bruce)
"Sherlock Holmes Faces Death," 1943 movie

Bill DeFoore, PhD (left), is an author, psychotherapist, consultant, and president of the Institute for Personal & Professional Development. He was the organizer and convenor of the September 1993 conference "Searching for the Soul in Business." He has taught psychology and sociology at the college level, and has designed educational programs for Native Americans, Montessori students, and inmates of federal prisons. DeFoore's work with individuals and businesses brings the body, mind, and soul of his clients into an integrated focus, resulting in their expanded self-awareness and higher levels of personal and professional integrity.

John Renesch (right) is editor and publisher of *The New Leaders*, an international business newsletter on transformative leadership, and managing director of Sterling & Stone, Inc. He has edited or co-edited a number of published collections including *New Traditions in Business, The New Entrepreneurs, Leadership in a New Era,* and *Learning Organizations.*

Renesch speaks publicly on transformative leadership in business and has addressed audiences in Seoul, Tokyo, Brussells, and various U.S. venues.

Introduction

Spiritual Insolvency: Insufficient Soulfulness in the Workplace

Bill DeFoore and John Renesch

With all the recent focus on the "soullessness" of commerce—in business books, the media, and trade publications—it would appear that many industrial visionaries are concerned over a different type of insolvency in the corporate workplace. While record numbers of large firms are struggling to avoid the various chapters and subchapters of formal bankruptcies, there also seems to be a "spiritual crisis" in business today.

Let's presume that the "soul" of a business resides, at least partly, in its values. The corporate culture, intentionally designed or not, can be more or less soulful in the principles for which it stands and the degree to which it operates according to those principles. We could say that many corporate cultures in the 1980s (the "decade of greed") lost their "moral compass" or co-opted and compromised their principles. You could say they "sold their soul," as has been often quoted in the pages of business periodicals and books which focus on a new paradigm approach to commercial enterprise.

Since the 1980s, forward thinking business enterprises have been recognizing that people are their greatest resource. While people have traditionally sought security from the corporate provider, we find that few jobs can promise it anymore. Without this "contract of security," meaningful work is being demanded, particularly by the most creative and industrious among us.

If the large corporations continue to lose good employees who want to be more entrepreneurial or more challenged in their work, they will be left with the least creative and the least courageous people—those who are holding on tightly and hoping they can survive the next layoff by remaining invisible and not making waves

Meanwhile, those individuals who leave involuntarily, or those who leave to start up new companies contribute to the rapid rate of growth of small entrepreneurial firms. Large employers continue to shrink—in numbers of employees, share of market, exports, creative talent, and adventurous leadership.

What vital human beings want is to have their work matter—for it to mean something, something they can take pride in. No longer is it sufficient to earn the bonus to buy the new car or second home; no longer is it enough to make the sale, or close the deal. The more creative and self-actualized people in business want to know how they make a difference in the world. Do we matter? Do we stand for anything beyond an improved bottom line? Are our values in alignment with our work? Is our soul being "fed" with our meaningful experience and valuable endeavors?

This type of "soul food" can postpone spiritual insolvency or even eliminate it —much like fresh capital can cure many of the ills of a cash-poor corporation.

While critics may argue that people's souls are the domain of religion and the clergy, individual responsibility for one's own fulfillment has a greater call for the modern visionary. Taking care of ourselves has been a rallying cry for the physical fitness buffs for a dozen years or more. How can we stop at our physical well-being, when our emotional, psychological, and spiritual well-being is in jeopardy? We pay a high price for ignoring these other parts of ourselves. Most thinking and vital people can't afford the cost and therefore will not continue this inner estrangement.

A company can manifest soulfulness in its culture without being religious. It can provide an environment wherein people can feed their own souls, having choices for meaningful work within the company. When this nourishment is minimal, or totally absent, it can be reinstated or created through intentional and competent leadership.

Spiritual insolvency need not result in bankrupting the

soul of a corporation. New energy, enthusiasm, and profitability often emerge within a business when it honors and cares for its soul. Whether it be lost, hungry, or neglected, the soul of business can be rediscovered through a myriad of creative and dynamic processes.

Twenty-eight authors and co-authors have collaborated with us to explore a variety of ways to recharge our work with soulfulness. Join us as we rediscover the values that comprise meaningful work and bring new life to this most central aspect of our human experience.

Part One

The Human Experience at Work

1
Evolution and Business
Gary Zukav

2
Personal Journeys
Ron Kertzner and Susan Jordan Kertzner

3
Stories of Shadow and Soul in Business
Bill DeFoore

4
Beadwork
Barbara Shipka

5
The Rediscovery of Anguish
Peter B. Vaill

6
Fear: The Juicy Part of Soul
Elaine Gagné

This opening section examines the personal experience of work, with its passions and voids, its intense highs and lows—the complete human experience at work. These six essays deal with shared experience, expressed and unexpressed emotions, and stories that bring the world of endeavor, toil, and creative effort down to a highly personal and "real" level. Compelling words touch people—not in the mind, as a concept or a theory—but in the heart and the soul, the focus of this anthology. Each of these essays addresses a different aspect of the soul and challenges the reader to look inward and reflect on his or her own experience as a person, and as a worker.

Best-selling author Gary Zukav opens this segment with an excerpt from his forthcoming book, providing a contextual perspective of business' role in the large picture of human evolution.

Enjoy the ride as you enter this segment and be prepared to be moved, provoked, and stimulated in many ways.

Gary Zukav is the author of *The Seat of the Soul,* a U.S. national bestseller, and *The Dancing Wu Li Masters: An Overview of the New Physics,* winner of the American Book Award for Science. His books have sold over a million copies and have been translated into fourteen languages. He is on the Council of Elders, Native American Earth Ambassadors, and is on the boards of advisors of EarthSave, Intuition Network, Humanity Federation, and Learnscience. He is a Fellow of the World Business Academy and recipient of its Pathfinder Award. He has served on the editorial board of *East-West Review: Business News for the Perestroika Era;* the literary advisory board, Earth Day 1990; and as chair of the Government and Politics Strategy Group, Campaign for the Earth. He graduated from Harvard with a degree in international relations and was a Special Forces officer in the United States Army with Vietnam service. He lectures internationally on the soul, consciousness, and evolution.

This essay will be included in a forthcoming book by the author and is published with his permission.

1

Evolution and Business

Gary Zukav

The challenges facing the business community today are far beyond those that are ordinarily thought to be the most fundamental. No analysis of business within the commercial framework that has been in place for the last two centuries will bring to light the underlying dynamics that are starting to shake the business world, and will soon transform it beyond the recognition of contemporary businessmen and women.

The long history of interhuman commerce from primitive barter through intercontinental trade through global multinational corporations has unfolded in a context that no longer characterizes the evolutionary path or modality of humankind.

In order to understand the next step in the development of the entire system of mutual support and assistance that has metamorphosed into contemporary commerce it is necessary to understand the changes that are occurring in the evolutionary development of the human species. Commerce as we currently experience it is a product of an evolutionary mode that is now obsolete. Commerce as future generations of humans will experience it will reflect the values and behaviors of a new humanity that is in the process of being born.

Since the origin of the human species, it has evolved through the exploration of physical reality—through exploring that which can be tasted, heard, smelled, touched, or seen. In this process, it has acquired the ability to manipulate and control those things that can be detected by the five senses. This is external power. The pursuit of external power, and evolution through the exploration of physical reality are the same thing.

During this period, humanity has been limited to the perception of the five senses.

The human species is now leaving behind the exploration of physical reality as its mode of evolution, and, simultaneously, the limitations of the five senses. Five-sensory humans are becoming multisensory humans—humans that are not limited to the perception of the five senses.

The magnitude of this transition has no historical precedent. Therefore, it is not possible to predict what commerce will look like once this transition has been accomplished. Nonetheless, it is possible to see the outlines of the economic system that the emerging humanity will construct by understanding the nature of the changes that are underway within humanity.

Authentic Power

Humanity is now evolving through responsible choice with the assistance and guidance of nonphysical guides and Teachers. It is beginning the process of moving consciously into partnership with nonphysical aspects of reality that are not accessible to five-sensory perception, and taking its place consciously in a larger fabric of Life than five-sensory perception is able to detect.

In place of the pursuit of external power—the ability to manipulate and control—humanity is now evolving through the pursuit of authentic power—the alignment of the personality with the soul.

Prior to the emergence of multisensory humanity, which is now underway, the distinction between personality and soul remained a theoretical, religious concept. As more and more humans develop the ability to acquire data beyond those that the five senses can provide, the distinction between personality and soul is becoming a more and more recognizable reality.

The personality is that part of an individual that is born into time, develops in time, and dies in time. The soul of an individual is that part of the individual that is immortal. Increasing awareness of the existence of the soul is emerging in many individuals as a thirst for meaning that cannot be filled with ordinary activities and accomplishments. Old victories no longer satisfy. Old goals no longer fulfill.

Intuition

Others acquire this awareness through different or more direct means. In all cases, intuition becomes centrally important, or begins the process of moving in that direction. To the five-sensory human, intuition is a curiosity. It is not taken seriously. To the multisensory human, intuition is fundamentally important.

Intuition is the voice of the nonphysical world. Since the nonphysical world does not exist for the five-sensory human, the five-sensory human does not take intuition seriously. The multisensory human depends more upon intuition than any other human faculty. The multisensory human does not deny the data of the five senses—multisensory humans do not walk in front of moving trucks—but the multisensory human acts on hunches about where trucks are more likely to be and where they are less likely to be.

In terms of commerce, this means that intuition will replace rationalization as the primary source of data in the development of long-term strategies, the means of implementing those strategies, and in the resolution of everyday challenges. The underlying requirements of efficiency, productivity, and profitability will not disappear, but the means of attaining them will no longer be the sole product of the intellect.

The intellect and its offspring—such as cost effectiveness analysis and statistical quality control—will be at the service of a higher directorate. They will have been demoted, in other words, from their current position at the top of the decision making hierarchy. They will no longer command, but instead will serve.

Values

Alignment of the personality with the soul automatically brings with it a set of values and behaviors that are different from those that are based upon the perception of power as external. The soul always strives for harmony, cooperation, sharing, and reverence for Life. As the deep and sometimes difficult inner work of aligning the personality with the soul through the mechanism of responsible choice begins to produce authentically empowered individuals within the business community, the values and be-haviors that these individuals bring to the community will both strengthen and foretell the major shift that is underway, and attract others in whom this process is becoming conscious.

These individuals will find themselves—and are finding themselves—in an arena of activity that is no longer satisfying or challenging: the sole pursuit of return on investment for stock-holders. Stockholders also are undergoing the same evolutionary transition, of which socially responsible investing is a manifes-tation. Natural alliances will form between those organizations that begin to move toward values and programs that reflect the goals of authentically empowered entrepreneurs and employees on the one hand, and similarly empowered investors on the other.

As entrepreneurs, employees, and investors move toward their own authentic empowerment, they will create commercial structures which reflect an economic reality that is strikingly different from our present experience.

The current economy is based upon scarcity and oriented toward exploitation. Its underlying assumption is that the Uni-verse does not provide adequately for all, and that deprivation, therefore, is a natural part of the human experience for parts of the human population. It is oriented toward the extraction of gain in all circumstances—either from other humans, from the Earth, or from both.

Success in an economy that is based upon the assumption of scarcity is the accumulation of surplus. This is called "profit." The same assumption that drives the entrepreneur to generate profit drives the investors that invest in the enterprise. The accumulated surplus is divided between the stockholders and the entrepreneur, or enterprise.

Within the enterprise, individuals also strive to maximize accumulation of surplus. They maneuver for ever-increasing salaries, bonuses, and options. Likewise, investors strive for ever-increasing returns on their investments. The result is competition within enterprises between employees, and between enterprises for investors.

The individual, or enterprise, that acquires the most sur-plus is most able to influence and control the market—the environment and others—through domination via economy of scale, threat of dismissal, threat of relocation, threat of hostile takeover, manipulation of resources, manipulation of product availability, and so on.

This economy and the activities that it generates reflect the perception of power as external—the ability to manipulate and control—which has been a part of our evolution through the exploration of physical reality.

So long as our species evolved in that mode, this economy and its activities served the evolution of humanity, although they were not necessary. Humanity could have chosen to explore five-sensory reality in a spirit of cooperation and reverence, as Native cultures around the world have. Instead, we chose to explore physical reality with a sense of conquest and domination. This produced the painful and destructive consequences that fill our world today and shape our institutions, including our economic institutions.

That mode of evolution has come to an end, and, therefore, so has the utility of the economics of scarcity and exploitation. Further pursuit of external power in the field of economics, and every other area of human endeavor, now produces only violence and destruction.

The economy that is emerging will be based on abundance and oriented toward contribution. The characteristics of this economy, therefore, are directly opposed to those of the present economy. This means that as the new economy begins to emerge, it will redefine all of the basic concepts that underlie the economy of today—ownership, productivity, and profit—in the process of replacing them with their successors.

Ownership

"Ownership" is a concept that is meaningful only within the domain of the five senses. Until now, the evolution of humanity has been confined to this domain. Beyond the domain of the five senses there is nothing to own except who and what a soul is. As humanity undergoes the transition from five-sensory perception to multisensory perception, the concept of "ownership" will at first become confusing, then questionable, and finally meaning-less.

Ownership is a means of exerting external power. To own property—a mule, a wife, a piece of land, a house, a Mercedes—in each instance is the ability to influence or control others. Every "No Trespassing" sign is an attempt to exert external power over another being. Every violation of such a sign is the same thing. By the number of slaves a person owns, or animals, or vacation homes, humans throughout their history have proclaimed the amount of external power that they have acquired.

External power can be gained, stolen, lost, and inherited. The lack of external power is a cause of anxiety to those who do not have it, because they fear abuse by those who do, and a cause of anxiety to those who have it, because they fear to loose it.

"Ownership" is the reflection of this dynamic.

With the development of contemporary commerce, ownership has become abstract. Ownership now extends to market share on the part of enterprises—wherein the transitory nature of external power is demonstrated daily—to stock holding on the part of investors—wherein individuals and groups challenge one another for board seats. Intangibles such as portfolio size and bank balance have replaced numbers of pigs or olive trees, but the dynamic beneath the drive for ownership of both concrete and abstract assets in excess of what is needed to support a comfortable life is identical—the pursuit of external power.

As individuals within the business community come to recognize themselves as immortal souls, and experience within themselves the shift from pursuit of external power—the ability to manipulate and control—to pursuit of authentic power—alignment of the personality with the soul—their understanding of the dynamic that lies beneath the concept of ownership will cause them to question the utility of this concept.

This is a natural development in the system of human values as the arena of human evolution expands beyond the material to include awareness of nonphysical dimensions of Life. This development will affect businesses as well as individuals. "Ownership" is a means of preventing cooperation, hoarding resources, and obstructing the aspirations of others as well as developing one's own visions, surrounding one's self in the environment of one's choosing, and protecting one's self from the unwanted intrusions of others.

As humanity moves toward authentic empowerment and harmony, cooperation, sharing, and reverence for Life replace competition, hoarding, focus on one's own needs, and exploitation of Life, the necessity for "ownership" will disappear. What was once a requirement for the acquisition of external power will become an obstacle in the acquisition of authentic power. Like an old technology that has been replaced with a new, it will loose its value naturally through obsolescence.

From the point of view of contemporary commerce, business cannot exist without ownership. All relationships between businesses are defined in terms of what is owned and what is not, what is controlled and what is not, and the desire to increase what is owned and what is controlled in every instance.

From the point of view of the emerging commerce, all relationships between businesses will be defined by the ability of each enterprise to contribute to Life, and to assist other enterprises to contribute to Life. Negotiations will center not over extending control, but over providing resources. Conferences will be held not to exploit the weaknesses of competitors, but to augment the strengths of friends. Assessments will be made to determine which enterprise is most able to provide the need of society that is under consideration, and how it can best be supported by others.

As cooperation replaces competition and mutual support replaces conquest, "ownership" of resources, access to markets, raw materials, and marketing potential will come to be thought of as "common," and then the concept will drop away for lack of use and meaning.

Productivity

"Productivity" within the domain of the five senses has come to be identified with the ability to transform material resources into products. As the economy has shifted from one that rests upon a manufacturing base to one that is primarily service oriented, "productivity" continues to mean the ability to transform raw materials—in this case human creativity and abilities—into profitable products. This shift reflects within the domain of the five senses the larger shift in the evolutionary path of humankind away from its original focus on the physical world toward increasingly conscious participation in the nonmaterial aspects of its reality.

"Productivity" is another expression of the idea of "product." While humanity was limited in its perception to the five senses, the only products possible were those that are discernible to the five senses. We understand that the "product" of love, trust, good will, and the intention to grow together can be a healthy relationship, but in economic contexts the term "product" refers to the material result of a conscious application of human will and material resources that, when produced, can be marketed.

Productivity is closely related to efficiency. As the products of a service oriented economy become increasingly labor intensive, and as the price of the educated labor that is necessary to these businesses increases, the ability to extract the maximum amount of product—service—from the labor force in the least amount of time is prerequisite to competitiveness and profitability.

Time is a concern of the personality. It is not a concern of the soul. The personality completes its life within a period of time. The soul is immortal. The personality sees its lifetime as the entirety of its existence. The soul views the same lifetime as one learning opportunity among many to gain the experiences that it seeks to experience, and to contribute the gifts that it seeks to give.

As humankind leaves behind the limitations of the five senses and multisensory perception becomes as central to the human experience as physical vision, hearing, taste, touch, and smell, the "productivity" of human enterprises will be appraised not on the basis of the material product or service that each produces, but on their contributions to the spirit.

Beyond the physical needs of a comfortable life are needs that are as vital to human growth and development as food and shelter. These are the needs of the soul. Productivity, until now, has been measured in terms of the ability to fill physical needs. In the emerging economy, "productivity" will encompass also the ability of enterprises to fill spiritual needs.

Spiritual productivity is measured by the heart, and only the heart can create a spiritually productive enterprise. We live in a Universe of maximal spiritual productivity. Each encounter, experience, and circumstance of each human life, including those that are painful and traumatic, serve equally the needs of each soul involved. The pain in each human life is a measure of the distance between the desires of its personality and the needs of its soul.

The spiritual productivity of the Universe flows not from the exquisite appropriateness of each experience to the needs of the experiencer, but from the compassionate essence of the Universe that, at every moment and in every way, serves the needs of each soul as it moves toward increasing awareness, responsibility, and freedom.

In the same way, the spiritual productivity of a commercial enterprise springs from the compassion for Life in all its forms that lies at the heart of the enterprise. Currently, this is extremely rare. Therefore, spiritual productivity measured in terms of the authentic empowerment of the individuals that participate in commercial activities is virtually nonexistent.

It is not possible for an enterprise to produce authentic empowerment. Each individual is responsible for moving into his or her own authentic power—the alignment of his or her personality with his or her soul. The alternative is pain. Pain results not because the Universe is cruel or vindictive, but because it compassionately provides for each soul the experience of what that soul has chosen to create through its own choices. Eventually, every soul will learn, through its own experiences, to create with wisdom and love a world without violence and conflict—a world without pain.

As more and more humans begin to see themselves and others as immortal souls involved in a learning process that entails the experiencing of consequences that each has chosen, they begin to choose their actions and responses to the actions of others more carefully, and, hopefully, more wisely. This is responsible choice. Striving to understand the circumstances of one's life and to live one's life from the point of view of the soul accelerates spiritual growth. This is spiritual productivity.

A spiritually productive enterprise, therefore, is one that reflects the same compassion and generosity of the Universe in which we souls evolve. It is one that honors the choices that individuals make; that allows the freedom to choose. It is one that celebrates the contributions of each individual and, therefore, enjoys the fruits of collaborative efforts made on the basis of conscious individual choices to allow others the same freedom. It is one in which freedom to choose and responsibility for the consequences of the choices that are made are not limited to the upper levels of a hierarchy, since, in the practice of Life, no soul is exempted from experiencing the consequences that it has created.

Individuals working together, each with the realization that authentic empowerment is an individual responsibility, and, therefore, each taking responsibility for his or her actions and interactions, creates an environment from which both material and spiritual productivity can spring in an abundance that is now only glimpsed by the emerging multisensory humanity.

Profit

As five-sensory humanity evolving through the exploration of physical reality becomes a multisensory humanity evolving through responsible choice with the assistance and guidance of nonphysical guides and Teachers, and the economics of scarcity and exploitation is replaced with the economics of abundance and contribution, the concept of profit as surplus will become meaningless. "Profit," or a term that replaces it, will still refer to benefit, to the successful accomplishment of consciously created goals, but the goals and benefits of the emerging business community will be those that enhance the soul.

The measure of success will not be growth of net revenue, but the spiritual development and physical well-being of all those whom the business touches. The bottom line for each individual involved will be the yield of fulfillment and gratification that cannot be threatened, versus the yield of dollars, marks, or yen that must be surpassed in the next quarter to remain a viable competitor.

As the goal of economic activity shifts from maximal extraction from the environment—human and nonhuman—to maximal contribution, the perception of humanity, the Earth, and Life will shift from that of "resource" to "symbol of Divinity." All that now appears as gist for the mills, ore for the smelters, and workers for the plants will appear as gifts of Life from Life to Life. As the objective of maximal contribution to Life—already emerging within the world's businesspeople as it is in the rest of the human family—becomes the magnet around which consciousness orients itself, the relationships between businesses and employees, vendors, customers, stockholders, host communities, the environment, and the world will change dramatically.

As the goal of maximal contribution is applied to each of these categories of partnership, the world of commerce will come to reflect the values of the soul just as it now reflects the values of the personality. As individuals undergo the task of aligning their personalities with their souls, businesses will undergo a transformation from the pursuit of external power—competition for market share and investors—to the pursuit of authentic power—ability to empower the individual and improve Life on the Earth.

Employees

In today's commerce, the purpose of the employee is to contribute to the growth of the business. The employee is seen as a resource, similar in nature to the other ingredients that are necessary to the success of a business—raw materials, subcontracted components, electric power, transportation outlets, and tax incentives. Just as more electric power is consumed when business is good and production is high, but is reduced when demand and production fall off, more employees are needed when demand and production are high, but fewer are needed when demand and production decline. The number of employees in a business at a given time is functionally identical to the amount of electricity the company purchases at a given time. Electrical expenses and payroll expenses are both necessary to keeping the business well and growing, but efforts to reduce both are continual and, essentially, identical.

This is reflected by the practice of paying employees by the hour. No other aspect of our current economic system reflects more clearly the relationship between a business enterprise and the humans that make it possible. That relationship is entirely functional and exploitative on both sides. There is no human dimension to the dynamic that determines it. Hours are purchased from the labor market just as kilowatt hours are purchased from the grid.

In the same way that high grade ore and low grade ore sell for different prices because of differences in the amount of value that can be extracted from each, skilled and unskilled labor sells, and is purchased, for different prices depending upon the value that the company can extract from it. When an assay office determines that ore is low grade or high grade, its selling price is based upon that assessment. Personnel offices in our world's corporations perform the same service in regard to humans.

In the commerce that is emerging, the purpose of business is to contribute to the empowerment and well-being of the employee. From the perception of the heart, no endeavor can exist for any other reason. In an enterprise that reflects the values of the soul, humans cannot be graded and injected or ejected from the enterprise like a physical commodity. This occurs today because the objectives of businesses, and the individuals within it, reflect the perception of power as external—the ability to manipulate and control. As individuals within the business community at all levels begin the process of aligning their personalities with their souls and acquiring authentic power, they will naturally become interested in serving each other and all of Life.

This will create the greatest gain in productivity since the recognition that collaborative labor produces more than individual efforts. The workplace today is an arena of competition, uncertainty, and fear that exist at all levels from CEO to hourly wage-earner. Each individual in a company of one hundred fifty employees, or three hundred fifty thousand employees, competes with one hundred fifty, or three hundred fifty thousand, co-workers. The explosion that will occur in the concrete manifestation of creative potential when the workplace becomes an arena in which each employee feels, correctly, that he or she is being actively supported by and cared about by one hundred fifty, or three hundred fifty thousand, co-workers is beyond the ability of today's businessmen and women to imagine.

When work, like Life, becomes engaging, stimulating, and fulfilling; when fear is absent; when the individual is present by virtue of choice instead of need; when co-workers, with all of their deep difficulties, lessons to learn, and gifts to give, are seen as souls that are learning together how to live and create together in harmony, cooperation, mutual respect, and reverence for Life, business will produce far more than the necessities of physical existence and physical pleasure. It will produce souls of increasing awareness, responsibility, and compassion.

This is the only goal that is worthy of business.

The Japanese model does not produce this type of individual. Unlike the Western model, it substitutes paternal care of the employee for overt disregard of the employee, but it does not empower the individual any more than a career in the military empowers individual soldiers. It feeds the need for security and the desire to experience a loyalty that is based upon fear of the unknown. It prevents rather than encourages individual empowerment. Further, it aims for the same goals as its less efficient and non-paternalistic Western counterpart: increased market share and profit.

Both the Western and the Japanese models of business organization are reflections of the perception of power as external, and, therefore, have a limited future. This does not mean that lessons concerning the increased creativity and productivity that come from a work force that is integrated into the organization that employs it are not valuable. The potential that the Japanese model releases, however, is a very small part of the potential of a collective of human souls that are awakening to themselves as souls living and learning together in a living Universe of compassion, awareness, and freedom.

As individuals within a business begin to care for one another as a natural result of aligning their personalities with their souls, the perception that they develop of themselves and others as souls will not be confined to the business. Our world is inhabited by five billion souls, all evolving together, each complex and remarkable. The desire to co-create will naturally expand the boundaries of the "business" to include individuals and organizations that co-create with it.

Customers

The relationship between businesses and customers is currently one of mutual exploitation. This is a reversal of the original impulse toward mutual assistance that was the basis of the activity that we call commerce, and which is natural among humans. What we now call "customers" were originally the recipients of good will. Help in carrying wood, assistance in picking berries, and care for the sick are some of the many ways that we have helped one another in our struggle for physical survival as humanity evolved through the exploration of physical reality.

Hospitality for travelers—at a time when each member of humanity was recognized as a relative—was a way of life that still exists for some Native Americans and aboriginals who have retained their traditional values and behaviors. Travelers were expected to enter a dwelling, even when the occupants were absent, to take shelter, and to eat. The table was always set metaphorically, and, sometimes, literally.

As the natural division of labor between men and women expanded to take advantage of the skills and aptitudes of individuals, specialization began to develop. Those who made the best arrows began to make them for others as well as themselves, and those who hunted the best began to provide food for the arrow makers. Specialization based upon unique abilities and interests, also a natural part of the human experience, came into being and with it, the system of exchange that we call "barter." "Barter" today refers to the driving of a bargain—an aspect of today's commerce that was not part of the original system of mutually beneficial interaction. What we now think of as "bargaining," obtaining the most for the least, was originally the process of assuring that the needs of the whole—the family, clan, or tribe— were met as specializations developed and the work of individuals shifted from one area of endeavor to another.

In times of abundance, surplus food, clothing, and tools were exchanged with other families, clans, and tribes to fill the deficiencies of each. Items common to one area, such as shells, were exchanged for items common to another. Trade developed and expanded as mobility increased. The result was an increase in prosperity for the whole. Early commerce was an example of the natural tendency of humanity to include ever-larger parts of itself into one family, and to provide for the material well-being of that family.

Customers today are sources of revenue. They are hunted with more efficiency than elk or buffalo. They are the target of psychological and emotional manipulation. They are courted and, when possible, pampered, but not for the benefit of the customer. They exist, from the point of view of the business, for the benefit of the business. If an individual does not qualify as a customer, he or she has no importance to the business. Values and benefits are offered to customers only when gain to the company is obtainable. Benefits to the individual that qualifies as a customer are offered not for the customer's well-being, but for the business' well-being and growth.

Products and services of value to the customer are the *sine qua non* of a profitable business. They are provided because businesses exist to make a profit. When a product or service is produced that customers perceive as marginal in value, effort and money are spent to alter that perception. The attempted, and often successful, manipulation always appeals to the pursuit of external power.

The relationship of the customer to business is also one of exploitation. "Doing business" with a business, for the customer, is the same as "doing business," for the business, with another business. Each seeks to maximize gain. The relationship is self-serving on both sides.

Customers shop for acceptable quality at the lowest price. They look for sales. They do not see a purchase as a conscious sharing of their wealth, but as the best investment. Their loyalty depends upon consistent extraction of maximal value from the companies to which they are loyal. If a company reduces its customer services, or changes its merchandise return policy, or increases its prices, customers take their loyalty elsewhere.

Companies are customers of other companies when they buy products and services, and businesses to other companies when they sell products and services to other companies, simultaneously filling both roles easily because there is no functional difference between them. Customers and businesses—consumers and suppliers—are interchangeable partners in a dance of mutual exploitation as each seeks advantage at the expense of the other.

From the point of view of a business, investors are also customers. The service that investors purchase is the ability of the business to increase the value of their investments. Investors, like all customers, shop continually for maximum value at minimum expense. If a business cannot provide the value and profit that another can, investors withdraw their funds from the first and invest them in the second. The effects of this upon the business from which funds are withdrawn and upon society are not considered.

As U.S. savings and loan companies became insolvent—a result of speculation with government insured deposits and/or mismanagement or fraud—they were forced to raise interest rates in order to attract more depositors. Depositors around the country and the world responded by moving funds—purchasing the service of—these financially unsound companies. This drained funds from solvent companies, forcing them to raise interest rates, thereby reducing their profits and threatening the health of the entire system.

This is the market at work. The relationship of customers to businesses and *vice versa* is currently determined by a market whose "invisible hand" is moved by the sum of the actions of the myriad of self-interested parties that comprise it.

In the commerce that is emerging, the relationship between customers and businesses will be the same as that between businesses and employees: Businesses will strive for the well-being and spiritual development of their customers. Customers will no longer be looked upon as a market to be exploited through the artificial stimulation of needs that has become the basis of consumerism, but as valued co-creators in the establishment of a system of exchange of human creativity and skill that reflects the values of the soul. The products that a company provides will no longer be seen only as those that appear on the shelves of stores. Each company will offer what it is, along with what it produces, to its customers, and this total is what its customers will choose to purchase or not.

This is already occurring as companies strive to advertise

their products as environmentally sensitive, publicize their community involvements, and increase the number of women and minority employees. The latter is mandated by law, yet when significant numbers of women or minority employees begin to find their places within a company, that company rightly presents this achievement to the buying public for its consideration.

Customers in the emerging commerce will consciously support those business that are contributing to the empowerment of individuals, the environment, and Life not only through their products, but also through their production processes and business practices. The customers that are emerging within this new emerging economy will consciously—without manipulation—pay what is needed when given the opportunity to support the conscious efforts of other souls, or collectives of souls, that are working to co-create a world in which Life in all of its forms is valued.

The customers within the economy that is emerging, in other words, will be empowered—willing to assume shared responsibility for consciously constructive business practices and products. They will look upon businesses as partners in the co-creation of a world that is desired by all, and respond in kind as businesses become endeavors of the heart.

Vendors

Vendors will also become part of the same enlarged family whose gift to society is an ever improving ability to communicate, or provide food, or transport goods and people, or meet the administrative requirements of running an organization, or any of the many other needs that each sector of the economy strives to supply. Cooperation with vendors and subcontractors will replace mutual exploitation. As each now strives to gain the most from the other through mutual satisfaction of their respective goals, each will strive to maximally enrich the other within the parameters established by the need for financial health, which, for each, will be the need to provide for the welfare of its employees, purchase raw materials and pay for physical facilities, and contribute to its host community or communities, the environment, and the world.

In the complex chain of product development, marketing, and distribution, companies now "carve out niches" for themselves. In the future, companies will continue to find ways to contribute to the needs of society, but the motivation for doing this will come from souls that seek to give the gifts that they have come into this world to give rather than the profit that can be gained from filling unseen needs.

Communities

The relationship of a business to its host community currently reflects the same orientation as the relationships between businesses and businesses, businesses and investors, businesses and employees, businesses and vendors, and employees and employees. Each seeks its own gain through interaction with the other(s). The aggregate effect of this continual and interactive seeking of personal gain is "the market."

"The market" determines the relationship of a business to its host community. If the host community, whether it is in Michigan, Alabama, or Malaysia, can provide labor cheap enough and tax incentives large enough to allow the business to produce its product cheaply enough to accumulate the maximum amount of surplus capital—profit—the relationship between the business and the host community remains good. Citizens are employed and the business pays its negotiated taxes and, perhaps, sponsors community projects.

If the living standard of Michigan, or Malaysia, rises significantly, however, and employees from the host community require more to meet that standard, the usefulness of the community to the business deteriorates, and the company may move. That decision will be based upon the projected comparative costs to the business of staying and relocating. It will not take into consideration the host community. This happens even if the increase in living standard is a result of the presence of the business in the community.

In other words, the increasing physical well-being of the host community is placed in opposition to the increasing well-being of the business.

The same thing happens if the market softens. Previously acceptable salaries will appear less attractive than labor from another community, such as one in the economically developing world, even if the location of that labor is more distant from the customers that the business serves, and requires more administrative effort. The decision to relocate or not will be based upon projected comparative costs, plus factors such as inconvenience, psychological difficulties attending relocation, and potential loss of managers who will not relocate, but it will not be based upon the impact of the relocation on the current host community.

In no case is the decision to place a business in a particular community based upon assessment of the needs of the community, and the ability of the company to provide them. In the current economy, the relationship between businesses and host communities is as mutually exploitative as the relationships between businesses and employees and between businesses and customers.

In the economy that is emerging, businesses and communities will attract each other based upon the symbiosis of their potential mutual contributions rather than their potential mutual gains. A business is a collective enterprise of souls. A community is a collective enterprise of souls. The collaboration of a business with a community is a collaboration of souls with souls, each immortal and striving to give special gifts to humankind; each learning through the complex circumstances of a lifetime how to become authentically empowered within the domain of five-sensory reality.

The productivity, both material and spiritual, of a business and an entire community each actively seeking ways to serve the other has not yet been tapped by the human species. Since businesses exist in every community, tiny or metropolitan, business has the opportunity to be the vehicle on both microcosmic and macrocosmic levels for the evolutionary flow of human development to flower in interconnected and mutually empowering ways that other spheres of human activity do not. The omnipresent influence of business currently is an encouragement to personal gain at the expense of others around the globe.

In the commerce that is now developing in embryo, each activity will be an opportunity for those involved to find the deepest sources of fulfillment and enrichment for themselves and others. Commerce presupposes relationship. The relationships upon which commerce is currently constructed reflect the perception of power as external. Each of these relationships serve the ability of individuals and or institutions to control and manipulate their environments and each other as each seeks to flee the fear that underlies every pursuit of external power.

The relationships upon which the emerging commerce is based reflect authentic power—the alignment of the personality and the soul. As humankind, individual by individual, moves toward authentic empowerment, the relationships that it forms and through which it expresses itself will be those that bring to consciousness and activity both those aspects of itself that require healing and those that are our most noble inheritance. Businesses, and the economy in which they are embedded, currently reflect almost entirely the former. The economic and commercial structures that are being born will reflect more and more the latter.

The Environment

As individuals align their personalities with their souls, they come to see not only themselves and others as immortal souls, but also the domain of the five senses as an exquisite learning arena that reflects at each moment to each individual the world that she or he is creating and, simultaneously, to the human species, the world that it is creating. This world now contains brutality, starvation, suffering, and exploitation because that is what the human species is creating. The environment is fouled and poisoned because humanity has chosen to use it as a reserve of resources for the benefit of humanity alone, and as a waste receptacle for the unwanted byproducts of human activity.

The Universe is a Universe of Life. It is not compartmentalized into living and nonliving aspects. There is nothing but Life. Life is everywhere and all things, including those that appear as inorganic to five-sensory perception. The Universe is conscious. There is nothing but consciousness. Nothing exists that is not a creation of consciousness. The assumption of humanity that Life and consciousness exist only as humankind knows and recognizes them is related to humanity's treatment of the environment.

While nonhuman consciousness and nonhuman Life are valued less than human consciousness and human Life, the exploitation of all that is nonhuman is a natural part of the pursuit of external power. Native cultures strove to attain external power in a context that values human Life and nonhuman Life equally, and that recognizes the Universe as living. This allowed them to construct hierarchies that reflect natural order in the physical and nonphysical world, but that do not reduce the value of the lower levels of the hierarchy in relation to the higher levels.

Non-native cultures, of which the contemporary form of

commerce is a fruit, have established hierarchies in which the higher levels are seen to be more valuable, and more powerful, than the lower levels. This perception is projected onto the realm of Nature, wherein the killing of prey by predator is seen as justification for the manipulation and control of the lower levels of the hierarchy by the higher levels, rather than as a natural sharing of energy between species.

By placing itself at the pinnacle of the hierarchy of Life from the point of view of the five senses, and assigning maximal value to that position, humanity has created a world in which exploitation of the environment appears natural. The results of this orientation now confront us in every aspect of our environment—air, water, soil, and everything that grows.

This is the learning domain of the five senses at work: We are facing the consequences of what we have chosen in the past, and, simultaneously, being given the opportunity to choose again. Each choice that we make now determines our experiences in the future, and so on. This process is continual, both for individuals, collectives, and the human family as a whole. At each moment, we are surrounded by what we have created, and, through our responses, creating anew.

The lack of reverence for all of Life that allows the CEO to be more important than his driver, the physician to be more important than her receptionist, and the engineer to be more important than the welder, also allows the needs of humanity to be more important than the needs of the other species with which it shares the Earth, and more important than the environment.

As individuals begin to recognize themselves and others as immortal souls, and as they begin to function as multisensory rather than five-sensory humans, they begin to see Life wherever they look, and to revere it wherever they see it. This leads naturally to an attitude of care and protection for the environment that is based not only upon the realization that our physical survival depends upon it, but also upon the desire of the soul to care for Life, to contribute to it, and to value it in all its forms.

As businesses and employees awaken to the deep bonds of Life that connect them to each other, they awaken also to the deep bonds that connect all of Life. The environment and the world—our tiny precious planet—become important not as resources, but as the home that we as immortal souls have chosen for our learning and that now terribly needs care and healing. As the human species awakens to itself as a collection of immortal souls learning together, care for the environment and the Earth will become a matter of the heart, the natural response of souls moving toward their full potential. Businesses will strive to heal the Earth, rather than to exploit it, because business will no longer reflect the pursuit of external power, but the authentic power of each of the individuals within the business community, now expanded to include all souls that the business touches through its activities, products, and services.

Women

Humanity's treatment of the environment is also related to its perception of women: We treat the Earth the way that we treat women. Women are second-class citizens in society and in the home. Their struggle to gain the vote in Western democracies was long and hard. In Western cultures, a woman who marries gives up her name—a fundamental expression of her identity—and assumes that of her husband. In parts of the third world women are expected to die with their husbands. In agrarian societies, and societies with forced population control, such as China, female infants are considered unproductive mouths to feed. They disappear often. In most Middle Eastern cultures, women are not allowed to show their faces in public, become educated, or drive. In virtually all cultures, women are treated as the property of males. In cultures where jurisprudence has evolved, their legal standing has been grossly inferior to that of males.

Sexual exploitation of women is the clearest parallel, among many, to humanity's treatment of the Earth. It is difficult not to see clear cut logging or strip mining as rape, because both are intrusive violations of an environment without sensitivity to or consideration of the effects upon the well-being of that environment. Both are taking without asking. There is no respect, much less reverence. There is only a perceived need, and the satisfaction of that need. That is rape.

Women are also second-class citizens in the business community. They receive less money than men for the same work; they are exploited within the business community in the same ways that they are in society and at home, if home includes a male; and their opportunities for advancement are severely limited compared to those of males. Beneath these difficulties lies a difficulty on the part of males to face the potential, power, and needs of their female counterparts consciously and directly.

This same difficulty in accepting the female principle on equal terms with the male principle that results in the abuse of females in the workplace also results in the abuse of the environment. Mother Earth is a female. She, like human women, is the strong and clear embodiment of the female principle. The imbalance between males and females, the female principle and the male principle, that has created antagonistic conditions between men and women within the workplace and outside of it has also created the antagonistic relationship between humanity and its needs on one hand, and the environment on the other.

This antagonism is clearest in the economic sphere, and will remain so while the economics of scarcity and exploitation continues to define the commercial activities of humanity. The economics of abundance is a direct reflection of the prolificacy of Life that is at the heart of the female principle. It will produce businesses in which the equality of the male and female principles is fundamental. As more and more individuals begin the journey toward authentic empowerment, and the economics of abundance and contribution replace the economics of scarcity and exploitation, the antagonisms between men and women and between business and the environment will be replaced with new, harmonious and mutually reinforcing relationships between men and women, business and men and women, and business and the environment.

The New Commerce

As the health of the environment, reverence for Life, and appreciation of the Earth as a living organism in a living Universe become integral to the orientation of business, business will become a natural champion of all that it now exploits—employees, customers, vendors, host communities, the environment, and the Earth. As a sense of family grows to encompass all of these, the distinctions between them will become less meaningful as boundaries that separate than as relationships that connect.

The emerging commerce of the emerging humanity will be a source of fulfillment to all who participate in it and a blessing to all who are touched by it. The evolutionary flowering of the human species into authentic power will find its reflection in the evolutionary development of the human activity known as commerce—the mutual assistance of humans to humans, humans to nonhumans, humans to the environment, and humans to the Earth. Just as commerce has reflected with precision and power the pursuit of humanity for external power, it will come to reflect with equal accuracy the pursuit of authentic power that is now leading humankind toward goals that it is only now developing the ability to comprehend.

Ron Kertzner partners with individuals and organizations in creating collaborative, learning environments. He works from the premise that there is a natural design for individual and organizational life that is unique to the individuals and groups involved. Practice areas for this work include dialogue, shadow work, conflict resolution and facilitative leadership.

He has served as a facilitator and consultant to numerous international and national initiatives including: Bretton Woods '94, Parliament of the World's Religions, The National League of Cities, and the Association for Responsible Communication.

Susan Jordan Kertzner is a partner with her husband Ron; they are facilitators, trainers, and consultants to organizations. Her orientation is toward building community so that the dignity and creativity of the individual, and the higher purpose of the collective, are simultaneously served.

She has also served as a facilitator and consultant to numerous national and international conferences including The Parliament of the World's Religions, the UN Taskforce on Overpopulation, the Democratic Caucus of the U.S. Congress, and the Dialogue Project at MIT.

Personal Journeys

Ron Kertzner and Susan Jordan Kertzner

It seems a bit presumptuous for us to write a definitive piece about rediscovering the soul in business since the process of discovering and listening to the soul is a lifelong process. It also seems difficult to write a conceptual piece about "soul work" because the very nature of the soul defies technique and technology. So what follows is a story of how we, individually, and now collectively, rediscovered our soul and the lessons learned while doing so.

The soul is fond of experience. Poet David Whyte speaks of the soul's thirst for experience as being part of "a veritable San Andreas Fault in the modern American psyche: the personality's wish to have power over experience, to control all events and consequences, and the soul's wish to have power through experience, no matter what that may be." The stories that follow may provide insight into how to deal with certain events in our lives. But their spirit is about the willingness to let go into experience and trust a deeper calling.

Susan's Story

Graduating with a master's degree in classical political philosophy, I found myself in the heart of corporate America at a large financial services company. The country was also in the middle of a large recession. What I encountered was a spiritual wasteland. As a management trainee, I had the chance to talk with many people in the company. What I discovered was that most people's lives were quite empty. Many embodied a hopeless atmosphere, appearing disengaged in their work. They felt management simply didn't care about them so why should they care in return.

I soon met an executive search person who, upon hearing my story, pointed out an alternative perspective. He started talking about developing the ability to create what I wanted in the workplace and beyond. The message I remembered was "you need to create what you love, and what you think would have meaning." I wondered how could I take my love for political philosophy and apply it in the workplace.

Through this search person, I met a senior vice president at a large computer company who thought my work in political philosophy gave me the ability to conduct deep conversations and to think clearly about structures of thought. He encouraged me to work with employees about what had meaning in their lives, what they wanted to create, and what career possibilities they envisioned.

The "wasteland" I first experienced began to show signs of life. This impulse for meaning and creating eventually led me to a course entitled Technologies for Creating, which focuses on the creative process and the principles behind creating one's life instead of reacting to circumstances. I soon began teaching these classes and started working with many of those I met at the computer company. Through exploring the nature of creating meaning in one's work, I began to comprehend that we all need to see our life as a blank canvas and to understand that we could create with it just as an artist would. Gradually, I began to work with people in career transition, coaching them on creating a worklife they wanted.

My passion for this work eventually led me to start teaching those who wanted to teach others about a creative orientation to life. Every two months, I worked with 120 people, many from large corporations, who wanted to teach this course. We focused on the questions, "How can my life truly be a creation? How can I live a purposeful life with a vision worthy of me?" These questions, which I discovered later have much to do with the soul, led to some magical stories. One involves an organizational development consultant, Michael, who was also a very talented and classically trained pianist. During the teachers' training, there is a moment when each participant must stand and say "I take a stand for my own greatness." If the course leaders did not feel the music behind those words, we would enter into a dialogue with that person and coach them into truly committing to their passion. It was during this time that Michael took a stand relative to his piano music. He is now a successful artist, having recorded numerous CDs and performed in North America, Europe and Asia. And, as the creative process would have it, he now brings his music to the heart of corporate America, assisting those in the workplace to listen to their own music, their own voice.

As I was working with individuals, I began to wonder whether organizations could also develop a creative orientation. This question led to work in organizational training and consulting. While working at one of the nation's largest training and management firms, Wilson Learning, I experienced the value of developing a transcendent vision for an organization and what can happen when you tap the power of purpose. The company's CEO modeled visionary leadership. He was "on fire" about spirit in the workplace and about work being a joyous, creative experience. When clients would come for public seminars, he'd greet them with a Mickey Mouse shirt.

One of our workshops was built around the story of a 3,000-mile run by Terry Fox, a man who had lost a leg to cancer and was running to raise awareness about and funds for cancer research. A video of Terry's run and his passionate commitment to his deeper sense of purpose was the center point of the day. What struck me about the video and ensuing discussion of the power of purpose was the profound impact it had on the executives who attended. There was rarely a dry eye in the house.

Through my work with Technologies for Creating and Wilson Learning, I saw the value of passion, purpose, and meaning. Beyond the day-to-day duties of the workplace lay a fertile ground for creation and deep nourishment of the soul.

Ron's Story

My soul started stirring during my college years. Without a full conscious understanding, I took courses that talked directly to the soul. I was a public policy major. The courses that captured my attention talked directly about people. "Policy Choice as Values Conflict," "Ethics and Public Policy," "Ethics and the Life Cycle," and "Humanistic Perspectives on Public Policy" asked more questions than provided answers, which I've since discovered is a crucial aspect of rediscovering the soul.

The questions related to how public policy affected those it was trying to serve, including ourselves. We reflected on issues of war and morality, death and dying, abortion, the environmental crisis, hunger and welfare. We heard the stories of migrant workers, coal miners, share croppers, the elderly, and those living under apartheid in South Africa and segregation in this country. We considered the unfolding meaning of our own stories while reflecting on others. Many of those stories came from paying attention to literature, yet another avenue for rediscovering the soul in business. What do we learn about ourselves and our culture when reading Walker Percy, George Orwell, Judith Guest, or Robert Coles?

These questions stayed with me as I entered law school. They soon disappeared. The new questions were: What are your grades? what is your class ranking? and what firms are you interviewing with? Only twice during my three years at law school did the old questions resurface. The first occurred during the semester I interned at the local legal aid society. While we won all the cases I worked on that semester, I couldn't help reflecting on the underlying quality of our clients' lives. It seemed as if our work barely scratched the surface on issues of class, race, and poverty. How much of a difference was I making? How do I respond to a culture of despair and anguish? How can I creatively engage questions of meaning, purpose, and hope?

The other came when I was in the process of interviewing for full-time jobs at corporate law firms during my final year. In the middle of what I thought was my 15th interview, I became uneasy. I began to ask myself, "Why are you even in this room? What is the social impact of what your talking about here? Is this what you really want with your life?" I found myself dutifully responding to questions about what type of law I wanted to practice, yet I felt detached from what was going on.

Upon leaving the interview, I realized that I had no interest in practicing law. Now what? The script had ended. Family and social values had pointed the way to a legal career. Yet, something compelled me to move into the unknown. My education had not fully prepared me to enter the space of uncertainty.

Gradually, I began to learn how to listen to that deeper voice: a voice that kept asking questions, that could not find satisfaction in the world of prestige, status, power, and money. Filled with moments of self-doubt and fear, I felt I had no choice but to listen to what was moving on a deeper level. There were no job descriptions that quite fit that deeper voice, yet I felt compelled to listen.

That voice led to questions about arms control and relations between the US and Soviet Union. At one meeting on the topic, I learned about the principles of conflict resolution and principled negotiation. There was a resonance with that deeper voice. During the next several years, as I studied and practiced in the fields of mediation, negotiation, and conciliation, I began to understand why this work nourishes my soul.

Principled negotiation, as described by Roger Fisher and William Ury in *Getting to Yes*, advocates separating the people from the problem. Beyond our differences of perspective on various issues, there is a deep underlying respect for people. We may not start out agreeing on an issue but there is room for listening to each other's perceptions and, if need be, emotions. The process values relationship, not above outcome but as an equal partner. I've found the soul receives nourishment through relationship.

In addition, the process encourages agreements to which both parties can agree. There is a desire to move beyond compromise, which is not satisfying to either party, to elegant solutions that meet the deeper underlying interests of both parties. The soul delights when two seemingly opposite viewpoints come together to create a third perspective that neither side alone could have come up with.

A key element of this approach is shifting the focus from what I say I want, my *position,* to why I want what I want, my *interests.* These include deeper elements of need such as a sense of belonging, recognition, respect and dignity. I see these as elements of the soul. As Fisher and Ury point out, there is a myriad of positions that can satisfy these deeper underlying concerns. When parties can speak about their interests and co-develop options that satisfy both underlying concerns, there exists a strong possibility of discovering solutions that work for all parties.

For several years, I had the opportunity to observe this process at work in a variety of settings—dealing with environmental and social policy issues, as well as interpersonal ones. Not all cases followed the process completely, yet I witnessed how this work can satisfy the need for creative results AND honor the soul.

And yet, there were still questions. While this approach worked in situations that had reached an impasse, how might one create an atmosphere that honored the soul even before conflict arouse? This led to my discovery of the power of collaboration and facilitation. It also happens to be the place where our stories meet.

Our Story

Our deeper questions led us, at different times, to work with David Straus and others at Interaction Associates, a Cambridge/ San Francisco-based consulting firm, who had refined the art of facilitating collaborative problem solving in both public and private settings. The magic of this work is that it potentially creates an atmosphere where all can share their insights and perspectives.

Early on in our work there, we were both asked to participate along with several other colleagues in a cultural change effort. The effort involved a New Jersey chemical plant which suffered from environmental safety and health problems. Morale was a serious problem stemming from the reduction of the workforce from 10,000 to 3,500 people in just under 10 years. In addition, the relationship between union and management had been adversarial for nearly 75 years. The question before us was, "How do we effect a plant-wide transformation?" Upon reflection our question was, "How do we re-ignite this plant's soul?"

We began by capturing the "collective voice" through employee focus groups. Our desire was to create space for people to speak openly and honestly, honoring their own "voice." A management group of 13 received the data from these focus groups in a special three-day off-site session. Several key focus areas emerged. First, the plant ranked last on environmental issues out of 70 company plants. This was a major revelation for an organization committed to global environmental leadership! Employees' pride was understandably low. In safety, it ranked 69th. Injuries were numerous and respect for human dignity, as reflected by safety, was low. People wanted to be involved more in shaping their future, in having a say in the issues that mattered most.

During the next two years, we, along with our colleagues at Interaction Associates, worked with a number of different groups within the plant that represented multiple stakeholder groups at all levels of the organization. Our purpose was to provide a safe atmosphere where they could collectively consider the deepest issues of meaning related to the transformation.

We also conducted numerous trainings so as to pass on the tools and mindsets for creating collaborative workplaces. Our intention was to educate people about their own process. DeToquville, in *Democracy in America,* emphasizes that the high functioning of democracy requires an educated populace. Likewise, a highly functioning workplace, that values the unique contribution of the individual, must equip people with the skills and awareness they will need to take charge of their own destiny: a destiny that enables them to bring all of themselves to the workplace—body, mind and soul.

During our two-year involvement with this plant, they became number one in the environmental area and number two in safety. There were no further layoffs and the union and management began to work together, using the conflict resolution principles outlined above. They also became a showcase of empowerment throughout the larger 70,000-person parent organization. While the results were rewarding, the larger sense of accomplishment came from seeing people taking back their own lives.

Yet, even beyond the success of creating collaborative work environments, questions still remained. Yes, it is satisfying to bring oneself fully to the workplace, to let the voices of the people speak, and together create meaningful results. What about those aspects of voice that don't neatly fit into an organizational change effort, that question the very fabric of the organization itself and the core assumptions about business?

This led to us to the work of Bill Isaacs at the Center for Organizational Learning at MIT. Inspired by the work of British physicist David Bohm, Isaac and others began inquiring into the processes and certainties that structure everyday experience. Beyond the cultural assumptions, beliefs, and opinions that guide most of our businesses is the possibility of listening to a deeper voice, a voice connected to the unfolding nature of life itself. Without the ability to think together, to reflect on the fundamental assumptions that guide our actions, our efforts at problem solving and reinvention merely add new problems to the ones we apparently solve.

We often talk about setting a "container for dialogue." We define a *container* as the sum of the assumptions, shared intentions, and beliefs of a group. As people begin to share their assumptions and beliefs in an environment that does not attack them, we can begin to inquire into the deeper questions of our purpose and meaning in organizational and community settings. The inquiry can often take us beyond the need for bottom-line results and more efficiency to the deep levels of the soul that asks us to reflect on purpose, meaning, and personal fulfillment.

The container develops as a group of people becomes increasingly aware of the initial guidelines for dialogue. These include: *suspending certainties* (the willingness to put forward one's point of view without needing to defend it or convince others of its "rightness"); *listening to our own listening* (not only listening to what others are saying but also being aware of our internal reactions, judgments, and responses to what is being said); *holding opposites* (the ability to hear different points of view without being pulled into agreeing or disagreeing with any of them); *slowing down the inquiry* (asking questions to evoke the deeper meaning of what is being spoken as opposed to interrogating others about their point of view); and *speaking to the center* (speaking to contribute to the groups new understanding rather than speaking to any one person to persuade or cajole).

We had the opportunity to see dialogue in action in two settings—one involving labor and management representatives from a Midwestern steel mill and the other involving urban professionals in a Northeastern city.

For the past 50 years, labor and management at the steel mill saw each other as adversaries. Through the process of dialogue, they began to question some of the deep underlying patterns of thought guiding their interactions. One union participant mentioned, "We have learned to question fundamental categories and labels that we have applied to each other....Labels like union and management."

Another union member said that the category "union" limited him as much as it protected him. "It's important to suspend the word 'union,'" he said. While there are still issues to be addressed between the two groups, they have transformed a 50-year-old adversarial relationship into one where there is openness to question deeply imbedded ways of thinking. This opens the space for the deeper impulses of the soul. It's as if the water flowing beneath seemingly solid structures of accumulated beliefs and opinions has a chance to melt some of the hardness and rigidity we face in the workplace. The energy released when this occurs, which we witnessed at the steel mill, provides the opportunity for greater innovation, creativity, and sense of bringing more of oneself to the workplace.

Our experience with dialogue in an urban setting, which involved a cross section of urban professionals from various parts of the city, was equally rich. While this group did not have a work setting as its backdrop to dialogue, we did have "life in the city" as the context for our being together. By the end of two years in dialogue, which consisted of meeting every two weeks for two hours (except during the summer), we had inquired into issues of gender, race, age, fulfillment in the workplace, the pace of urban living, urban versus rural living, and the spirit of community in our communities. All these issues touch the fabric of our lives in an urban setting.

We came together not to fix problems and find solutions but simply to inquire together into the nature of our living. As deeply-held assumptions surfaced, there was often personal and group experiences of pain. When we gave ourselves permission to go deeper, we often found ourselves participating in a "pool of common meaning." People would remark about how others were thinking their thoughts, speaking their words. Often we fell into a deep silence, a silence rich with meaning. The best way to articulate this experience is through the poet, Rumi, a 13th century Persian poet, who wrote:

> Out beyond ideas of rightdoing and wrongdoing
> There is a field
> I will meet you there
> When the soul lies down in that grass
> The world is too full to talk about

As we continue on our journey of the soul, we are finding our passion in creating space for people to discover their individual sense of purpose and meaning while also creating the context for greater collaboration, shared meaning and coordinated action. While there are specific tools to assist in this work: technologies for creating, principled negotiation, collaborative facilitation, dialogue, there is also the larger context or "field," as Rumi would say, in which this work unfolds. Just as there is a gravitational field or an electromagnetic field, there is a "field of meaning" that exists between us as individuals and in our organizations and communities. We may not see it but we can sure feel it.

We've discovered that the cultivation of the field requires

the deepest levels of dignity and respect, what M. Scott Peck calls "civility." It lives through literature, poetry, and music and is refined by following the deepest impulses in our hearts, including our desire to serve others. It ultimately is about love—for oneself and for others. In this field, the soul thrives.

Our stories tell us about the importance of following one's own voice, not knowing where it will lead, of experiencing the power of a creative orientation in life, of seeking perspectives that integrate seemingly opposite viewpoints, of empowering others to speak their voice and of listening to the deeper meaning emerging through a group. All this provides a rich context for learning, for creating, and for honoring the deepest reaches to the soul.

Bill DeFoore, PhD, is an author, psychotherapist, consultant, and president of the Institute for Personal & Professional Development. He was the organizer and convenor of the September 1993 Dallas conference entitled "Searching for the Soul in Business." Bill speaks and conducts workshops internationally on topics dealing with the healthy power of human emotion in personal and professional relationships. He has taught psychology and sociology at the college level, and has designed educational programs for Native Americans, Montessori students, and inmates of federal prisons. Bill's work with individuals and businesses brings the body, mind, and soul of his clients into an integrated focus, resulting in their expanded self-awareness and higher levels of personal and professional integrity.

3

Stories of Shadow and Soul in Business

Bill DeFoore

Until about six years ago, the business world was for me a dark and cold aspect of life where I felt lost and somehow out of place. I was convinced that business was something that only bored and boring people did, and I wanted nothing to do with it. It never occurred to me that it is as basic and central to human existence as our language and our culture. I equated business with money and, in view of my personal history, that required that I reject it as an active part of my life. Not surprisingly, this proved very costly. In retrospect, I realize that for the first half of my life, I avoided money and thoughts about money. It actually seemed somehow dirty or evil to me. I made it, spent it, and gave it away, but I never kept it. These were unconscious attitudes and behavior patterns, until I slowly began to realize I had been creating the same financial situations for myself all of my life.

Consciously, of course, I had a completely different set of values regarding business and financial stability. I thought that it was just fine to make money, and I assumed I could always get someone else to manage my business for me. After living with the devastating results of these attitudes for most of my life, I decided to explore my relationship with money and the world of business. One of the most important lessons I have learned in this process is that I am the creator of the business world that I experience. I realized further that each of us individually and all of us collectively are creating the business world as a whole through every exchange, transaction, and negotiation we make. I began my individual creative process in business at the age of twelve.

Cold and Dark Beginnings

It is four-thirty in the morning. The world outside is dark and cold as I crawl from the warm comfort of my bed, struggle into my clothes, and go downstairs. The house is quiet as I open the back door and step into the early morning air. On my bicycle with the biting chill of the wind in my face, I feel a paradoxical mix of a sense of adventure and a longing to go back to the comfortable warmth of my bed. Though it's the farthest thing from my twelve-year-old mind, I am beginning my career as a business man. As I enter the small, rickety wooden building near my school where we roll our newspapers for delivery, no one looks at me. It's too early to be friendly, our brains are still asleep, and nobody really wants to be there. I walk to an open spot on the shelves along the wall and lay out my papers. The guy to my right is incredibly fast. He can roll four papers to my one, and he gets them tighter and neater. This is a big deal to me, but it doesn't seem to matter to him. That familiar feeling that I'm not as good as others and don't know what I'm doing is strong in me, as I strain to act like I'm on top of the situation.

I'm the last one to leave the building, being new and slow. The basket on my bicycle is loaded, and I'm off to deliver my product to my customers. It is still cold and dark. The papers are big today, and maneuvering corners with 40–50 pounds of dead weight hanging in front of my handlebars is no small task. It never occurs to me for a moment that I am bringing stories to my customers about the world and its pain, suffering, excitement, and opportunity. I'm only aware of the strain of my body and mind against this task that seems too big for me. I was doing what my father wanted me to do....Uh-oh, that curb was higher than I thought, and there go the papers all over the street. My little guy emotions are vibrating at this point. As I scramble to pick up the papers and reload my basket before the next car comes along, my heart is pounding and I feel small and helpless. But, of course, these feelings must be stuffed inside me, just as I am stuffing the newspapers in my basket. The job just has to be done.

Actually throwing the papers, on the other hand, is a blast.

Now I'm in my element. I'm a kid with an imagination, riding through the night air on my trusty steed, throwing my tightly rolled papers onto the porches (into the flower beds, under the shrubs and occasionally through the windows) of my customers' homes. This is true adventure. There's the hook shot over the head, the sidearm, and the overhand bullet. The bullet is the one that gets me in the most trouble, of course, and is also the most fun. This is what kept me going on the job, the thrill and excitement of adventure coupled with the feelings of worth and value at having accomplished a difficult task. All of these themes have stayed alive in me to this day, and have been driving forces in my professional career.

The part of the job I had the greatest difficulty with was collections. It makes sense, I guess, since I had not yet learned to value money. I just did not want to go and ask those people for money. I dreaded, and therefore avoided, collections. It seemed that many of my customers acted as if I were begging for something I didn't deserve. The good feelings I received from the few who were friendly and paid on time didn't make up for the pain I felt at asking for something I didn't value from someone who didn't want to give it to me. In spite of all this, I earned pretty good money on that paper route. I had no idea at the time, however, how much I was really earning or what I should do with it. It never occurred to me to do anything but spend it. So that's what I did.

All of my jobs were like that. I did them because that was what I was supposed to do, and then I spent the money. Saving was not of value to me nor to my family at that point. The unspoken myth in our family was that it was far more spiritual not to have money than to have it. As a Baptist preacher's kid, I somehow got the message that God's chosen ones were poor, or if they had money they quickly gave it away. So if someone had money, they were not truly good. This was not an overt message, but it was there and it was powerful. Although it was unconscious on their part and mine, my family gave me my basic foundation and training for life in the world of business. Like those mornings when I was delivering papers, the world of business seemed dark and cold, just as home and family seemed filled with light and warmth.

To follow my sense of internalized values, I had to be without money. At one point in my adult life, I even took this to an illogical extreme and went into debt. Perhaps the unconscious reasoning was, "If God blesses those who have no money, then maybe I will be even more blessed if I'm in debt." At the time, I consciously believed I was making good business decisions. Going into debt was not accomplished by overspending, but by using my money to take care of others' emotional needs. Nobody loved me for it, not even God. The word "business" had always been a dirty word for me, and I was unconsciously reinforcing this personal mythology in my adult business life. I don't remember hearing the term "good business," and if I had, it probably would not have registered for me. At that point in my life I could not imagine how the two words "good" and "business" could fit together.

Myths of Business

As I have explored this mysterious phenomena we refer to with the seemingly innocuous word "business," I have discovered that I am not the only one with biases and beliefs regarding money and acquisition. There appears to be a powerful mythology associated with the world of business, and we are all a part of it. When we boil it down to its most basic nature, we find that business itself is innocent. Objectively, it is simply the exchange of currency, goods, and services between and among individuals and groups. These basic exchanges have taken on the life and meaning they have for each of us today through the manner in which our families, communities and cultures have transacted them. We formed our moral and professional value systems accordingly. The deep mystery of the soul in business begins to emerge as we explore the combined effects of the many and varied systems and stories that have come to life for each of us in our daily lives.

The combined effects of our individual stories have become a vast and rich mythology, which we see unfolding in the epic saga of our global business scenario today. It seems to me that we can only accurately explore this complex realm through first becoming familiar with our own original story, which created our primary perceptual framework. Our personal story is a sort of lens through which we view the world around us. When our lens is clouded and smudged with unexamined biases and beliefs, our vision is faulty, causing us to see and react to shadows and illusions as if they were real.

As a young man, I saw the shadows of cold and dark forces at work in the world of business. It seemed that the "sharks" and "barracudas" were indeed using cut-throat tactics, and had no humanistic or moral scruples governing their actions. Somehow in the world of business it seemed permissible to walk on people, ignore their feelings, needs, and sensitivities and "go for broke". Further, it almost seemed to be a sign of superiority if a business person were cold, unemotional, and never swayed by the needs or sensitivities of others. The rewards were certainly there, since this type of person seemed to be the one who "rose to the top" and made the most money in the shortest amount of time. I had no idea how to function in that kind of world.

From my perspective, the trick in business seemed to be to ignore feelings and act as if you knew what was going on even when you didn't, just as I had on my first job. The world of business appeared as cold and hard to me as that pavement I had scrambled around on, picking up my newspapers as a boy. I only saw the part of it that was as dark as the shadow my family and I projected onto it. At home and at church, we seemed to be filled with light, goodness and sensitivity to others. We were the preacher's family, after all. Our shadow was the only place for our own cold, hard and insensitive aspects, so that's where we put them, along with business and other "purely secular" aspects of life. The concept of the human shadow was originally developed by psychologist C.G. Jung, and is described as the place in the human psyche where we put everything that is unacceptable in the light of day. We then unconsciously try to reconcile with these abandoned aspects of our soul by projecting them out into the world to get a better look at them.

The Business of the Shadow

It is much easier to see our shadow in others than in ourselves. Robert Bly gives a wonderful perspective on how this occurs in *A Little Book on the Human Shadow*. The problem is that when our shadow shows up in a competitor, associate or business system, we don't recognize it as a disowned part of us. Upon seeing what we detest "out there," we feel a tremendous passion inside, and have the mixed desires to learn more about it and to destroy it. We want to destroy it, because it would not be in our shadow if it had not originally been found to be unaccept-able within our value system. We want to learn more about it, because at a very deep level we sense a connection with it and long to bring it back into our psyche where it belongs. Projected shadow contains the abandoned parts of the soul, seeking to find their way home. When we see what we have rejected in ourselves showing up around us in our lives, it frightens and infuriates us. We then try to solve the problem by fixing or changing that person or system out there, which usually makes matters much worse. Until we reclaim and reintegrate our shadow, we find ourselves chasing it, and chased by it, everywhere we go.

Having failed to solve the problems of the world around me, I have been getting to know the sharks and barracudas of my own soul. As I have explored and embraced these aspects of my shadow, a process which Bly calls "eating" the shadow, I find new perspectives evolving in my view of the business world. I now see heroic images emerging in a colorful world of organizations which recognize the responsibility each of us has for the shape of things in business. I see a network of interconnecting lines of commerce that literally spans the globe. These lines cross boundaries that no other single system seems to have managed to penetrate. No language, culture, religion, or belief system has the pervasive influence of trade and commerce. This new image of business thrives when communication lines are open, as the consistent growth of international commerce during times of improved global communication would indicate. The institution of business may just be the vehicle for global transformation needed to correct our dangerously self-destructive trends. I now see the soul of business as holding not only the problems of the world, but the potential for their resolution as well. You might say that I now project light as well as shadow when I look at business, providing a clearer and more accurate picture.

I still see the dark images out there, which tells me that biased though it was, my perception was not completely inaccurate. If there weren't some good "hooks" out there for me to project my shadow onto, none of it would have stuck. The terms "shark," "barracuda," and "dog-eat-dog" as applied to business are not mine, but they did provide excellent material for me to project my disowned shadow onto. There is no question about the destructive forces at work in the business world. We have all had permission to project and act out shadow elements in business, provided by such prevalent attitudes as, "This is strictly business" and "The business of business is business." These statements imply that business is devoid of anything having to do with human sensitivities, needs, and emotions. With no room for humanitarian concerns in business, we give ourselves license to commit cruel and heartlessly self-centered acts that would be unthinkable in other arenas. This is how we seem to have wound up with separate values for our business and personal lives. There are those of us who have taken advantage of this license to act out the shadow, and there are those of us who have stood and watched in horror. We are finding that both positions have dire consequences, and involve projection. We are further discovering that human emotion, need and sensitivity are very much business concerns, and can no longer be "put aside" or neglected.

The Prevalent Power of Fear

Think of the greatest villains you know of. Whether they be tyrants, greedy corporate moguls, or violent gang members, they are more powerful and dangerous the more you fear and hate them. It is difficult not to feel negative emotion toward these perpetrators of destruction, but however we may dislike their activities, we certainly do not want to add to the problem. By fearing or hating something we automatically project an aspect of our shadow onto it, thereby giving away part of our emotional energy or personal power. Villains want to be feared. The hated often become more "hate-full" the more they are hated. Hating and fearing add to the problems we hate and fear.

We must courageously honor and examine the dark shadows of our own souls, rather than compulsively trying to solve the problems we see outside ourselves. If I know that the evils I have always detested and feared live at least potentially in the depths of my own psyche, then I can begin taking responsibility for my part of the world's shadow. If I am in the process of making allies of my dark and disowned aspects, I will project less fear and judgment onto the people and systems around me, and my vision will clear as my personal power grows.

The emotion of fear is all too prevalent in business. Fear-based action may be seen as the primary force at work in the destructive aspects of business. This would include greed, as motivated by the fear of never having enough, and retaliation and revenge as based on the fear of being overpowered by others. Managers who use fear to motivate employees, advertisers who use fear to sell their products, politicians who engender fear regarding their opponent in order to win elections, religious leaders who perpetuate fear in their followers, and movie moguls who make millions stimulating fear in their audiences are a few of the most significant fearmongers in our world today. Any astute observer has noticed how fear drives the stock market, and if extreme enough, can even cause a major collapse. The impact of these forces on the business world and the global economic scenario is substantial. As we fear, we "shrink away" from the object of our fear, become small minded, and lose sight of the global picture.

When we are lost in fear, we find that community service, socially responsible business practices, and environmental consciousness are out the proverbial window. When afraid, we forget that the bottom-line practical truth of our physical reality is that we are all human beings on the same planet, completely dependent on it and each other for our survival. Fear literally causes tunnel vision, a shrinking of consciousness that makes us want to separate from the persons or systems we fear. On the other hand, awareness of the common ground of our being ends this separation and brings us together. As we develop the courage to examine the fears we all share and the impact they have on us, we are moving to common ground. We are each responsible for the projections we carry into our next transaction. If indeed the world around us is a reflection of the world inside us, then it is apparent where our first priorities for problem solving must be. By exploring and absorbing our own shadow, we allay our fears and clear our psychological viewing "lens," allowing us to see the world around us as the beautiful, tragic, and magnificent mystery that it is.

A Return to our Divine Origins

When we see ourselves as originally divine beings, separated and thrown into life's struggles and in search for a way to reconnect with our divinity, the collective human story starts to make sense. The soul of business both embraces our struggle and provides a vehicle for reconnection with the natural divinity of life. Soul, as used here, refers to that part of an individual or organization which contains our stories and a deeper sense of meaning, and which also may seem confusing, emotional, or even dark. When we separate the spiritual from the secular (as I did in my childhood), we may actually be losing touch with soul and with the opportunity to honor this aspect of our businesses. Perhaps there is no truly secular, and perhaps business is at its essence sacred. The concept of the secular creates a hole in our perceptual field into which we can throw our personal refuse and avoid the difficult task of taking responsibility for it. At the 1993 Renaissance Business Associates conference entitled "Searching for the Soul in Business," Thomas Moore stated that soul can often be found in the inferior aspects of life, the things we throw away. It could be that exploring our personal refuse is a valid way to explore the soul of business. When all of life becomes a part of our spiritual awakening, our holes are filled, and there is no more cause for fear or projection. We become whole containers for the powerful emotional and spiritual energy that is our birthright. When we learn that the vast mysteries of the universe reside within our very being, the journey within becomes as important as our ventures into the world around us. We thus learn to embrace all of life, with its pain and ugliness, as well as its beauty and joy.

If business is to be seen as a form of life, which it no doubt is, we must conclude that it has a soul. Business seems for many of us, however, to have been thrown away into our perceptual holes with other disowned aspects, and therefore often reflects the dark, cold and destructive components of our nature. Perhaps this is why we need a book about rediscovering the soul of business. We must reclaim all of our abandoned and disowned aspects, and in the process, we would do well to reclaim business, and reconnect it with its own divine origins.

The first swap of animal hides for weapons by prehistoric beings, the first lemonade stand, or the first paper route provide a possible glimpse of the divine child of the business world. Business is innocent in its origins, as is all of life. The rest of the story is one of separation from innocence and the struggle to reconnect. In the separation phase, there is much chaos, grief, and turmoil, for each of us individually and for all of us collectively. By honoring what was once rejected and projected, we find value in our "garbage" and revive the disconnected and dying elements of soul. Undertaken on a large scale, this type of process might facilitate a renaissance of healthy values by which we can live and conduct business in a harmonious fashion.

When our primary motivation is respect for life and a sense of personal responsibility, we find the world to be a wide open arena for incredible varieties of positive action. Freed from turmoil and the tyranny of fear, we can travel freely in the inner and outer realms and take advantage of the incredible opportunities that lie before us. As we wake up to the reality of our existence, life does not necessarily get easier. We certainly find, however, that we become much more energetic and expansive within in. The rich color of life's mystery in its multifaceted manifestations becomes a world in which we feel honored to live. Business is a powerful vehicle for moving through and creating within the world as we know it. It is an essential part of the fabric of our existence on this planet. We would do well to re-build and maintain this vehicle with great care for its soul.

So tell your story of acquisition, loss and learning. Tell it to your families and friends, and to your business associates. Listen to their stories. This is an important way in which our personal soul speaks. The soul of business speaks through the collective voice of those individuals who create it, those who conduct it, and those who utilize its products and services. These are the voices of the soul. This voice comes through the most clearly in an atmosphere of emotional freedom, where our passion can be permitted to emerge spontaneously without fear of judgment. Tell of your first dollar earned, your first bad business decision and your first feeling of success. Tell of your experimentation with deceit. Tell of your first love and your first heartbreak. Tell of your dreams, even the ones you have given up on. The art and craft for rediscovering the soul in business resides within each one of us, and the substance of soul is in our stories. A renaissance of values will spontaneously occur as we align ourselves with the creative energy in our own individual soul.

Barbara Shipka consults to corporations primarily in the arenas of creating a global orientation, anticipating increasing interdependence, leveraging growth and transitions, working with differences and diversity, and developing resilient work roles. Among her clients are Cray Research, Honeywell, IDS Financial Services, Levi Strauss, Medtronic, The Pillsbury Company, and Wilson Learning.

Shipka serves on the Board of Directors of The World Business Academy and initiated the Minnesota Chapter. In addition to the corporate sector, she has worked with the United Nations, government agencies, the non-profit sector, and the education sector. She has lived and worked in Lebanon, The Dominican Republic, Somalia, Ethiopia, The Sudan, Czecho-slovakia, and Switzerland.

Shipka is a contributing author to several business anthologies including *When the Canary Stops Singing, Leadership in a New Era,* and *Community Building.* She is profiled in *Merchants of Vision* by Jim Leibig and *Who We Could Be At Work* by Margaret Lulic.

4

Beadwork

Barbara Shipka

They had moved beyond the anxious beginning in the off-site teambuilding process when people often feel they might not make it. Thus, they were less concerned that clashes between conflicting agendas within the team might cause the entire effort to fail. Throughout the day there had been several breakthroughs, insights, and clarifications related to why, in the past two years, they thought what they had thought and did what they had done. The feeling and mood in the group was improving but it was still constrained and cautious.

They had not yet connected at the level of soul. They had not yet had the sort of experience that would allow them to notice their common ground—that understanding at a deep level that connects individuals like a string connects beadwork. When that kind of connection occurs, people recognize it in the same way they recognize, for example, that beads do not make a necklace without the string. They know that the beads are the necklace they see but that the string provides the invisible connection between the beads.

Like the string of the necklace, a connection on the level of soul is deep inside—through the very center of our beings. The breakthroughs that create this connection become the essence of people's ability to serve as community for each other while they do the difficult work of achieving their goals together.

For a necklace to be formed, the holes in the beads must be revealed. One single string must then be threaded through the holes. Thus, a whole new entity is created without dimming the beauty of each specific, differentiated bead. Each bead maintains its individuality while the collective emerges as a magnificent new entity.

To add to the complexity of their task as a team, this group was far more diverse than a handful of beads. This was a group of jewels of every kind—a diversity task force. So, the necklace had to have special composition, special balance.

Beyond the anticipated complexity of attempting to focus on the same goal, they had a mixture of backgrounds, colors, and beliefs that ran the gamut of taboos, sensitivities, and learned prejudices about others who are in some way obviously different.

On a diversity task force, by definition, there are always many agendas and much passion about which agenda is most important and most urgent. When individuals feel they have to compete with other agendas for air time, resources, and action, what shows up is conflict and some amount of confusion, despair, and fear.

We were in a room together now because the glimmer of some of the jewels had become dim on the surface. This had occurred as they tried to work together without deep connectedness, while walking on eggshells and skirting critical issues. To their credit as individuals, they had already demonstrated the strength of their passions for progress because, in spite of the conflict, they had hung in there. But as a team they were faltering.

Some members were considering leaving the task force if this teambuilding process didn't "work." And why not? These people were volunteering their time to make their organization a better place for everyone. No one was picking up the slack for them on their already more-than-full-time jobs upon which their performance was judged. In fact, it cost some of them a lot to be part of this task force. Many were actively struggling against their managers' perceptions that what they were doing, this "diversity stuff," was a low priority.

Following are two of many revelations that occurred within this group of people.

Mark's Story

I could feel Mark's fear all the way across the room. I knew exactly what it was about. I had interviewed him and everyone else in the group before the teambuilding session. The information I received would allow me to glimpse the overlapping themes of their individual concerns and dreams.

In our previous interview, Mark told me that he felt compelled to tell the group that he is gay. He felt it was necessary if he was to work with the others at a high level of integrity. He talked about what a big risk it was and how terrified he felt. Yet, this was a diversity task force and his deepest concern was about what it was like for gays and lesbians to work in this organization.

I offered to support him. I was also clear that, no matter what he said in the interview, I would leave the final choice, responsibility, and timing of his disclosure up to him. I encouraged him to trust his intuition and his heart.

Now we return to the actual teambuilding session. Everyone was nervous. Living amidst the challenge of diversity is not abstract. It requires personal risk and breaks conventional rules. Because everyone else was nervous too, they didn't notice Mark's high level of anxiety.

I was fairly certain he wasn't hearing much of anything that was going on. I saw him wipe the perspiration from his hands onto his pants. I saw him breathing fast and shallow from above his Adam's apple. Having little or no air in his lungs, he would occasionally breathe deeply in the form of a gasp or a sigh.

I, too, was nervous. I was thinking, "Now what have I gotten myself into? Am I prepared enough, skilled enough, to help him and the group through the conversation that needs to occur if he chooses to risk it? Had I advised him well? Should I have discouraged rather than encouraged him?"

That last self-doubting question helped to shake me back to my Self, my own awareness. I may not always like the truth, but I know that truth works. I may not like the risk of vulnerability but I know it leads to connectedness. I may not always like the reactions of others, but I know that the truth and risk of vulnerability bring integrity, depth, trust, and connectedness. This is how we reveal the holes through the center of our jewels so the string can form our connection.

These thoughts helped me to remember that "I"—the apparent ego part of me—does not do this work alone. I remembered that if I stay as close to completely present as I am able and if I trust my own intentions, I will know what to do. Whatever I do in those moments will be coming from the center of me where I am deeply and invisibly connected to the whole. These thoughts helped me to remember that something major was at stake here. We were gambling with Mark's vitality, his creativity and his breath, his very lifeforce.

As I watched Mark barely breathing, I reminded myself to breathe deeply. Then I reminded myself of what Angeles Arrien suggested in *The Four Fold Way:* Stay present; listen for what has heart and meaning; speak the truth; be open to outcome rather than attached.

I have no memory of what was actually happening prior to Mark's disclosure to the group. Whatever it was, it was going well. Some safety net had been established and the precedent for taking risks had been set.

Mark cleared his throat. He said, "Ah......" He fidgeted in his chair and his voice quivered. "Ahm, this is......this is going to be......this is very difficult for me." Now tears streamed down his face. "This is very difficult for me because I'm scared. I'm scared of what you'll think when I tell you what I need to say." He couldn't go on. He bent his head forward and wept. Then, as the tears subsided for the moment, he took several labored, deep breaths.

Others were watching him, and more, they were with him. These people had been working with him for months. My guess is that many of them already knew his secret. But it had not, until now, been anything that could be openly noted or talked about directly.

He tried again. "You see, I'm......well, I'm gay." Sigh. "There. I finally said it. It's the very first time I've ever said it to people I work with. I'm sick of keeping it a secret. I'm sick of hiding and wondering who knows and whether it matters. I'm sick of fearing I'll accidentally disclose something, offend somebody, or miss a detail.

"And I'm scared. I'm scared you'll think of me differently or that you'll put distance between us. I'm scared of being rejected because of something that is important to me and part of who I am. I'm scared of being rejected here, by you, for something that has nothing whatever to do with my work."

When he was finished, a "silence that connects" filled the room. He had opened the space for the soul of the group to fill.

What followed is best described as a nonphysical, gentle reaching in. It was as though Mark was in the center of a circle and others were reaching in toward him.

Someone asked permission to ask him a question. He said, "Okay." She asked. He answered. Tender and gentle. His breathing changed. He began to relax. Someone else said something compassionate. Another expressed support and acceptance. Someone else said, "Thank you," and admitted his own naiveté about the gay experience and his resulting awkwardness.

Every—and I mean every—comment was appropriate. Actually, appropriate doesn't begin to express it. We sat together in an absolutely perfect moment. There was nothing else in the whole world beyond what was going on in that room among this particular group of people.

Then Mark began to weep again. This time the tears were not based in fear and anxiety. Rather, they were based in gratitude. He cried and said, "Thank you." And again he said, "Thank you." And again he said, "Thank you." And again....

I don't remember what else happened that day. I do remember thinking that while we had experienced a euphoric moment, none of us knew what might happen next as a result of the risk Mark had taken. A moment of risk is one thing, but living in the world with the consequences of that risk is something else entirely.

A year and a half later I was invited to work with the task force again. They had been doing some wonderful work. In fact, they had accomplished all of the goals they had set for themselves. Now they had a new set of problems, but this time the problems were sweet. First, their membership was changing. They had become so close and had done so well at breaking taboos around language and experience that they requested assistance to help in letting go of old members and integrating new members.

As an ad hoc group they had created recognition for the issues and needs around diversity in their organization. Now it was time to figure out how to transfer their work into the mainstream organization and to decide what their new role was to be—even if it was to be.

Before they could begin work, however, they needed to check in with each other. Mark, now the designated co-leader of the group, waited until near the end to speak. Again he had trouble getting started.

"I don't know why this is so hard for me. I just get so emotional. I'm just going to jump in." He took a long breath and let out a sigh. "This last year—since I came out in this group—has been the best year of my life. I can hardly believe it. Your support gave me the courage to come out to the organization as a whole. I remember the day I signed my name to an e-mail notice that was going to every person in the organization. It was announcing a meeting of the gay and lesbian network and inviting anyone who wished to join us to do so. I actually had a friend stand behind me for support as I pressed the 'Send' key. And then I thought, 'Oh, God!' But also I thought, 'There! It's done.'

"None of the things I feared have come to pass. In fact, quite the opposite has occurred. I have actually been rewarded. I have been able to spend time with our president talking about what it's like for me and others who are gay. I know he's interested partly because there are a lot of gay people in this organization. But also, he seems genuinely interested in his own learning and growth.

"My work has blossomed. I am so much more creative and productive than I have ever been before. I can't believe it! Now I can notice just how much energy was going into worrying and covering my tracks—such a waste!

"Each time I come out to someone new or in some new situation, it's still a risk. But it will never be the risk it was with you. I thank you all for that." He spoke these words with his eyes glistening and his face glowing. "It's an honor and a privilege to know you and work with you."

Vision

Because of the delicate and complex circumstances of this group, and because of my own passion for human relationships and differences, I chose to articulate a possible vision for them in that initial teambuilding session.

First, my vision was that they would allow their differences to be present; that they would hold differences not as conflict but rather as precious art to be viewed with love, examined in detail, admired for creativity and beauty, and handled with care.

At the same time, I suggested that they give themselves permission to have conflict—lots of it. My vision was that they would *really* get into the issues and learn from each other; that they would drop the facade and the language taboos; that they would speak and listen to each other. What a rich opportunity!

Secondly, my vision was that they would model within themselves individually and within the task force as a whole whatever it was they envisioned for the organization at large; that they would commit to learning and integrating for themselves what it was they wanted to teach others. In other words, that they would live together in the way they wanted everyone in the organization to live together. I suggested that if people in the organization saw them doing this, it would teach far more than any training program ever could. And, further, I imagined for them that the measurement of success would be that people wanted to be on the task force rather than out of it.

Third, my vision was that they would find a common, higher-order goal that encompassed, but also transcended, their individual and "special interest group" agendas. I proposed that when they found a higher-order goal, not only would they work toward it, but also that they would entrust their individual agendas to each other. In other words, the black person would work the gay person's agenda, the working mother would work the disabled person's agenda, the Hispanic would work the white male agenda....

And now, it was their turn to share their visions. I had asked the members of the group to draw pictures representing what they individually felt passionate about. I thought it would be a useful step forward for them to articulate their own and witness each other's visions of what this group could be and do; of what the broader organization would look like and become as a result of whatever they chose as their work.

People were sharing crayons, pastels, and other art supplies. They were working in twos and threes, engaging in casual, lighthearted conversation. Having witnessed some of the previous clouds of suppressed or misdirected anger and frustration, this engagement was, in and of itself, significant. It was heartwarming to see their eyes connecting and to hear laughter as they critiqued each other's artistic skills and apologized for their own. As I wandered around, I saw that their drawings were laden with rainbows and flowers and stick people. One person's drawing was different, however.

Andrea's Story

Andrea was sitting very quietly by herself. She was not drawing. A large, clean, white piece of poster board sat on her lap.

In her hand she held a pencil. She had no other art supplies near her. Her face was somber, her eyes had the glossiness that precedes tears.

In situations such as this, I know people do what they need to do—no matter what task I suggest. Also, given the freedom and the safety, people do what needs to be done for the group as a whole to move forward. That's what happened in this situation.

People began sharing their drawings. The pictures were naively sweet and simple, while the thoughts behind the drawings were touching, profound, and—most importantly—universal. The common desires of the heart were showing up.

But it was Andrea's response to the activity that really moved us forward at the level of soul. What she gave offered the group a quantum leap—out of time. Months of hard work at the head level could not match the few moments when she spoke from her heart and gave of her soul's suffering.

She sighed and said, "Well, I didn't do the assignment. I'm sorry, I just couldn't do it." She very deliberately put her pencil down and slowly held up her large white piece of poster board. She pointed at the center. "Do you see that small black pencil dot there in the center of this white paper?" she asked.

"That black dot is me. And the white paper is our organization. I feel like that black dot in this organization—alone and small and unseen." Tears streamed down her face.

Everyone in the room was quiet. Even breathing seemed to have stopped. She wept and talked about her first days in the company; about how people said she only got the job because she is black; about how being black never goes away; about how people pretend not to notice; about how white she is expected to act. She spoke about how, at lunch, the conversation doesn't include her and is outside her experience. She felt that no one wanted to hear about her background—like how she was shot at in high school.

Andrea was quiet for awhile. Everyone respected the interlude. Then she spoke about her vision. She described what it would feel like for her if this organization really valued her. Her vision was larger than that, however. She spoke about her children and how her vision of the workplace was that it would become more open and inclusive, and not so hard for them as it has been for her.

Silence emerged once again. It was not an awkward or disapproving silence. It was a beautiful silence. It was the kind of silence that warms rather than isolates; a silence of compassion and wordless comprehension; a silence that accompanies the process in which the many feel equally vulnerable with the one. It was a silence of connectedness at the level of the soul.

Bridges

Mark, Andrea, and each of the other members of the group, as they were moved to do so, offered up individual, personal arenas of pain. Each spoke of places within them that seemed to be the holes through which the previously unknown, unclaimed string was able to link them as a precious, priceless group of jewels.

Through risking vulnerably, they were able to touch both their own and each other's souls. They had the opportunity and privilege of caring for each other's pain without fixing it. They were able to simply notice and to be with each other. They came to more fully understand each other, and to feel and be who they truly are together.

Risking changed everything. Bridges were created that crossed the deepest, most painful parts of human experience. These bridges allowed everyone in the room—no matter what color, creed, gender, sexual preference, or nationality—to be linked over chasms that had previously seemed too broad to ever be traversed.

The results of the team's process relative to its productivity were stunning. In very little time, the group developed a common vision and strategy, divided the tasks and went to work. They were aligned!

Consequences

Almost four years later, I spent time with both Mark and Andrea separately. I wanted to see how each had interpreted our experience. What I learned was beyond what I had expected. The experience was a watershed for each of them, as it had been for me. I also learned how each is currently living with the ramifications of having taken risks and of having participated in such a soul-filled experience at work.

Not all of the results have been positive—as in "they lived happily ever after." Yet, in the context of soul work, all that happens is positive. As David Whyte says in *The Heart Aroused,* "We think we exist only...when our sense of ourselves is growing and getting larger, when we are succeeding or stepping up to the line for promotion. If things are dying or falling away, we...think there is something 'wrong' with us." And, further, "The soulful approach to work admits and allows the yeast of loss into our work lives."

Mark left the corporation. Now, two years later, his appearance has changed dramatically. He is broader in the shoulders. He looks more mature and dresses much more originally.

In his words, "There was something about being so closeted that actually forced me to be physically smaller than I am now. The pressures to fit in, to be a certain way, were so enormous. I'm physically bigger now. I would have to shrink to go back to where I was before.

"I felt young—like a kid—inside the company. My feeling was that there were adults to please and I was the one who had to please them."

He spoke of being angry. "I can't tell if the anger I feel when I think about that time is a result of where I am now or of how I felt then. Maybe I was angry then and only now can afford to notice it."

He also commented, "Eventually my coming out at work stopped my career. I applied for supervisory positions five times and I didn't get any of them, even though my reviews had always been exemplary. In my perspective it was because of homophobia. I finally got the courage to bring it to my manager's attention. Shortly thereafter I was offered a promotion. It was too much."

Finally, he noted the transcendent level of his process. "Part of what I did was to lay the path for others to come out, to bring their whole selves to work."

Andrea still works within the same corporation but has changed her job. "I've changed jobs and location. Yet, to this day, I can pick up the phone and call people from the task force and they are there for me. The connection is still there." It probably always will be.

She muses, "It's amazing how much stuff got articulated with a little tiny dot. I think about that and the impact I've seen within the group. If only we could bottle it and carry it out into the rest of the world. Then I could hold up my piece of paper and say, 'This is the way I feel' without having to hear, 'No, you don't feel that way. You can't be feeling that way. We are a corporation that supports diversity.'"

Further, she reminisces, "There were absolutely no barriers after that. I'm still hearing about stuff that got resolved between people that I didn't know existed at the time. The process we went through is still being talked about. It came up in a management meeting just two weeks ago.

"Each and every boundary and barrier was erased. We all spoke. We were heard and listened to. So we got stuff done."

Andrea also laid out her new pain. "The thing that happened in the group was so wonderful. However, I had to go back out into the real world. I saw people not being promoted, and being fired because of style—when we were supposedly *encompassing* differences in style.

"I now find myself unable to directly say anything when I feel prejudice. As a black woman I am seen as manipulative, as serving my own agenda, and as acting in reverse prejudice.

"The openness and honesty in the group gave me a new sense of what work relationships could be. I had a new sense of hope in the group. But that's also when I began to feel a true sense of hopelessness as well."

The soul within each of us in business longs to be seen, felt, and heard. Preventing this from happening consumes enormous amounts of our energy. We have to work very hard to hide and protect the deepest, most vulnerable parts of ourselves—the parts that, paradoxically, need the most care and nurturing.

It is the hole through the center of each bead that allows each to be inextricably and intimately connected with the others. It is the hole—which metaphorically represents vulnerability— that gives each bead an opportunity to experience and offer meaning in a new way—as part of a larger whole, the necklace. It is the soul—which *is* vulnerability—that gives each of us as individuals an opportunity to experience and offer meaning in a new way—as part of a larger whole, be it the relationship, the team, the community.

Peter Vaill is Professor of Human Systems and Director of the PhD Program at George Washington University's School of Business and Public Management. He is the former dean of this school. He has also served on the management faculties of the University of Connecticut, UCLA, and was visiting professor of Organizational Behavior at the Stanford Business School. He holds a Bachelor's degree from the University of Minnesota and MBA and DBA degrees from the Harvard Business School.

He is the author of numerous articles and books, including *Managing as a Performing Art: New Ideas for a World of Chaotic Change*. In 1985 he was described in the *Training and Development Journal* as one of the top ten organization development specialists in the country.

Vaill has worked with many well known corporations and with most of the major agencies of the U.S. government. From 1985 to 1988 he was editor of the American Management Association's journal, *Organizational Dynamics*. He has been a member of the Board of Governors of the Center for Creative Leadership since 1990.

5

The Rediscovery of Anguish

Peter B. Vaill

I have been thinking quite a bit about anguish—how our glitzy, technocratic, can-do society and culture seems to have a hard time with anguish and, in particular, that there does not seem to be a real public ethos of anguish except on just a few subjects such as the Kennedy and King assassinations and the Vietnam War. There was public, sustained anguish about civil rights in the 1960s, but there has not been any recently. Pollution of the environment has yet to achieve any national consensus of anguish, nor has the towering public debt. Peace and disarmament probably have a consensus, but not an anguished one. Aging is as yet invisible in terms of a public ethos of anguish. The drug and AIDS epidemics are contemporary examples of our nervousness about public anguish.

We agree these are problems and that someone ought to do something, but we would prefer that it were not so *public,* so graphic, and so frustrating. As Carly Simon sang in the 1970s, we would prefer to "close the wound, hide the scar." The marital agony that she was writing about, by the way, never developed a public ethos of anguish either. Abortion is an issue on which a great deal of private anguish occurs. But note how, in public, all we can do is scream at each other. There is little, if any, shared anguish over this tragic, stubborn predicament we are in as a result of the combined implosion of moral and religious values, individual rights, medical technology, socioeconomic factors, and ideas about the proper role of government.

There is something in the original notion that our national spirit suffers from our inability to communicate meaningfully with each other publicly about our fear, our pain, our sadness. We keep thinking we're going to solve these problems once and for all and that there will be no more anguish in need of caring, ministry, and healing. We continue to ignore the wisdom of Gerald Ford's Secretary of HHS, David Matthews, who dubbed ours the Age Where Things Have Not Turned Out The Way We Thought They Were Going To, as well as many far more penetrating social critics who are trying to understand how such pain and such awful problems can apparently be relatively invisible to the optimistic, can-do, problem-focused American soul.

Anguish in Organizations

I believe the only organizational issue I have encountered where consistently there is real personal anguish accepted as part of the issue to be dealt with is in the area of layoffs and downsizing and plant closings. That people are *really hurting* as a matter of *fact* is accepted on that particular issue. But I can't think of any other where it has been accepted—not certainly the stresses and strains of such things as new product introductions and new technologies, not around intense competition for plum promotions, not with respect to changes of command at top levels—although occasionally that can get emotional.

Every personnel counselor and plenty of loan officers in the organization credit union are privy to what people are going through personally, but there is little or no recognition or acceptance of it publicly in the system. Reorganizations might properly be matters of anguish, but we tend to lather our feelings over with cynical humor—that's what I mean, in fact, by the lack of a public ethos. We can't just share our pain and confusion with each other. We have to transform it. There is massive suppression of anguish going on in the organizations and communities of the developed world—no one's fault in particular; just a fundamental part of the culture.

When worry, pain, confusion, trapped feelings, and fear become intense enough they are what I am calling "anguish." I think there is a lot of collective but unexpressed anguish in our modern organizations, judging at least by what individuals say, by such stress symptoms as turnover, substance abuse, interpersonal conflict, and hair-trigger litigiousness.

My basic point is that we cannot talk about change to alleviate these feelings if we cannot be more open about them in the first place. In these anguished feelings lie the spiritual meaning and spiritual energy that are central to their transcendence and to their healing.

Anguish: Spiritual Loss

Anguish suppressed is anguish displaced. If people can't show openly how sad or worried or frightened they are, the anxious energy puts on masks. Anguish puts on the mask of workaholism and attacks the substance of the issue in a frenzy. Anguish puts on the mask of political astuteness and adroitly maneuvers around the system, sniffing constantly for danger or for an advantage that might bring greater security. Anguish puts on the mask of technical rationality and searches diligently for optimal solutions—solutions that by virtue of their elegance, their comprehensiveness and their scientific grounding, will supposedly alleviate suffering. Of course they never do; they always promise more than they deliver and bring with them in the bargain a whole new set of issues and costs which did not exist before the rationalistic optimal solution was adopted—and anguish is compounded.

Suppressed anguish self-medicates with drugs and alcohol. Suppressed anguish grasps at magical cures and esoteric visions. Suppressed anguish, most tragically, even puts on the mask of passivity, indifference, and depression.

All these masks are endemic in the "developed" world. We see them everywhere and they are so common and accepted that they are hardly seen as worthy of comment. The world is full of workaholics, technocrats, wheeler-dealers, depressives, and stressed-out substance abusers. "Shit happens," the bumper sticker says with its own mask of worldly wisdom. So what?

We cannot talk about change to alleviate these feelings if we cannot be more open about them in the first place. They are fundamentally feelings of spiritual loss, I think—that is what makes them matters of genuine *anguish* and not just annoyances and minor disappointments. As people like us try to do more and more with organizations—as we strive for higher levels of performance, deeper relationships among organizational members, greater degrees of personal self-realization for individuals—we come more and more into the realm of the spiritual meaning of life. We are talking, after all, about helping to bring out the best in persons and groups, and in organizations. We are talking about helping people to manifest the most beautiful and precious human characteristics we know—trust, care, creativity, joy and exuberance, courage and perseverance. The human beings who are going to manifest these qualities are going to be spiritually quite developed—both personally and in their collective norms and values.

How are they going to get this way? Are they going to be "engineered" into this consciousness and mode of action by some behavior technocrat? I doubt it. In fact, I am sure they will not. People are going to develop spiritually by some other kind of spiritual program than something designed and administered by a rationalistic problem-solver. That is why it matters that we have to help anguish come more clearly and publicly into the open in groups and organizations—so that people can find out who each one really is, what is really on each one's mind, and what each one really has energy for.

Fundamentally, it is so that people can more clearly experience each other's capacity to love and be loved. One feels the most anguish over that which one loves most deeply—when it is lost, or not what one yearns for it to be, or in mortal danger.

People do love their organizations. The love their products and services. They love their industries and they love their stakeholders. They love their work colleagues and they even love their bosses. Or at least they sometimes love these various people and things. In the highest performing systems, they clearly love all these things intensely. So when things go wrong, they feel anguish; they wouldn't call it this, but they feel spiritual pain. *That is what anguish is—spiritual pain.*

Anguish and Values

I wish to connect anguish and spirituality to the situation people are in at work. Organizations are value systems. This is not something we hear as often as we should. We hear that they are economic entities. We hear that they are instruments to pursue objectives. We hear them described in terms of their technologies and transformation processes and in terms of inputs, throughputs, and outputs. We hear them likened to the nervous system and we see them modeled as information systems. But organizations are also value systems. They are relatively stable expressions of human priorities, i.e., values. Whatever else they are, however else they can be modeled, they are expressions of this—of what people want and don't want, value and don't value, attach meaning to and don't attach meaning to.

I call them "relatively stable entities" and that is what they are supposed to be. However, increasingly, in the modern environment, they are not. They are undergoing chaotic change—in technologies, in markets, in membership and leadership, in expectations of stakeholders. The changes are in large increments, they are uncoordinated in their number and magnitude, they are threats as much or more than they are opportunities, and so they don't breed pleasurable anticipation. They are changes requiring new values and priorities, not just change in actions and policies and physical equipment.

In addition to all these characteristics of modern change— large increments, uncoordinated and crosscutting, threatening, and challenging values directly—modern organizational change is also *continuous*. The modern organization and environment is a *novelty generator* and this characteristic strikes at the very essence of what an organization is and what it means to be organized.

No matter how beautiful the combination of values and actions we discover along the way, we have to be prepared to let go of them in favor of new combinations which will be more adaptive under new conditions.

So organizations are destabilized value systems in our world. The changes *we* would like to introduce are only some among many that are going on.

Values are our grounds of meaning. They tell us how the world ought to be for us. They tell us whether we are in a place that is good or not good for us, in a place that is getting better for us or getting worse. Valuing—preferring—is part of what it means to be human. We do not have to just take things as we find them, for our minds guide us to introduce changes that will be better for us, our communities, and our species.

As our grounds of meaning, values are one of our primary ties to whatever we consider to be the larger meaning and purpose of the world and the universe, and of what we consider our role in it all to be. We say we value what we value *because* . . . and then we put a reason behind the because.

The interesting thing is that *all* values—and for most Americans, our initial reasons for valuing what we value and believing what we believe are materialistic and quasi-scientific— all values, regardless of what their initial "becauses" are, ultimately trace to some supernatural or mystical vision of what the universe is about. This is a fairly commonplace observation among philosophers, even though you don't hear it so often in the worlds of the behavioral sciences and management and organization development. All values are ultimately grounded in a supernatural, mystical, or divine vision, whether or not the person has made it explicit to her or himself. This says, then, that all values are profoundly matters of faith, because another name for the supernatural or divine is the invisible and unknowable. Faith is indeed a mode of knowing, but a very different one from the one valued and trusted by the culture we have all grown up in. Yet it seems to me fairly clear that actions in organizations taken by managers, members, and consultants are matters finally of faith.

Anguish and Faith

Now it is easier to see why anguish is such an important matter in human affairs, and why its suppression is such a dangerous and misleading matter. In the chaotic world of the modern organization, values are under constant challenge, which means whether we realize it or not, our faith in the rightness of our actions is constantly challenged. Regularly and frequently our values do not withstand the challenge. Sometimes they are merely defeated, as when a competitor finds a way to pursue the *value* of quality more effectively than we do, or where the *value* of a careful search for a new key employee turns up someone who proves to be unable to do the job. But sometimes the very value itself that we held is negated. We valued the long term; short-term thinking won the prize. We valued merit and evenhandedness in cross cultural dealings; knowing the right people and greasing the right palms turned out to be the governing values. We value means over ends; we find ourselves losing to one who values ends over means.

Where the very *values* one holds dear are negated, anguish is often the result. Anguish can also attend the situation where all parties agree on the values but some parties cannot seem to successfully pursue the values and must face the despair of not being able to achieve what one values.

Because the organization is a value system, and because modern conditions constitute a nonstop process or challenge and negation to our values, and because anguish is the result of the loss of the persons, ideas, and things we hold dear, it *must* be possible to discover the nature and working of anguish in the modern organization. Otherwise we are deep in denial, playing a game of mirrors and let's pretend. Furthermore, if we do not deal with the anguish that accompanies the pounding our values are taking, we will not be able to reflect on what values are possible under the emerging conditions, and on how our faith in the idea that there *is* meaning in life can be kept robust and forward-looking and inspirational to those around us.

Notice that what I am talking about does not apply just to an organization that is undergoing an unusual buffeting at present, such as an assault by the Japanese, a power struggle at the top, or a major lawsuit. What I am talking about applies to all social settings, no matter how superficially tranquil or sheltered they seem to be. We are living in a time where people are being pulled from their cars on a highway and shot. No one is immune from surprise. A terrorist, by definition, is someone who intends to harm you in a time and place and manner that you never expected, and the world is full of terrorists, some with Uzis, yes, but some also in three-piece suits sitting at terminals or lecturing before a flip chart.

Anguish and Creative Change

It seems to me that "creative change" under the conditions I have sketched, has to involve the spiritual pain, the spiritual condition, and the spiritual development of those who are in-volved in it: those who are the objects of it, those who authorize it, those who lead it and those who consultatively facilitate it. I don't see that it is a matter of *choice* if values and spirit, change, and anguish are related in the way that I have described.

Without rapid change, it may be possible to maintain the illusion that spirituality is not involved in the conduct of human affairs. But it is, indeed, an illusion. The truth is that spirituality is there, and it has always been there. Americans are both privileged and cursed to be the first society to discover that thorough and extensive introduction of science and technology into every corner of society does not diminish the presence and significance of spirituality one iota.

The pervasiveness of spirituality means that the ideas we have about leadership, management, organizing, and facilitating change are *incomplete* to the extent that they do not recognize the spiritual basis of working with human beings. They are *inadequate* in times of change to the extent they do not recognize this spiritual basis, and they are simply wrong if they try to argue that the spiritual condition of the people involved is of no importance to the way things proceed. And these methods have been wrong for all time—wrong for as long as there have been human beings involved, because spiritual *feeling* is such a significant part of what it is to be a human being.

A management that tries to engineer structure to guarantee the actions it wants and suppress actions it doesn't is wrong. A strategic plan which assumes the adequacy of a purely secular mission to define the meaning of the organization is wrong. A scoring system for assigning merit pay raises on "objective" criteria is wrong. A leadership style which does not appeal to followers' spiritual qualities and yearnings is wrong. In calling them "wrong," I mean they are in error. They misvalue the person. But I guess I must also own up to a moral judgment in my use of the word "wrong." I mean both a mistake and, yes, I mean *improper* in a moral sense. This is the moral stand I take—and of course I am not alone. But it is getting to be time to speak up, first on behalf of the reality of anguish, but more importantly, on behalf of the need for spiritual development.

Since the situation I am talking about has been around for a long time, and since we are by no means the first society of humans to be struggling with our anguish, can we learn anything from other human communities who have struggled similarly? I think we can.

Anguish and Professional Practice

There are three things I want to call attention to in particular which seem to have occurred rather consistently in earlier ages, and, indeed, which can be seen around us today, although so far as I know, they are not interpreted as direct attempts to cope with anguish. All three of these broad developments are matters that I hope can more and more become part of our practice as men and women who are interested in fostering spiritual growth and "healing our home."

Time

First is the matter of *time*. We must be one of the most impatient societies in human history. Rush, rush, rush. It is no wonder that another name for workaholism is "the hurry sickness." I am talking about dwelling more fully in the time of our anguish. The anguished feelings we have are going to be around for years. Which social condition or type of condition that was a matter of anguish in 1960 no longer exists? Our troubles last for years—and, in fact, America's troubles may be just beginning, if you believe some of the apocalyptists there are around. To care more about time gives us more time to ground ourselves in what is really going on. We become more sensitive to the emptiness of quick fixes and temporary palliatives. It is said that the alcoholic or drug addict finally takes action to begin recovery when he realizes this rotten situation is going to go on and on and get worse and worse. That is what I mean by finally coming to dwell in one's anguish. This is when, too, it becomes clearer and clearer that nothing on earth is really going to save us once and for all, and that realization is a giant leap forward in spiritual awareness.

We can help our friends and clients *take time*. We can help them listen to just what kind of pain they are in and evaluate more thoughtfully just what might constitute a real resolution to the mess, as opposed to a shiny and attractive temporary cover-up of the pain. We know that in the midst of all the pressure and the anguish, people often don't think too clearly; they grab at superficial solutions just so they can feel they have done something.

We can work with our colleagues to help them deeply experience the feelings of pace and progress. Any change process is a collage, not a linear "course of action," despite our mythology to the contrary. As a collage, with many fronts involved, impatience is an easy mood to fall into, especially for people with power to command others and who may be in the grip of the hurry sickness. Impatience is an attempt to relieve anguish. The reason patience is a virtue is that its companion in the soul is anguish.

Networks

There is more to the question of groups—and it constitutes my second main avenue along which we can help with the rediscovery of anguish. Where there are no solid groups, where at most we are ethereal networks of superficial acquaintances, there can be little or no healthy, public expression of anguish.

Everyone is too cautious. Many foreign students have told me that one of the most surprising things about America is that when we say "How ya doing'??" in a loud, jolly voice, we don't mean, "How are you really doing?" We don't expect an answer, they are astonished to discover.

Philip Slater called our basic organizing principle *The Pursuit of Loneliness,* and little has happened in the succeeding seventeen years to reverse that indictment. Our psychic bonds to each other become more and more attenuated and anguish becomes more and more private as a result.

A popular magazine recently suggested that *compulsion* is the disease of the 1990s. A compulsion, of course, is an uncontrollable attempt to relieve anxiety and anguish by some stereotypical piece of action, be it work, food, drugs and alcohol, sex, cigarettes, gambling, shopping video games, or jogging. When the person cannot *not* engage in the activity without noticeable agitation and/or guilt, compulsion is at work.

Many of these compulsions already are being addressed by the Twelve Step program that was originally developed by Alcoholics Anonymous. The most significant things about these programs is that they are deliberately and intensely spiritual programs, and they are clearly conducted as fellowships. The anonymity principle was probably originally intended to avoid publicity and embarrassment and it still achieves that. But it also focuses attention not on the externals of who we are, but the internals—the things about us that transcend the superficial. In other words, the spiritual things.

Beyond the Twelve Step programs, we need to keep working on ways to bring people together. Networks don't always form automatically, and they certainly don't run themselves. Yet there is wide agreement that there is something called "networking" and that some people do it pretty well.

Becoming Theologians

This rather heroic vision of our practice of leadership and facilitation leads to my third broad area of development and deepening. Given that there is so much unease about spirituality in society, and given that there is such a proliferation of gurus and of spiritual ideas and methods, I think one who is going to navigate all this in a sane and spiritually sound way has to be something of a genuine theologian. It *is* a ministry I have been describing in these remarks, but it is a ministry that is itself subject to all the confusion and all the temptations and all the distractions that everyone else is subject to.

When I say we must become theologians, I do not mean we must become abstruse, otherworldly contemplatives who periodically issue densely reasoned and essentially unreadable tracts. I mean we must become more down-to-earth, more personal and robust, more everyday.

We need to learn to think flexibly and freshly about spiritual matters. I see no reason why spiritual insights should turn into dogma, though that is what has tended to happen over the centuries. Maybe it is because some spiritual insights are, indeed, so shattering and engulfing that it is natural to try to freeze the essence of what happened to some person or group into a dogma for all time. In times of rapid change this won't work. For dogma to really take hold, it needs decades of enough tranquillity to repeat itself over and over. That won't happen in the world of our foreseeable future. What *will* happen is that spiritual pain—anguish—and spiritual questions will keep arising in new conceptual garb and in reaction to the cornucopia of new events and experiences the world holds. It will take a genuine theological consciousness to understand, and help others understand, what is happening; it will take a true sense of ministry to create and sustain the relationship wherein spiritual growth can occur.

The subject is not one for dabblers or for those who would catch the latest trend in consulting and training, but I believe there are thousands of professionals who are ready to explore what a spiritual practice, in both senses of the word "practice," may be. Such a spiritual practice may start with the rediscovery of anguish.

Elaine Gagné, EdD, has been designing and implementing seminars (presented on four continents) for over twenty years in corporate, government, and private settings. She has inspired thousands of people toward a new experience of organizational and individual effectiveness through experiential and practical presentations in leadership development, team learning, and essential communication skills. Her most recent publication is *Designing Effective Organizations: Traditional and Transformational Views*. Sage Publications, CA. 1995 (co-authored with Dr. David Banner).

Gagné is a presenter and consultant with the Covey Leadership Center and a visiting Assistant Professor at the University of the Pacific, School of Business. She is co-founder and ex-officio President of Renaissance Business Associates (RBA), an international association of people dedicated to the demonstration of integrity and excellence in business.

Elaine and her husband, Don Dinwoodie, share a love of gardening, hiking, and their small ranch in Colorado. They have four adult sons: William, Stuart, Luke, and David.

6

Fear: The Juicy Part of Soul

Elaine Gagné

> Who ever shall see through all fear shall
> always be safe
>
> —Lao Tzu
> Translated by Stephen Mitchell

I recently explored this statement in depth and learned a lot about what is really important to me. I was reminded that values drive our behavior in all aspects of our lives and that personal choice creates my experience of reality. I saw how fear in business dealings can be a barometer of value systems.

One week, I was remarking on a regular basis just how great things were. Then it happened...the kind of thing that "can never happen to me" but, in fact, can happen to anybody. My husband was a party to an accident that changed our lives forever. In early 1994, he was driving down a peaceful residential street when a six-year-old boy darted out into his path chasing a ball. The car struck the boy in a way that caused massive injuries—to the extent that the doctors considered amputation of his arms.

My husband was traumatized. He still bears the emotional scars of this horrible accident. Contrary to what often occurs when parties to an accident become fearful and allow others to come between them, we expressed our regret directly to the boy's family and became regular visitors at his bedside. We have become very close to this boy and his family, despite warnings from the legal and insurance people. We have been intimately involved in his recovery, trying to be as useful as possible in his caretaking and the healing of his injuries. To date, his progress is considered miraculous by many of the hospital staff.

At one point in the early weeks following this tragedy, I began to experience sleeplessness, anxiety, and fear. I was forced to look at the cause: fear over being sued and of losing assets which represented a lifetime of my study, work, and service as well as that of others. My demeanor, effectiveness and ability to focus were all impacted by this event.

It was a powerful "red flag" for me: My fear was orchestrating my experience. I believe that the universe collaborates to make me whole and that anything in my path is an opportunity to grow. This had been no exception. What I "saw" through my fear helped me to reorganize myself at a higher level of function in business. Fear can be a teacher that can help us assess our value system.

The Learning Process

Here are the three basic steps I moved through relating to this event and the subsequent learning:

> Step 1. The stimulus, or event (stressor—"good" or "bad").
>
> Step 2. The experience associated with the event.
>
> Step 3. Choice.

Step 1 is any event that carries meaning and stimulates a response or reaction (a "stressor). For example, a television advertisement promoting a particular make and model of automobile might be an event for the person who created the ad or a person who is looking for a new car. The person who has no need for a new car, or no interest, may not even notice the ad; that is, the advertisement would not be an "event."

Regarding Step 2, different people have various experiences in response/reaction to the same event: This is a clear indication that fear, and our beliefs and values, greatly determine the nature of our experience. Fear is a mirror of one's personal value system and "real" beliefs. Here is a simple example of this: Two people are walking through the woods enjoying a spring day. They come across a snake; one person is delighted and wants to collect it for his son's reptile garden; the other person freezes in fear. The first person believes he can be safe with snakes and that they are fun to have around. The second person does not believe he or she can be safe with snakes and that snakes are *not* fun to have around.

Another example of this might be the rise and fall of the stock market and the different reactions that different people have to that occurrence. Here are two extreme cases: For the first-time investor who has invested a recent inheritance, the fall of the stock market might result in severe depression; for a seasoned player who has a balanced investment portfolio, the fall of the stock market might be just another day.

Step 3, choice, won't happen if one is unaware that there *is* personal choice. In that case, one is left with the raw experience whatever it may be. Conscious choice is the difference between being a *victim* of one's circumstances, or the *master* of one's circumstances.

The Power of Choice

Choice is the heart of the matter. I remember my first conscious choice when I was a small child. I was enjoying "kids' day" at a local amusement park in the early 1950s. I was taking my first roller coaster ride and had absolutely *no* idea of what I was in for. The sounds and smells of the day and the vision of huge mounds of cotton candy filled me with excitement. As I approached the rambling, rumbling roller coaster, my excitement heightened. I sensed the fever pitch awareness of all the children around the area. I was first in line for the next ride. I couldn't see very much, but the sounds of screaming eerily burst forth and diminished. Then it was my turn to lead the new batch of riders on to the waiting cars. I sat in the front with two other children. I remember the sounds of scraping metal as we inched up the first incline. We began to level off high on the first "hill"— higher than I had ever been in my young life. I felt frozen as I sensed what was happening: We were going DOWN—and down we went! I couldn't breathe; my heart beat wildly in my chest, my grip on the bar in front of me was so firm that it seemed that I was part of it and it was part of me. I barely had time to recover from one searing descent when I would have to endure another. My fear was debilitating and I thought I couldn't stand any more. When the car finally rolled to a stop, I started to get my balance again.

I had been so involved in recovering from the shock of the experience that I didn't see the cars filling up with more excited children...and we were off again with me still sitting in my front seat torture chamber! I knew that I could not survive another such trip, yet it was too late to get out. I felt frozen in terror as we ascended. As we neared the crest, I took in a deep breath and deliberately breathed out as we flew down the other side. I felt my body relax. What a thrill! I was in control. I repeated this process over and over and enjoyed a wonderful ride. I have no idea what inspired me to do this breathing process, but, to this day, I'm convinced it saved my life! The end result was that I experienced dramatically different effects from the *same* stimulus! I never forgot that moment of realization that I had the *power* to manage the effect of my circumstances. I guess it's true that when we're really pushed to the wall, the genius of our unconscious takes over.

This powerful realization made even more sense for me during a high school physics lesson. In this class, I heard that "energy is never lost, it simply changes form." If the event, the stimulus, was a form of energy, could I somehow affect what forms that energy would take through me? If I 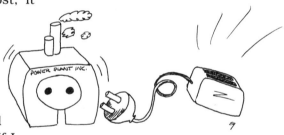 were to plug directly into that energy, just as if I were to plug my toaster directly into the electrical power plant, I would burn out.

Choice: The Transformer

Value-driven, personal *choice* acts as the transformer for any energy perceived. Choice determines the nature of the experience. Through personal choice, I can determine if I will experience a state of dis-ease or ease. Ease, in this case, is not necessarily synonymous with comfort, but rather is indicative of a state of mastery and control in one's life.

The more value-driven conscious choice a person makes, the more personal mastery he or she demonstrates. This seems to work to a degree, regardless of what these values are. A classic example of this is Adolph Hitler, who valued Aryan supremacy so

passionately that he exterminated entire segments of the population for his cause.

I would underscore the relationship between value-based choice and personal mastery. Here is an example of such value-based choice: I recently had the all-too-common dilemma of wanting to be in two places at one time. Making a decision on where to be was easy because I based my choice on a priority value. I felt empowerment, mastery, and control in the situation. An interesting side effect was that, in sensing my own feeling of confidence, others involved accepted my decision with ease. So, what can keep us in that state of choice?

The Creative Process

We can stay in the state of conscious choice if we can intercept our habitual and automatic reactions and deliberately embrace the creative process. One way I interpret the creative process is in four steps. These four steps, while outlined in sequence, in fact, may occur simultaneously. There is no "end" of one step and "beginning" of another. Briefly, here are the four steps:

Being	Achieving
1. Stillness	3. Pro-Action
2. Connection	4. Creation

Step 1: Stillness—the internal state of quiet mind and emotion. This is not necessarily the absence of external chaos, but rather the art of being still regardless of the external state,

much as an athlete would be still prior to the start of an athletic event. This is the step in which we are most likely to intercept habitual and automatic reaction. It is out of this stillness that the next three steps flow.

Step 2: Connection—honoring the relation to the important factors in the situation. Connection includes tangible as well as intangible factors, for example, other people's perspectives, machines, and one's own attitude regarding the situation. Before appropriate action can be taken, it is important to be aware of the current circumstance—as it *is* rather than how it *should* be. Connection is more a matter of consciousness than of time. An example of this might be considering a situation from another's point of view or realizing that the machine really will not work any faster if you slap it hard.

Step 3: Action—*pro*-action rather than *re*-action is what is required here. Pro-action is based on an internal source of control; re-action is the knee-jerk re-action to the circumstance, that is, the external circumstance is in control. Pro-action is based on value-driven, personal choice. It is the antidote to the victim-state consciousness.

Step 4: Creation—the difference between creation and results is the mastery of the person moving through the first three steps. Anyone can achieve results, but only the master can infuse his or her artistry in such a way that *results* evolve to *creation*. A classic example of the difference between results and creation are the two orchestra conductors. One conductor does his job, getting the right parts of the orchestra to come in on cue, but without a passion for the music. The other conductor is passionate about the music and inspires the orchestra to give outstanding performances. The magic spreads to all who listen. While the outcome of the two conductors is that the same music is played— and all in a timely way—there is clearly a difference between the two performances.

The Foundation

Because the last three steps emerge from the first, let's look at Step 1: Stillness. We all have our ways to maintain stillness in our lives. Otherwise, we would not be able to withstand the stress of our work and our world. Drugs, smoking, drinking, and other escapist modes give a temporary, false sense of stillness which is really a "numbed" consciousness. Rest and sleep are obviously healthy ways to maintain stillness. Other methods are walking, meditating, music, reading, art, play, dance, and yoga.

The Stress-Emergency Kit

In my own experience of staying in stillness at any moment, I discerned four potent and readily available resources, which I call the "Stress Emergency Kit." This four-part Stress Emergency Kit for the "in the moment" stillness works for me: Breathing, Humor, DSFS, and Gratitude.

The Stress Emergency Kit
1. Breathing
2. Humor
3. DSFSQ
4. Gratitude

1. Breathing. My terrifying childhood experience with the roller coaster taught me about this one. My later learning about deep breathing augmented that learning. Herbert Benson from Harvard University coined the "six-second relaxation response" as a way to alleviate stress. His theory is that you can create a conditioned reflex of a deep breath that exhales tension from the body. This is totally available at all times. Notice what happens to your breathing the next time you are stressed about something. For most people, their breathing stops or is constricted. If you develop a habit of releasing tension through breathing in times of stress, it can happen automatically.

2. Humor. I've heard it said that laughter is "internal jogging." I have certainly found humor to have the magical effect of lifting my mood. I recently heard a stand-up comic explain how he reads the newspapers. He looks at the news from the comic's perspective. What a way to keep from being depressed by what bombards us daily. This does not mean that one goes about laughing at problems (although some of them are pretty laughable, at least in retrospect). This tactic does, however, give encouragement to find the humor in a situation.

The first time I experienced humor as a reflex to stress was on the first day of a week-long speaking tour. My colleagues and I had just pulled into the motel where we would stay our first night and were unpacking the car. My suitcase was not in the back of the van in which we were traveling. I began to chuckle to myself as I envisioned myself washing out my clothes every night and brushing my teeth with my fingers! I started to tell my colleagues that I had forgotten my suitcase when the driver interrupted me to say that he had already taken my case to my room! I thought of what a bad time I could have given myself. A bad time, even for a few moments, is a bad time, and takes its toll on our overall well-being. Since the topic of my presentations was "Stress Management," I'm glad I didn't show up at the evening presentation all stressed out!

Humor can become a conditioned reflex, an "inside job" that no one even needs to know about. It can make the difference between a moment of living, ease—or a moment of dying, dis-ease.

3. DSFSQ. "Do Something For Somebody Quick." I once heard an old folk song that included those words. An experience with a colleague motivated me to actively experiment with this technique. I was coordinating an international conference which involved more detail and stacks of paper on my desk than I had bargained for. I worked alongside my key assistant, David. It seemed that whenever I was feeling overwhelmed and stressed out, David would show up and say something like, "What can I do to help you right now?" Now, David's desk looked as chaotic as mine did and he handled even more detail than I, but his gesture always effected a calm in me.

I noticed that when I would extend this same kind of gesture to someone else, I would immediately feel in control and on top of the circumstances. Offering to do something for someone else takes me out of my own victim state and into a proactive state. I have found that even little anonymous gestures have that impact, such as wiping out the sink in the airplane lavatory. The person who created the "Random Acts of Kindness and Senseless Acts of Beauty" campaign was really on to something.

4. Gratitude. To me, nothing seems to preserve sanity and youth as much as an attitude of gratitude. One of my greatest teachers told me a story which exemplifies this point. Chiropractors Bill Bahan and his brother Wally Bahan were on their way one dark rainy New Hampshire night to make a house call. They had a flat tire and pulled off the road. Bill walked around the car surveying the scene and said to his brother, "Look, Wally. Three good ones!" They had a good laugh, fixed the tire and were on their way. How many times do we let the "little" things get blown way out of proportion. Now, it may be hard to *find* something for which to be thankful in a circumstance. There are some pretty grim happenings these days. But how about being thankful that you know ways to *be* in the circumstance to minimize the troublesome effects. Perhaps an attitude of gratitude for what IS working in the situation is a way to stay grounded in the truly important factors.

What fear can teach us:

(A) *What I fear spotlights my values.*

After my experience with the accident involving the little boy, I took a look at the source of my fear. This examination revealed that I was acting as if property and other assets were more important than my health and relationships. I was appalled at this recognition and something shifted in me immediately. I was able to chart out a clear and effective action plan based on consciously chosen values versus being driven by unconscious ones.

(B) *Making decisions based on my values empowers me.*

Knowing what values I really want to support for myself facilitates decision-making. I am alert to the values that my behavior indicates and make deliberate choices based on what I *choose* to value. For example, in waiting longer than expected for an appointment, do I fidget about and complain? If so, is this an indication of my value to always be "in a hurry"? Do I value my time enough to call ahead and confirm the appointment and ask if there will be any variances from the schedule? Do I value the "found" time to do some extra planning or reading? My experience with fear opened all of this up for me, teaching me much about what I can control and what I can't.

(C) *There is power in accepting what is and moving on to creative action.*

Another lesson I learned from fear is that of where I put my trust. There is value in assessing the situation carefully, taking the necessary steps, and then letting go! When there is nothing more that can be done in a situation, it is time to put my energy somewhere else. It is also a good idea to have a tickler reminder to continue to check on the progress of the situation at timely intervals.

I call this form of trust "acceptance." Acceptance of the situation as it *is* is not necessarily liking or agreeing with it, but accepting the way it *is* at *this* time. Denying the situation or raging into blame is not the best use of energy. At the risk of tired comparisons, I've heard that if something goes wrong in an Asian business, the first question asked is, "Where do we go from here? How do we fix it?" In contrast, in a Western company, the first question in such a problematic situation may well be, "Who is responsible for this?" that is, who do we blame. When there is a problem, do we automatically stop to determine who to blame or do we get on with the job of solutions?

(D) Effectiveness increases when I recognize and avoid self-sabotage.

An additional lesson that fear provided for me is the awareness of self-sabotage. I understand that the word "sabotage" originated from the practice of French factory workers throwing their wooden shoes (sabots) into the machinery as a form of protest. The period of time when I was experiencing the debilitating effects of fear was a crucial period for me. I failed to meet two important deadlines. In a sense, I threw a shoe in the machinery. The problem was that it was *my* machinery! This gave me cause to look at why I would want to obscure the meeting of my own goals.

My reflections were valuable. I now habitually give myself time buffers in my goal-setting and I look at what I will have to "give up" if I am successful at meeting my goals. For example, if I am in a situation in which success at my goals means that I need to go on to another project which I am resisting, then what I have to give up is the project that I am enjoying. This is an irrational line of thinking, to be sure, but then, the subconscious mind is not always rational. When I am clear about what is going on, I can either make arrangements to change or adjust the future projects, or I can come to terms with the fact that I am going to do that undesirable project. To fail at the project that I am enjoying is sure to cost me in the long run—both in reputation and future prospects to take on similar projects. Obviously, there may be more complexity to what a person has to "give up" in order to succeed. That is cause for deep personal reflection.

(E) Fear can be a healthy part of growth and safety.

Healthy fear is another consideration. The world is a dangerous place for one who knows no fear. I used to think that it was important to be brave—to never show any fear. One interaction with a zip line on a "ropes course," and a game played at a school for entrepreneurs changed that for me. In the first case, I was taking my first high-ropes course in the country north of Toronto in 1981. This was part of the curriculum for a course in experiential-based learning. I was first up on the "Burma bridge" to cross the spans from one tree to another. The platform was about 40 feet above the ground and the zip line was a fast descent to the ground. As I was being harnessed in, I couldn't take my eyes off the ground below, feeling a growing fear rise in my belly as I was challenged by my belief that I was not supposed to be afraid. I missed two of my cues to jump and went on the third only because my belief that I was not to be afraid took over. I didn't even remember to breathe! On the descent, however, I realized that I was safely harnessed in and that nothing could happen to me. I had been so fearful, I imagined danger!

The second part of this lesson occurred at the School for Entrepreneurs at Tarrytown, NY in 1984. We were playing the ring-toss game. Again, I thought I was not supposed to be afraid and took the greatest chances for the highest return. What I learned, indeed, the same thing that the people who developed this game at Harvard University learned, is that those with the healthy fear took reasonable (vs. crazy) risks and were the ones who ultimately had greater success at what they were doing.

These two experiences taught me that 1) it is O.K. to be afraid—it's what we *do* with the fear that counts, and 2) denying fear and taking unnecessary risks can create loss.

Renaissance of Values

What does all of this have to do with soul and the renaissance of values in business? Fear is a juicy element of soul. I've heard it said that fear and love are the two core human emotions. We can either let these two emotions define *us* or we can define *them*. The choice we make at this crossroads ultimately colors our character.

In such times of choice, I learn over and over again the truth of these words: *No power on earth can disturb the strength of my reality or the effectiveness of my being.* I see that my business and other aspects of my life continually challenge me in this belief but, ultimately, I agree with Benjamin Hoff (*The Te of Piglet*) who writes of his appreciation for the face of *soul:*

> Before we start crying and praying to the Uni-
> verse to take away our Trials and Tribulations,
> we might more closely examine what it has given
> us. Maybe the "good" things are tests, possibly,
> rather difficult ones at that, and the "bad"
> things are gifts to help us grow: problems to
> solve, situations to learn to avoid, habits to
> change, conditions to accept, lessons to learn,
> things to transform—all opportunities to find
> Wisdom, Happiness, and Truth.

To quote William Blake:

> *It is right it should be so'*
>
> *Man was made for Joy and Woe;*
>
> *And when this we rightly know,*
>
> *Thro' the World we safely go;*
>
> *Joy and Woe are woven fine,*
>
> *A Clothing for the soul divine.*

So, if I want to experience life fully, I have to do it at the depth of myself: my spirit, my uniquely creative expression; and my soul, which is the home of fear and love. The following guidelines, highlighted from my recent soulful experience with fear, have helped me to do just that:

1. Look beyond the fear to what it says about your value system. For example, do you value "getting the job done" at the expense of people, integrity, or personal health?

2. If you don't like what fear has to say about your value system, make some positive choices to change that.

3. Look at the part that fear may be playing in creating personal or business loss and determine how you want to handle that.

4. Make a positive choice about what you will give up in order to succeed at the goals that you set for yourself and your company.

5. Remember that there is really no such thing as "good" and "bad"; it's all food for the soul.

Fear has been food for my soul. *Seeing* through fear is at once the challenge and the joy. The result is, as Lao Tzu implied, ultimate safety.

* * *

POSTSCRIPT: I am happy to report that Zack, the little boy who thrust himself into our lives, has made a very strong recovery and is almost "as good as new." All legal matters are settled. He and his family have moved and, though we will not be likely to see him very much, Don and I believe he will remain a part of our lives. We're glad for that. And we're thankful for the thoughts and prayers of friends from many parts of the world during this significant time.

Part Two

Metaphors for Transformation

7
The Tin Man:
Putting the Heart Back in Business
Richard J. Biederstedt

8
Quest for Spirit
Magaly d. Rodriguez

9
Soul Transformation:
Learning from our Dreams
Michele Bleskan

10
Soul Loss in the Kingdom
of Great Busyness
Colleen Burke and Lois Hogan

This segment of our collection contains metaphorical approaches to soulful work. Through the use of storytelling, dreams,
and fairy tales, these four chapters each contribute a unique
perspective to the reader's heart and soul.

These essays and stories appeal to the less linear part of
us—void of charts, models, and processes. They offer the reader
an unusual passage to understanding the human needs of

work—the needs that exist so as to satisfy the complete human being—body, soul, mind and heart.

This segment can be an adventure—like when a child is read tales of princes and princesses—so you may want to begin it in an open and receptive state of mind, similar to the innocent child who hears the classic fairy tale.

Richard J. Biederstedt has fifteen years' experience in streamlining and reorganizing companies, ranging in size from Fortune 100 to start ups, to improve their profits and increase employee satisfaction. This knowledge led to the creation of his own company, Transformational Business Solutions, which was designed to improve a company's operations while creating a positive environment for employee involvement. It utilizes combinations of business theories and common sense to create lasting changes.

His writing career started when he composed music review articles for a newspaper within the Knight-Ridder group. He is currently working on three soon-to-be-published books, *If Common Sense is so Common, How Come I Can't Find It Anywhere?*, *Ten Steps to Problem Solving*, *The Tin Man—Finding a Heart in Business*, and *Shaman—The Inner Journey*.

He is a graduate of the United States Air Force Academy and received an MBA from the University of North Dakota.

7

The Tin Man:
Putting the Heart Back in Business

Richard J. Biederstedt

Like the Tin Man from the Wizard of Oz, business has seemingly lost its heart. Decisions affecting the lives of each employee are made based upon stockholder opinions, executive management hunches, or the politics of the boardroom. Too often, these decisions are spurred on by the desire to increase corporate profits or maximize executive earnings at the expense of the individual worker. Not that profits or making a lot of money are bad—but at what cost?

The real heart and soul of any business is the nonmanagement employee who comes to work and performs the same tasks day after day. Typically unknown by anyone higher than their immediate supervisor, these workers bear the brunt of dealing with processes that are out of control, management that is out of touch, and a system designed to ignore their input.

This has to change if companies want to mean more than just a paycheck for their employees. Employees want to feel needed; they truly want to make an impact and know that what they do counts for something. Letting them participate in the business decision-making process will not only increase the loyalty an employee feels towards the company, but will help give the company a collective "heart."

Given the nature of the business world today, this is what

would happen if the Tin Man went to visit the Wizard of Oz in today's business climate.

Tin Man: I'm looking for the Wizard of Oz; he's going to give me a heart.

The Royal Guard: Do you have an appointment?

Tin Man: No, but I'm long overdue. I desperately need to get a heart.

The Royal Guard: Okay, fill out this appointment request form, go over to the Munchkin Building and have a seat. They'll give you a client identification number, a priority class, and a tentative meeting time.

Tin Man: Can't I just see him now?

The Royal Guard: You could if you were Someone. Let's face it, you're just a Tin Man. Maybe if you were like this Dorothy character we saw a few years ago you could get in. The Wiz saw a return on investment with her immediately; man, that girl could sing. Not much fashion sense though. Seems like no matter what style or color outfit she wore, she always used those same fancy ruby colored shoes. Anyway, do you have any special talents?

Tin Man: Not that I know of. I am a loyal, hard working person though.

The Royal Guard: Yeah...you and everyone else. Now move along, looks like an impatient lion behind you, don't know why he keeps cowering though.

Trudging over to the Munchkin building, the Tin Man thought about the conversation with the Royal Guard. He became filled with self-doubt. What did he really have to offer? Are the days of people being appreciated for who they are really gone? He hoped not. As he arrived at the building he saw a line two blocks long. Patiently, he took his position at the back of the line. Six hours later he finally talked to a clerk.

Tin Man: Hello, I'd like to make an appointment to see the Wizard about giving me a heart.

Clerk: Your name.

Tin Man: The Tin Man.

Clerk: Your occupation.

Tin Man: Self-employed.

Clerk: Annual salary.

Tin Man: What does that have to do with getting an appointment?

Clerk: These days, the higher the salary the more important you must be; therefore, the sooner the Wizard will talk to you. It's standard policy. Salary?

Tin Man: I don't work for salary, I do what I do because I want to help people.

Clerk: Too bad. You'll be waiting quite a while. Let's see, no salary, no REAL job other than helping people. Okay. Looks like your client appointment number will be 11063452.

Tin Man: What number is seeing the Wizard now?

Clerk: Eight thousand seventy-two. It should be about 12 months, give or take a couple of months. Depends on how many more important people than you come in and bump you further down the list.

Tin Man: Isn't there anything you can do to get me in sooner? The rainy season's about to start. I could be all rusted by the time I get in to see the Wizard.

Clerk: Listen, pal, I'm just doing my job. I get paid to follow the rules, not think. Just take your appointment slip and wait for your time to arrive. Geez, like I have time to listen to all you whiners.

The story of the Tin Man is representative of how many workers in today's society are viewed by both themselves and their management. The feeling that employees are nothing more than a resource needed to fulfill a larger business need is rampant. This attitude towards the very people who are crucial to making a business successful has created a work force without motivation, a management group without feelings and a business collective without heart.

So how do we change this attitude? It begins by going back to the basics of what life is all about. Not the basics of business, but the basics of life itself. No matter what the social status or income level, everyone on this planet is simply trying to get through life the best way they know how. We all struggle with the ups and downs of our existence on Earth and hope that somehow—through it all—we manage to do some good for the world. Remembering that we are all trying to cope will help us to understand why the people around us do the things they do. Understanding that life is not about what company makes the most profit, or who has the most money when they die, will help us create a better environment for both business and the employees.

It was 16 months before the Tin Man was able to finally get his appointment. While he waited for his day to arrive, he thought long and hard about what having a heart really meant. It struck him that he seemed to have more heart than either the Royal Guard or the Clerk at the Munchkin Building. They didn't care about anything except doing their job as they were told without regard for the other people they came in contact with. "What happened to their hearts?" he wondered. Were they born like this or did their jobs steal their very essence from them? And if they lost their hearts, why didn't they go to the Wizard themselves and ask for another one? These thoughts and more raced through his mind as he approached the Royal Guard.

Tin Man: I'm here as scheduled to see the Wizard.

The Royal Guard: Let me see your paperwork. Okay, everything seems to be in order. Come on in, but don't touch anything, don't talk to anyone, and no matter what you do, don't contradict anything the Wizard says or you'll never get your heart.

Tin Man: Thanks for your help. This means a lot to me.

The Royal Guard: Just doing my job. Frankly, it doesn't matter to me if you get your heart or not; I still get paid the same amount of money.

Tin Man: Don't you get any joy out of knowing you're helping people fulfill their needs?

The Royal Guard: At first, I guess so. Now, it's just a job. I'm not even sure the Wizard or anyone else here even knows my name, no one has ever asked me what it is. I remember when I first started this job, everything was exciting. I enjoyed meeting the people who were coming to see the Wizard. We'd talk, I'd get to know them and understand their hopes and dreams. The job was fun, I felt like I was part of something good. Then, after a couple of months I was told that I was spending too much time talking to people. I was told that if I only spent 30 seconds talking with each person and no more, that I could get through another 150 people a day and maybe get a promotion. My desire to advance took over. Now, I've got it down to spending only 18 seconds with each person. Probably just a coincidence but the number of people coming to see the Wizard has decreased by 40% since I quit talking to the visitors. At least I'm more efficient, even though now that customers know I can't take the time to talk to them they don't come here anymore. I'm still waiting for that promotion, though. Maybe I've lost my heart, too, and don't even know it. Anyway, good luck, Tin Man. You know, I'm not sure which one of us needs a heart more.

Tin Man: Thanks. By the way, what is your name?

The Royal Guard: It's Gabriel, thanks for asking.

Tin Man: You're welcome…Gabriel. It was nice talking to you, even if it was for more than 18 seconds. Seems I blew your average for today, but I enjoyed talking to you. Deep down, you're still that same man who likes talking to people; you just forgot, that's all.

As he turned to walk down the hall the Tin Man thought he saw small tear drops forming in the eyes of the Guard. The Guard somehow seemed softer, more human than he had before. It gave the Tin Man hope.

Putting the heart back in business is not as difficult or as hopeless a task as it might seem. A good start would be for a business to acknowledge that their employees are not mindless drones, and quit treating them as such. To do this, employees must be considered an integral part of the decision-making process as it affects their jobs. Unilateral changes that affect a person's life should not be made without, at the very least, an explanation of what is being changed and why. Too often, these types of decisions are implemented and the person who is most affected is the last to know or understand why changes are happening.

No one knows the details of a job like the person who must deal with it every day. Unfortunately, the further a person gets from the "line" jobs, the more decision-making power their position has over those jobs. This distance creates a lack of understanding about the consequences decisions will have, and creates an attitude in the mind of the employees that management simply doesn't care about them. This "management doesn't care" attitude creates the same "don't care" attitude in the employees about their jobs and the company. Soon, the employee has slipped into a "working only for the money" attitude, with no sense of loyalty, respect, or camaraderie for anyone or anything.

Several attempts at reversing this trend have been suggested. Employee empowerment is one of the most recent approaches in use today. The reason empowerment isn't as effective as it should be is not in its ideals, but in its execution. For many companies, empowerment means putting a suggestion box on the wall or asking for employee involvement in issues that have no real consequence or importance. The key to making an empowerment concept work is to provide not only the input into recommending changes but the power to actually make the changes suggested. When people are asked for input to a process and their input is ignored or constantly rejected, they will eventually stop contributing ideas. Once this switch from contributor to worker takes place, it takes a lot to win that employee back. Mistrust has replaced trust.

Too many of us assume that the higher the salary of an individual, the more intelligence and decision-making ability that person has. This is not the case. Ask those who have even been in the military and they will tell you that the people who make it work are the non-commissioned officers and enlisted personnel, who make far less money than their officer counterparts. The same is true in business. Executives may set the overall course for a business, but the company would go nowhere without the people who perform the daily tasks necessary to complete the job.

The Tin Man walked down the long corridor as directed. He couldn't help but notice that everyone he saw inside the building had a blank, emotionless stare about them, the same look the guard had at their first meeting. The employees all went about doing their jobs but said nothing. Occasionally, someone would look the Tin Man in the eyes, but then quickly turn away. Perhaps, he thought, they sensed his lack of a heart and it made them nervous.

The Tin Man finally reached the doors to the Wizard's office. They stood over 20 feet tall and had very ornate wood carvings all over them. "A great man must be behind these fancy doors," the Tin Man mused. Carefully he knocked on the door. With a loud creaking noise the doors parted and the Tin Man entered.

Tin Man: Hello your Wizardness, I'm here to see you about a heart. You see I need one very badly and...

Wizard: Silence! Say no more or I'll throw you out of here. Now, let me see your papers.

The Tin Man hands over the paperwork and waits.

Wizard: So you think having a heart will make you a better person? Better in what way?

Tin Man: It would allow me to have more understanding about people. I'll be better equipped to deal with people, motivate them, have more compassion, and be better in business or whatever else I do.

Wizard: There is no room for a heart in business. It's a cold, cold world. The goal is to be better than your competition, to beat out your peers for the next promotion either through hard work or politics, and to work your employees until they can't give any more to anyone. That's business! If you want to do something where a heart is needed, go be a starving artist, not a business person.

Tin Man: But look at you. You must have a heart to help all the people you do and run this city.

Wizard: All show, Tin Man. But you're right. I have plenty of heart, or should I say hearts. Anyone who works for me must give me supreme loyalty and put this company and me above all else, especially their own free will and their families. So yes, I guess you could say I DO have plenty of hearts...theirs.

The Wizard let out a deep, almost evil laugh. The Tin

Man turns to walk away.

Wizard: Where do you think you're going? We're not through talking. Say, you might be just the person I'm looking for to run my new marketing department. I need someone to soften up my image and make me more appealing to women and children. I haven't had much luck with those demographics since that Dorothy girl took her little dog and left town. Bad public relations, that one. Soon after she left I had every woman in town looking to go back home. Lost a lot of my workforce that way.

Tin Man: I don't think you can help me. Any heart you could give me would probably be stripped of the qualities I want.

Wizard: What qualities are those?

Tin Man: You know, compassion—a genuine desire to make people's lives easier, more fulfilled. Letting people know they are important to me and that everyone can make a difference. Giving back to people the kind of loyalty that they give me. You know, the more I think about it, the more I believe I already have a heart, I just didn't realize it.

Wizard: It's illegal to believe anything unless I authorize it first. You're in Oz now. If you aren't careful I'll have the guards take you away. A man like you is dangerous. But I'll make you a promise. If you leave and don't spread any of this needing a heart talk around, we'll call it even.

The Tin Man nodded his agreement and left the room, shutting the great doors behind him. On his way out he managed to speak with everyone he met. He told them he was starting a business of his own—one that was based on mutual respect and a willingness to let the people get involved and determine their own destiny on the job. He wasn't sure anyone was listening but by the time he got to the front door there were 603 people behind him.

So how do we put the heart and soul back into business? Like the Tin Man, all of us need to understand that, without basic compassion for each other, we are doomed to a society bound by class, salary, race, gender, or any other designator we choose to differentiate ourselves from our neighbor. Until we start to look at each other as members of the same family we will be doomed to an unfulfilled work life.

Ask yourself this: If I were only getting paid half of what I am today to do this same job, would I? Chances are, you answered "No." If this is true, then you understand why we have such a big problem. At the very least, work must be something that makes us feel good about ourselves and what we do. Have you ever found yourself looking at someone who makes more money than you but is in a job that is so miserable you wouldn't want it—even for the extra money? It's not the job that's bad, it's the environment surrounding the job.

So, what are some of the things that need to be changed to bring about a better environment and get businesses' hearts pumping again? Here are a few suggestions:

- Employees need to be considered an asset, not merely a resource. There is a difference. An asset is something that is valuable to the company, something that adds to the bottom line. A resource is simply the raw materials to be used to get the job done—a material to be used up and reordered when it's no longer useful. Unfortunately, most companies consider their people a resource, not an asset.

- Management must remove roadblocks for their people, not become the roadblock. Too many managers become so enamored of their titles that they assume they suddenly have supreme knowledge and power. Instead of being a help to their employees they unknowingly add stumbling blocks. Reports, job requirements, or reorganizations added just to show they are the boss only serve to diminish the employees' feeling of importance. Typically, when management does things that hurt a job's efficiency or productivity, it's the workers who are blamed. The usual reaction is for management to tell the workers to work harder.

- If your people are consistently having to put in overtime to get the job done, the problem is one of two things: Either the staffing for the job function is too low, or the processes used to fulfill the job's requirements do not work properly and must be corrected. The wrong approach is to require the workers to continuously work the extra hours, assuming that the employees will do it forever because they are happy just to have a job.

- Companies need to treat ALL employees with respect, consideration, and basic human dignity, not just those who are highly paid and wear fancy suits. There shouldn't be a direct correlation between the title or salary of an individual and the amount of respect we afford that person.

- Employees at every level must be provided access to making inputs and changes to the processes that affect their worklives. Without the ability to contribute to creating the job, how can we expect the employee to have ownership in it?

- Feedback on employees' ideas, even if it's negative, must be consistently provided. Employees don't mind being told that their ideas or suggestions were not implemented if they are told why not, and shown that some other way of doing the job is preferable. When the employee sees that some other way will make their life easier it won't matter whose idea it was as long as the understanding of what is happening is conveyed.

- The work environment has to become more employee friendly and less sterile. I've heard of companies that have a "No Plants, No Pictures, No Music, and No Personal Effects" rule. Talk about creating an environment where the employees feel like they are nothing more than a faceless cog in the wheel! If the work environment is warm, open, and friendly, the employees will be also. As the environment goes, the attitudes of the employees will follow. It's a direct mirroring relationship.

* * *

The Tin Man was determined to implement these types of changes into his business. On his way past the front door the Tin Man knew there was one more person he had to talk to.

Tin Man: Gabriel. I'm starting a new business. One that appreciates the individual. Would you like to come work for me? I can't pay you much, but I can give you back your freedom and sense of purpose. I'd like you to be in charge of ensuring that all my employees get back their hearts. Teach them to care again. Can you do that?

Gabriel: You know I can. Just give me a second. I need to leave a note. I've been waiting for this for the last 12 years.

As he left the Wizard's complex the Tin Man turned to see the hundreds of people who were following him out the door. "I may be on to something," he thought.

The following day Tin Man Enterprises was born. The company started into direct competition with the Wizard's business. Within the first 3 hours of operation Tin Man Enterprises managed to grab a 64 percent market share of the people looking to fulfill their desires. By noon the Wizard's business was placed in Chapter 11 bankruptcy. Upon hearing this news the Wizard stormed out of his office and went up to the front gate where the guard was supposed to be. No one was there. Instead, all he found was a note tacked to the inside of the door.

> *I've gone to find what you took from me so many years ago...*
>
> **My Heart**
>
> *You can send my final paycheck to Tin Man Enterprises. Or better yet, keep the money since it's all you seem to care about.*
>
> *Signed, Gabriel*

The Wizard clutched the note and sank to the ground. As he studied the note an awful feeling came over him. He had no idea who Gabriel even was.

In the background, the Wizard could hear the sounds of a song. It was "Tin Man" by America. Appropriately, the verse he heard had something to do with the Tin Man realizing that his heart was not something the Wizard had to give him but was there all along.

* * *

Business, like the Tin Man, needs to realize that its heart is still there. We just need to rediscover it, and let the magic of Oz take effect.

Magaly d. Rodriguez, MS has a varied background as a nun, missionary, mother, community builder with migrant workers, director of programs for race relations and the prevention of violence and drug abuse, and as a corporate founder/CEO.

Born in Cuba, her graduate work was in human resources, specializing in bilingual/bicultural education and counseling. Her expertise includes creating competitive environments that encourage creativity, diversity, business excellence, conflict resolution and intuitive, authentic leadership. Her corporate clients achieve significant turn-arounds in surprisingly short periods of time.

Rodriguez currently serves as CEO of Creative Breakthroughs, Inc., which she co-founded with Carol Ann Cappuzzo and Karen D. Lundquist. The trio specializes in accelerating values-driven corporate change.

8

Quest for Spirit

Magaly d. Rodriguez

No one could be more surprised than I at the turns on the path of my life's journey. I set out as a nun looking for global remedies for people in poverty. I wanted to eliminate hunger and build global peace and community. I searched for tools that would help people liberate themselves through strong working and caring relationships. Today, in manufacturing plants and senior management groups in global corporations, my colleagues and I address corporate spiritual hunger, create peace where there is conflict, and build community or teams.

One of my biggest learnings is that some of the same liberating tools that were effective at raising the quality of life in communities in poverty can quickly resolve serious conflicts, improve working conditions, and transform the bottom line in a struggling business! Breaking the strangle hold of hate-based factions over people in poverty, for example, is quite similar to breaking oppressive control mechanisms in manufacturing sites. Since operators appear to hold the same position in a company as people in poverty hold in society, what works with one works with the other. Only better, for there are tangible rewards for making effective change in a business.

Some of the tools my colleagues and I use to facilitate rapid change don't look corporate—nor do they look "serious"—for some may see them as too "feminine." *Though counterintuitive, these feminine/creative approaches have worked where nothing else has.* What our team has learned is that the soft intangibles of business life, things like trust, caring, and recognition, can speed change and improve the tangibles. When skillfully nurtured, the "software" of a business can bring surprising results in improved processes and bottom lines. Ours is a "disciplined feminine" approach that weds the arts and imagination technologies to cutting edge business systems and quality tools. Neither the creative side nor the business tools alone worked as well as both together. And, although it is a challenge to do so, we begin with the "soft" stuff.

Some years ago I was asked to help design a management conference for a business that was losing millions of dollars each month. The company participants were depressed and felt helpless to stop the hemorrhaging. In addition, the CEO of the parent multinational company had hinted at a possible sale of the business on Wall Street a few weeks prior to the conference. Participants arrived at the conference with spirits drooping. Given the seriousness of the challenge, the managers were quite surprised when I opened the meeting by reading a longer version of this fairy tale for them:

A Fairy Tale: The Compassionate Ones

Once upon a time there was a kingdom under siege from new enemies. They realized they were losing more of the challenges to their dominion than ever before. Those who advised the king ordered the use of all the known and proven approaches to solve the problems and regain the confidence of the people, but those approaches failed. Then they started new initiatives, using the logical consultants. And those new programs also failed. Through many cycles, efforts were redoubled. People exhausted themselves trying. Although ever more gold was thrown at the programs that were supposed to remedy the problems, nothing worked well enough, nor fast enough.

Now, the advisors did not inform the king of the seriousness of the situation, for they secretly questioned the king's ability to rule. They blamed him for getting them into this mess and were exceedingly afraid of the career consequences for themselves if they brought him bad news. Things continued to grow worse until the people of the realm were desperate. Would no one hear the pleas of the suffering? Would no one come to their aid?

Fortunately, the king had a dream. It happened after one of his anonymous walks (attired in peasant clothing) to talk to the people of the realm. He returned to the castle angry at his advisors who had not told him how serious matters were, and was extremely worried about what they should do. That night he fell into a troubled sleep and dreamt the answer to the Kingdom's ills.

In the dream he met a Wise One who assured him that the Kingdom could still be saved, but the measures that needed to be taken would be far different from any journey they had yet to imagine. Success on this journey would not come from using the old ways, weapons, and tools, nor from using old maps and beliefs. Success could only come from using the skills of "the Compassionate Ones."

The king—even in the dream—argued vehemently that neither he, his advisors, nor his subjects had been able to find a solution as yet. How could old legends of an enchanted people be of any aid? But the Wise One simply responded that even with an unlimited supply of gold, the old measures would not work. Even the new tools and strategies, though obviously good, could not work yet because they did not address the real problem.

"Then what is the real problem?" the king demanded. The Wise One smiled, saying that the king might find it hard to believe, but the problem was really a "matter of the heart." The kingdom was in trouble because it did not have the hearts of enough of the people anymore. The Wise One said that the missing ingredient, the activating agent that could make all the new strategies work, was the human heart. True success could only come from capturing and engaging the hearts of the people. "Contact the Compassionate Ones, for they know what to do." With that, the dream ended.

Because the logical ways were obviously no longer working, the king was open to the message of the dream. The next day he called his advisors together and told them about the advice of the Wise One. The king wanted them to immediately discover how to find these Compassionate Ones. After relating his tale, he waited for their response about capturing the hearts of the people.

The advisors were silent. Though their faces were passive, some were now totally convinced that the king was incompetent to rule. No one even knew if the Compassionate Ones were real! To be sure, there were legends—stories of individuals who once practiced a simpler, yet more disciplined way of life; stories of people who had found great joy in just being alive, in relating and working together, and whose word was sacred to them. The stories were of unconditional love, and listening ears, and people whose hearts were always open, yet were firm in their values and masters in their crafts. But the legends stated that these Compassionate Ones had hidden themselves, feeling sad and useless in a world that had turned from the disciplines and the magic of the heart.

The advisors were not impressed with the dream. How could these fabled people be of any aid—even if they could be found? The kingdom's problems demanded measures of power, money, and force, not soft, mushy approaches! Anyway, the advisors did not know what to do. This was certainly not their specialty. Why didn't the king ask for the creation of a new weapon, a new strategy for battle, a new steed to carry them to victory? Those things they felt they could manage. But the things of the heart! Who knew anything about that anymore? And of what possible use could it be?

So the kingdom and the advisors and the knights (the advisor's direct reports) simply went back to doing what they knew how to do. And there was no heart in it.

Though the king was saddened that no one supported him, he decided to act before things grew even worse. He sent messages to every part of the realm saying: The king searches for the Compassionate Ones, those who know of the ways of the heart. *He knew so little about these special people who possessed the ancient gifts, and he hoped they could be found in time to save the realm. The king sent his messages and waited.*

As long as the kingdom had existed, there had been fables, but no one now seemed to know how to find the Compassionate Ones. But the king persisted and, in time, his patience was rewarded when an old and wise woman who knew about the Compassionate Ones came to him. Studying with his new teacher, the king learned about the silent, secret call that could move the Compassionate Ones to come out of hiding and gather. Though he had feared that they were just legends, the king chose to act on faith and hoped that they would see the sign as it flashed across the sky. The wise woman had told him that the Compassionate Ones had an inner signal seeker that would alert them to the sign, so the king waited and hoped that they would respond.

When the signal flashed across the sky, something wonderful happened to more than just a few of the subjects in the realm.

Something happened inside. An inner door seemed to open, and a chord was struck in their hearts, stirring to the signal in the sky. The surprised ones felt new courage and strength, remembering things they never realized they knew. They found themselves moving toward an ancient meeting place to gather with the Compassionate Ones! That could only mean that they were a member of the ancient healers, the powerful ones who could change the course of history! They were Compassionate Ones!

"How could this be?" they asked one another as they traveled. "I am just a cook!" or, "I am a carpenter!" they protested. "I can't do anything special! I don't have any power! How could I be a Compassionate One?"

But the answer came as quickly as the question was asked. Sometime, somewhere they had opened their hearts to mystery as well as history. That opening had made a channel to a deep inner source of power. When the signal came, the door was already open and they responded joyfully. The new—and untrained!—Compassionate Ones realized that they knew of ways to access their power and could learn what to do from both outside coaches and inner knowing. But they needed to trust, for impatience or skepticism seemed to close the door again. Their new insights and power seemed to retreat in the face of stress or negativity.

Slowly, the early responders moved toward the gathering place. Among them were women and men of every race and nationality, as well as some who had never succeeded as knights and a sprinkling of leaders who loved risk taking and listened for both feelings and facts. Then came all manner of resourceful, sensitive and caring ones to plan what could be done to save the realm.

And as the group gathered—seeing the magnificent diversity and talents of those who came from every region and every occupation in the realm—there arose a great realization: Everyone in the kingdom had the power to be a Compassionate One! Those who did not respond to this first call simply had not yet opened the door to their hearts, but they possessed the same inner power as well.

The insight brought laughter, and dancing, and fun! In spite of being battered and bruised from their former lives—for their gifts had been considered unimportant—the new Compassionate Ones dreamed of a time when all people would open their hearts and learn its mysteries. They hoped that all people could feel their true inner power and become energized with spirit and enthusi-

asm. They saw visions of people really connecting, trying to understand and to work together. They saw lives changed and safe havens set up so that people didn't want to go back to the islands that they had once been. They saw strangers welcomed and women empowered....And they knew that there were many more potential Compassionate Ones and that there was much more magic available....But we get ahead of our story here. Let's go back....

As the Compassionate Ones made their way to the meeting place, the people of the realm hoped against hope that the kingdom could be transformed. They knew now that the legends were true and that there were many new members among the healers. This was unexpected—Compassionate Ones that had little experience. Would the new ones activate their powers quickly enough? Would they be open to what was already inside of them and willing to learn from exacting teachers? Would they be willing to practice in order to master the new (yet ancient) magic of the heart? Would they work to develop and maintain the environments required to trigger the gifts? The kingdom held its breath with anticipation, for the new disciplines were known to be quite demanding.

What happened? We don't know yet. The Compassionate Ones have only just gathered, and some of you are only now reading of your own hidden magic. *May your eyes see beyond the surface, and may your hearts remain open, for the destiny of the realm depends upon you.*

To be continued....

Results

Though this fairy tale may sound "touchy-feely," it got the attention of the amazed high-level managers attending the conference. Following the example of a values-driven senior vice president, they participated in experiences designed to stimulate imagination, reduce stress, bond teams, and clear toxic relationships. The very next month saw an "unexpected" five-million-dollar improvement. *The month after that, this business that had been losing millions for several months broke even.*

Although the emotional benefits of the conference could not be sustained without additional support systems, the experience proved that liberating-heart approaches could work. Since then, I have teamed with a set of talented colleagues and committed senior managers in selected businesses and have tested many new learnings. We've named the methods that liberate the heart "rapid change technologies" and have used them to help our clients engineer some amazing corporate transformations. A few examples are as follows:

> **Challenge:** Midsize company showing poor productivity.

> **Result:** In less than six months, productivity grew from 60% of total requirements to 98%.

> **Challenge:** Manufacturing plant faced with a ten-year-old hostile union–management environment, a pending strike, low productivity, and a planned closing within 5 years.

> **Result:** In less than one year, productivity soared 50%, quality service was at 98%, safety noted only one minor injury, and new products ensured the existence of the plant beyond the year 2000.

> **Challenge:** A large plant in a Fortune 10 company facing a hostile environment and a possible phase-down of activities.

> **Result:** Within nine months, the plant was benchmarked as having the second highest rate of positive change in the world. Inventory and hazardous waste were both reduced by 30%. Fixed costs were reduced by 20%. The union–management relationship became one of cooperative involvement in the turn-around.

> **Challenge:** Managers in a mill in the South feared a work stoppage as part of negotiating a new contract .

> **Result:** Within weeks, they achieved a mutual agreement in the contract for cooperative employee involvement in High Performance Work Systems.

Returning to the story of the Compassionate Ones, you might think, "Surely a fairy tale can't do all that!" True enough. When the emotional high wore off, managers who had tried the new ways found that under stress, they went back to the old track of power struggles and control, far from the path of the heart. Soon, people lost faith again and the losses returned. Though many factors were involved, evidence seemed to support a strong correlation between morale and the bottom line.

Discouraged, I asked myself how traditional managers who seemed open to change could learn faster.

They needed more empowering behaviors for credibility to support a challenging new business paradigm. Though I was skilled in emotionally moving crowds to action from my community days, at the time of the fairy tale I had not yet solved the question of what to do when the emotion wore off. The daily toxic behaviors of leaders undermined the new path with abuses of power—often quite unconsciously!

A Retrospective

Probably inspired by the romanticism surrounding the Cuban Revolution in the 1950s and heartbreaking experiences on the border of Haiti, I had always wanted to make a real difference in the world. I wanted to make large-scale, fast, and irreversible change where it seemed impossible. Originally, I sought remedies that were powerful enough to significantly improve violent, hostile, or severely impoverished regions. Later, the goal was expanded to include tools for transforming corporations, due to their critical position in the world. I searched for remedies that:

- are quick and effective in healing small groups, large organizations, or geographical regions;
- are accessible to everyone, not high-cost, and don't require "experts" or formal education;
- are globally acceptable, easy to learn and share;
- strengthen courage, caring, and community;
- reduce hostility and violence;
- are portable, not dependent upon a location, a structure, or a machine;
- are deep, transforming, and not easily reversible.

Impossible? Perhaps. But I knew they had to exist, for the quest had already unearthed many tools that sparked interest and hope in depressed people, though they did not yet work well enough to sustain beneficial change.

Fortunately, the continuing search had prepared me to meet Carol Ann Cappuzzo in 1981. She opened a whole new world of human possibilities. As a gifted intuitive and master teacher, Carol Ann's work was cited in both the national television program "That's Incredible" and *Superlearning,* a book by Sheila Ostrander and Lynn Schroeder. In her "Project Blind Awareness," Carol Ann taught blind adults and children to "sense" more. Sharpening innate skills gave blind participants greater awareness of their surroundings as well as a greater sense of safety and self.

Carol Ann's experience in personal transformation seemed a logical fit with my experience in group transformation. Our combined skills were soon adapted to helping managers and employees in corporations embrace deep change.

Though we needed credibility in corporations to support global transformation goals, we were still quite handicapped, for Carol Ann and I had no business experience. Our clients were much like the Compassionate Ones, with antennae to hear our messages in spite of the exclusively rational (and male) environments they worked in daily. Though we could accelerate deep change in people, it was hard to explain our methods to those outside of our client circle.

Thus, when Karen D. Lundquist appeared, we were ready for her. With Karen we now had a trio that could credibly and creatively facilitate transitions in any size business we chose to serve. An engineer by training, Karen was a top-rated manager in one of the largest corporations in the world. While a plant manager, she called me and Carol Ann into a mid-sized manufacturing plant experiencing severe labor–management challenges. With her courageous insistence on the use of the rapid-change tools, as well as her considerable skills in engineering, quality, and business systems, that midwest plant leaped onto a whole new level of functioning and 330 jobs were saved. We were thrilled when the plant overcame questions about its future, became a benchmark even for a Japanese manufacturer, and surpassed other, much newer plants as well.

Karen left a promising fast track in that multinational company, and joined me and Carol Ann in the consulting world. Karen's arrival marked a dramatic improvement in the success rate of our work, for she brings outstanding business disciplines and the skill to explain our methods to business people. In addition, she demonstrated the power of the disciplined feminine tools in the face of extreme challenges. The rapid-change technologies sped good ideas into action at her plant and channeled the energy of teams into the work rather than into resisting change. The results included improvements in the lives of the workforce and the generation of more than seventy-five million dollars in additional sales.

Today our team follows a plan for business transformation that uses rapid-change tools at every step.

The first issue faced in making transformational change in a company is how to send a "signal" that alerts people to a new "work magic" business paradigm and to the "more" inside of each of them. People in business have been through change before. Many feel burned and have seen enough "programs of the week" to question and ignore even important initiatives. We find that the proposed change must be based in deeper values and have staying power beyond the times and into the eternities, to paraphrase Henry David Thoreau. Somehow we must gather the corporate Compassionate Ones who may not know how to activate their own magic yet, or who have been squelched when they tried to use it.

It's a challenge. Whatever is done must be heard above the cacophony of information overload, communication static, and long standing fears. The signals, the skills, and the tools we use underline:

- that people can learn and change faster, easier, and with more fun;
- that each person is responsible for the human environment around them and for excellent work;
- the power of the mind and intuition;
- the importance of intangibles such as love, trust, truth, and beauty in business life;
- that we all have a purpose and that it can benefit our families, our businesses, and the world;
- that empowering one another works better than enemy-making; and
- the benefits of personal depth change.

Five Steps to Rapid Change

After years of testing, we have concluded that there are five steps to meaningful rapid change:

1. Relieve distress by creating emotional safety. We share tools and facilitate inspiring experiences that allow managers to demonstrate their commitment to changing their own dysfunctional behaviors. Employees often shake their heads, saying, "I would not believe this if I had not seen it myself!"

2. Enrich people's environments. Business environments become more colorful. Visuals decorate the walls, communications are more interesting and honest. People discuss feelings openly, diversity adds energy to the workplace, and meetings are more inspiring and fun. Training is more learner-centered and presenters are encouraged to "spice up" and involve participants in their presentations!

3. Grow leaders bigger. Leaders in one company took the risk of developing their passionate, disciplined, and authentic sides. Learning how to live their values and "hold their centers" under stress, they insist upon responsible behavior and excellent product from both themselves and others. The workforce responded with higher productivity and breakthrough accomplishments. These managers continue to learn how to both inspire and set appropriate boundaries.

4. Commit to sound business *and* people practices. Managers are challenged to adopt state-of-the-art business disciplines that complement the people disciplines of the first three steps. One company that uses business systems tools on the tangible side, and imagination technologies and creativity tools on the intangible side, healed the rift between employees and management and turned a profit in five months—after seven years of losses!

5. Take ideas to action quickly. Action must include both tangibles and intangibles, supporting both the recognized, concrete approaches of quality, for example, as well as addressing areas such as feelings and morale. One site that clearly honored intangible values, as well as numerical goals, made dramatic changes in less than a year while having a lot more fun! Managers prioritize emotional safety and contrary opinions, and they value ideas that improve tasks as well as relationships. With improved morale, managers find that excellence and discipline are more easily embraced.

One of our clients saw how matters of the heart can empower or destroy the workplace. In just six months, there were more than $110 million of bottom line improvements. The identified intangibles which added energy to the environment included optimism, sincerity, honesty, bonding, and enthusiasm. Then leaders addressed what drained the business of its vitality:

intangibles that included manipulation, suspicion, inflexibility, negativity, and prejudice. It had been hard to change red to black on the balance sheets without a good spirit in the organization. But with heart, even very difficult tasks became a rewarding adventure and the business is now out of danger.

At this point on my quest for spirit, I enjoy a partnership with powerful women who also believe in the human soul. When heard and responded to, the soul has a way of healing itself and its surroundings. At first, people seem to grow quiet inside, considering. Then excitement builds and they change. When this change is reflected in the behavior of enough individuals (or shown significantly in the behavior of even a few), groups can transform and their interactions become healthier and more effective. With success based on a heart paradigm, business leaders can more easily commit to values that transcend profit.

The work of helping people become accelerated, joyful learners is truly a matter of the heart—whether in families, communities, or corporations. It is important to me. I am grateful for the opportunity to work with colleagues and clients who are committed to the soft, compassionate side of life. We delight in engaging the hearts of people in a business—and then watching those numbers turn around!

Michele Bleskan is the principal of Partnership for Transformation, a Minnesota-based company specializing in executive development, individual and organization transformation, and change management.

Bleskan has 15 years of experience designing and incorporating humanistic processes, most recently as a senior consultant at American Express. Previously, she held management positions at First Bank Systems and Dayton Hudson Corporation. In her role as a spiritual teacher she also conducts workshops on anger and grief, nature retreats, and an executive development program entitled The Essence of Leadership, A Spiritual Journey.

A graduate of the University of Minnesota, Bleskan has studied psychology and industrial relations and is now preparing for advanced work in transpersonal psychology.

Soul Transformation: Learning from our Dreams

Michele Bleskan

Dream Time Part I

In the car with Elizabeth and my son Ryan, heading to the career counselor's home, I took a wrong turn. The town was not far from my childhood home, and I thought I would remember the way. It was not long before I realized that this was a difficult trail and we were not on the right road.

The trail led up and down steep dangerous ravines. We came upon some sort of mine or rock quarry, with people wandering and working. I spotted a woman and I called out to her but she kept on walking. A man came toward me but I said, "No, I want to speak with the woman." I needed to ask her where we were and how we could leave this place.

She had on headphones, the type to muffle harsh sounds and intrusions, as the noise from the rock blasting and the machinery grinding was horrendous. She reluctantly approached the car and I asked, "How can we be released from here?" She responded with disdain and contempt. Angry that I had interrupted her from leaving the quarry, she blurted out bitterly, "I have to get home." Then she stomped away.

Cars began speeding out of the quarry like a scene from the Dukes of Hazard. I became certain there was a way out of here if

I just followed the workers back to the town. As I stepped back into the car, men approached in a menacing manner, and we fumbled to lock the doors and sped away.

Around the sharp bend in the road, directly in front of me, was a huge rock wall, man-made with large sharp slabs of granite, in a steep and narrow pitch—life-threateningly steep.

I made one attempt to drive up the rock wall but my four-wheel drive was not engaged and we rolled back. Terror filled us as we expected to topple over. We did not, and I regrouped at the bend in the road. I thought to myself, "If these workers got out this way, so can we." I spotted one car taking this road and I was convinced it was also our way home. Once again, I attempted the wall, locking in the four-wheel drive this time. We climbed straight up the wall, still fearing it would crumble beneath us and we would tumble to our death. It worked. I steered my way along the wall by being clear on my intent and not distracted by other aspects of operating the car. Amazingly, I did not have to operate the gas pedal or shift gears. It appeared that the car was self-powered. Most importantly, I was not to think of how big a feat this was, or fear would overtake me and we would fall off.

It occurred to me how well this was going, how effortless. "Just steer," I said to myself, "keep it on the narrow path and you will make it." Then I thought of my passengers, captive on this adventure: Ryan committed and engaged, seeming fearless; and Elizabeth huddled in the back seat frozen in terror. I had led her on this dangerous journey rather unintentionally, or so I thought. "How are you, Elizabeth? I am so sorry you are afraid." She said nothing. I stopped the car and we embraced, relieved to have escaped. We were shaken but unhurt.

Soul transformation can often occur when one takes a wrong turn. We think we know the right road home to our authentic self, but it often is our ego's deception of fame, glory, and power. Can a wrong turn become a right road home to the true self? Arduous and frightful at times, it can certainly transform us.

But what is soul? Words are meaningless to adequately describe it. By its very nature, soul is beyond words. Viewed as the essence of who we are, soul lies outside time and space, with no form except its physical manifestation through human beings. Soul is that part of us that extracts experience and meaning out of our daily events. It judges not failures or successes as the ego personality does, but considers all events and outcomes as rich material for composing life.

Dreams help reveal our inner life, our deep unconscious and conscious workings. They serve as a mirror to our deeper needs and desires, claimed and unclaimed. Honoring your dreams honors your own unique process as a complex human and spiritual being. This dream mirrored many aspects of my journey. A journey to find my place and my Self, within the stone and granite walls of organizational life. So many of our inner resources are required in our work roles. And, while the organization exhausts the narrow parts of us we do bring to its door, it paradoxically does not ask enough of us. Time is the largest apparent sacrifice as we spend the majority of our waking hours within the organizational structure. Every day, we bring our skills and abilities, our professional expertise, and our political savvy to the hallowed halls of our jobs.

Corporate Qualities of the Untransformed Soul

Why is it so important to heal and transform at the soul level at work? Repressed emotions and fears can be seen in very visible ways within today's corporations. Fear of failure and judgment lead us to check our talents and gifts at the gate each morning. The corporation does not know how to deal with such diversity. Issues of unresolved separation from our parents translate into dependency within the workplace, justifying hierarchical, paternalistic management systems. Repressed childhood abuse yields elaborate control and defense postures between colleagues. In fact, at the heart of organizational dysfunction is the elusive attempt to regain this lost safety. Shame and unworthiness lead to the sense that we will never measure up— leaving us to struggle for interconnectedness through seeking status and power. These are just a few of the many examples of why vitality and aliveness are absent for many in the workforce.

These unhealthy behaviors are demonstrated over and over again, in spite of the organizational trends toward wholeness: holistic principles of empowerment, quality, accountability, models of team formation, core process redesign, and renewed client service. The true behaviors that should manifest from these principles do not. For within those granite walls, the prevailing norms and behaviors are to conform, not create; to deliver results regardless of the cost to the individuals; and to maintain collective denial instead of acknowledging the truth. Fear and anxiety run high. The balance between work and home life is elusive. The double message to share power and authority within the hierarchy is disconcerting. Individuals are forced to find or create their own unique paths to fulfillment.

Restoration of the Natural Resources

As the dream so crudely depicted, the organizational machinery and methods to extract the richness from the natural resources were primitive and harsh. So, too, are the measures employed to mine the human potential in today's organizations. Companies have not learned the valuable lesson of expending reasonable effort to replenish their most valuable resource—the people.

Elizabeth, a business communication professional, found she could no longer deaden herself from hearing, nor digest the greed-based messages instilled by the culture where she was employed. She hungered for a higher level of integrity in her environment than that which was demonstrated by the large regional bank where she had worked for seven years.

Elizabeth endured great pain as she struggled to find the path home to her true self. Transformation required her to brace against the harshness of the company, use it as a force to shape, define, and fire up her soul as she struggled to claim her gifts. Eventually, she left the bank to form a consulting practice. She never gave up hope for her former employer—who is now a client of hers. She is now a better teacher from the outside and has helped the bank create the humane culture she had always desired. The noise of the machinery is no longer deafening in Elizabeth's world—now full of vitality and authenticity.

The dream mirrored my journey to authenticity. For many years of my career I found myself behaving as one of the men, separated from my feminine self, seeking validation from external measures and power structures. I dressed in the corporate male uniform, a navy blue suit with a button-down-collar shirt. More importantly, I masked confidence with aggressive enforcement of company policies and practices. I was a hardened administrative bureaucrat. Getting up in the morning and coming in to work was brutal. I was so internally conflicted, not realizing I had betrayed my true self in this pursuit to become a successful corporate citizen. This internal struggle continued for some years. Only later did I realize how bitter and hardened I had become. As in the dream, rock quarry walls within and around me shielded my true identity.

Forced Transformation: A Major "Wrong Turn"

If not for a personal health crisis, I may never have confronted the aspects of my self that were separated from my feminine self. Working in a patriarchal system, I had learned to deaden myself from the harsh environment. Yet, feeling alienated in the world of male patriarchy, I continued to receive deep intuitive and physical messages from my body: This was not the right place for me. "Seek your true path and identity," they whispered. How long could I ignore their urgings?

Being unaware of the personal cost of denial was dangerous. Like the woman in the dream, I needed the courage to move forward to find the road home. I had to traverse the rock wall, not once, but twice—achieving success only when I engaged my power and intent.

These men and women in my dream were my unformed Selves awaiting transformation. At first glance, that seemed so far from possible.

If organizations are unable to foster or support the human soul in their current restrictive environments, how can those who remain hope to enable such a transformation? Certainly those who yearn for authenticity and self-actualization do not all have to leave their jobs and start their own businesses. Some men and women can and do remain inside, and are fully engaged working to make a difference, but from the inside out. I've worked with two such people: Rick and Kris.

Rick and Kris are creatively talented professionals who have engaged their superb skills and expertise to redesign how their financial service firm meets and exceeds the needs of its clients. For them, the structure of corporate life provides a powerful force of energy from which to create and innovate. They clearly see the obstacles, and the deficiencies, of their firm. The machinery and methods of the organization are seen as transformable, given time and ingenuity. What makes them or their story different from Elizabeth's and mine?

Kris is quite a fireball—a woman with light and spark in her eyes. In her role as a manager of client advisory boards, she uses her creative flair to better understand what her clients want and expect. She is as quick to burst out in laughter as to explode in outrage. Kris demands a fresh look at all she touches, and the organization more than tolerates her, they leverage her passion for the client.

Only from a position inside could she play such a pivotal role in awakening and redirecting the internal focus. She serves as a challenger of assumptions by bringing in real clients and prospects to comment and critique the marketing and sales practices and products. Maybe this is not the cutting edge in today's world, but it has transformed her organization and her livelihood.

Rick is one of the emerging new leaders, engaging and warm, the new male role model of the '90s. A family man with strong traditional values, Rick was involved as a member of a hand-selected team. In that role, Rick worked to redesign how the company interfaces with its clients. Beyond redefining the organization's systems and processes, he helped struggling leaders recreate relationship-oriented business practices. The transformations were painful for these task-oriented leaders.

As leaders redefine themselves in the coming decades, through role models such as Rick and Kris, we can expect much to change, and have hope that the emergence of soul will be nurtured and fostered by these new leaders and the power structures they form.

Dream Time Part II

A group of women was held captive in the same area of the quarry. We were required to receive our work instructions and directions from a man acting as the gatekeeper. He was vigilant about his role and I was irritated with having to ask and wait for him to allocate what I needed and wanted.

On one occasion I grabbed a package addressed to me before the gatekeeper could handle and distribute it. He found out and confiscated the package to punish me, and would now prohibit me from receiving any further deliveries. I was furious, then apologetic. Neither approach was successful. He refused to have his eminent role be questioned or circumvented.

An old man approached me and I began telling him about the treatment bestowed upon us by the gatekeeper. The old man owned the land where this quarry stood. He explained how jealous the gatekeeper was of my closeness to the old man and that the gatekeeper was really a very insecure and unhappy person who takes his role and function as his identity. "Well," I said, "he's also cruel." Often he kept essentials like food and nourishment from the women. Our own unique gifts would be screened and judged, more often than not unfavorably. The old man assured me that this behavior was beyond his role at work and not acceptable.

He then drew my attention away from my complaints and changed the subject to a more serious matter. For it seemed our next assignment, a critical mission for mankind, was here in front of us. It appeared that underneath us, at this very spot, the planet was building up such pressure that we needed to drill deep and release the pressure. The planet at any time could implode beneath us, and our very existence would be threatened. The group of women working in the quarry were requested to go on this mission. But I wondered, what did we know about the earth's pressure and how to release it immediately and effectively?

The old man asked us for something of much greater significance than we envisioned for ourselves. My feeling of inadequacy immediately surfaced, and I tried to avoid this deeper engagement in life by whining about the injustices we had experienced in our workplace. Some of the common expressions of suppression of our soul's vitality are just such bitterness, blame, complaint, rationalization and pity.

Neglecting my inner transformation only damaged me in the process. I did not fan and keep alive the flames of my interior fire; thus my vitality and aliveness smoldered deep within me. Like the earth's pressure, it was required that I dig deep and relieve the pressure, making room for the fire below and my fuller expression of self.

Process of Transformation

If the deep personal work required to discover soul and define self is not facilitated by the organization, or is marginalized at best, how does one follow the quest to satisfy this yearning for purpose within the granite walls and still fulfill work obligations? The process I followed, and observed in others in the workplace, was simple at first glance, but difficult to do and powerfully effective.

Emotions

Reaching the soul level requires acknowledging and expressing what we feel. For me the journey into this place was the most painful passage I had encountered in my lifetime. The tragic death of my daughter in January, 1993, catapulted me into the deepest emotional wounding and healing imaginable. My emotional healing from childhood neglect and abuse had begun years earlier, but culminated in this darkest of pains—the loss of my child.

For most, such tragic losses do not occur, but, sooner or later, the trapped energy of unresolved emotions will emerge and run your life in unconscious ways. We may hope that we can keep old emotions all trapped and contained forever, but healing past wounds is a prerequisite for emotional health, and being present to the emotional realities of your current life is the daily homework for emotional well-being. When our true feelings are suppressed, we lose touch with our real needs.

Being emotionally connected to what I was feeling was the beginning of my soul transformation. Emotional health is the ultimate goal for the following reasons:

- The heart, not the intellect, provides access to an authentic soulful life. Being truly who we are, and true to our emotions, is acting from the heart. One caution here is, misuse of emotions without the balance of objectivity can distort reality and drain us of our vitality and peace of mind.

- Feeling our emotions enlivens us, restoring vitality and the love for life. Releasing emotions in healthy ways is a lifelong process, expressed clearly without manipulation or control.

- You can no longer separate yourself from the pain and injustices in the world, nor the pain of others, when you are emotionally healthy. You will seek to alleviate others' pain in clear and healthy ways. Furthermore, because you now own your own feelings, you will be more likely to give assistance selflessly versus selfishly.

Since I began this conscious journey to wholeness, I have realized a new level of happiness and fulfillment never before present in my life. I feel radiant and alive. Not everyone is comfortable with my self-actualized behaviors. Yet, as I become authentic, more people connect with me, making my life richer and deeper.

This newfound access to my Self, and to those in organizations in which you live and work, will have far-reaching implications for furthering organizational change. When one operates from the heart, daily existence is full of color. No longer are events and experiences just black and white. No longer will decisions be made without fully considering the human implications. Results will be weighed against the human cost required to deliver those results. Blending this heartfelt approach with the well-developed intellect can unleash unlimited human potential for the world at large.

Being vs. Doing

The path to transformation requires a great deal more solitude and self-reflection than is popular within the American culture. In addition to your public and private life demands, the time for Self needs to be diligently allocated and cherished. In this state of BEING, you produce nothing concrete, but free something of much greater value. Allow yourself this time. Create space for the bigger you to emerge. It is in these quietest of moments that your soul will speak to you.

A close relationship with silence and stillness is critical to creating vitality in our life. Eastern culture has long honored the traditions of contemplation and self-reflection. In that culture, inner silence is valued and necessary to achieve emptiness, which for Westerners can be seen as psychological death. Our strong attachment to individualization does not appreciate the feeling of "not knowing" who we are, which emptiness brings. Paradoxically, it is often through experiencing the non-self that we begin to learn who the real self is.

The emptiness and unknowing conjures up the sum of our fears of the personality. Our illusions of safety and immunity from death shatter. We are forced to see what's in our present life and grieve for what's not. Only then can we have the possibility of awakening. Only then can we embrace BEING unsure of who we are.

Depending upon your life circumstance, this reflection time may be one day of one week, one week of a year, or one weekend each month. Go alone and give yourself permission to experience the silence. Allow the fatigue to sweep over you—the exhaustion that is so deep and submerged that you hardly are aware of it most of the time. Allow the questions to emerge, even the most difficult ones. Remember that your discovery of true self is not a problem to solve, so just allow the discomfort to BE. There is nothing you have to do but to breathe, feel, and heal. These are all very tangible acts, though none are concrete or measurable. At first return, you will feel more uncertainty than you've ever let enter before.

Connections to the Earth

Many of us live in urban settings and commute to concrete jungles, where we fulfill our daily work requirements. For me, the separation from the natural settings of forests, farmlands, lakes, and streams of my childhood was unnatural and artificial. The separation from my true self paralleled this separation from the earth.

It is as important for us to know Self in relationship to the earth, as it is to know Self relative to our workplace. Unless we do, our separation and disconnection from the earth can devastate us and the planet. When one perceives the earth as a treasure—upon whose viability we depend—we then know our lives are as intertwined as the air we breathe and the ground we build our lives upon.

My journeys to solitude and self-reflection, for the most part, took place in natural settings outside of the city where I work and live. In these places of grace and beauty, I felt the pain of the earth. I became more aware of my needs and dreams as I became more aware of the planet's. I would lie upon her mantled breast, and feel the warmth of her surface envelop and draw me closer for healing.

When there is no kinship with the earth, policies and mandates with world-wide implications can easily be made which negatively impact the earth's sustainability. As you heal and go deeper, the earth plays a significant role in the journey; then, and only then, can you authentically reach out to impact your community, your nation, and the planet in a soulful and caring manner.

Corporate Qualities of the Transformed Soul

Organizations are powerful forces of manifestations. As institutions, their ability to harness ideas and energy and create concrete products or processes are unparalleled. Their role in the world cannot indefinitely choose profit over stewardship of the planet. Organizations are a collection of individuals who, en masse, can heighten the consciousness and awareness of this larger organizational purpose. Organizations have a collective soul awaiting transformation, as an aggregate of each individual's quest for purpose and meaning. My view is to transform the organization by transforming the individuals who make up the population, one person at a time.

It takes a solid foundation of trust in Self and trust in others to truly empower the workforce. Personal insecurities and feelings of inadequacy often preclude a leader from sharing herself in any real manner, let alone sharing critical information that might foster independence versus dependence.

A colleague of mine, Catherine, did justice to herself and her organization by enabling such information sharing. Catherine's vision for the electronic media department she leads is to provide the necessary technology to communicate information to the masses of employees. She understands that information is power and that, historically, this information had not been widely shared. But she also knows that employees need critical information to make sound decisions. Catherine was wise enough to know that her vision needed senior management sponsorship; so she strategically educated senior management and gathered that support. This vision will have dramatic results within the organization over the next three to five years. She is a master in her field, but more so a transformative leader in her understanding of the human need for information and communication. Sharing of power is a quality of the enlightened leader.

Another associate, Rebecca, has no problem acting from her heart. As a leader in executive development, Rebecca is required to design and deliver leadership programs with impact. She is only too aware that to impact leaders in a meaningful manner, her designs need to embrace the heart of the leaders she teaches, so they may further impact and reach the hearts of the employees they lead. It is a delicate balance for this audience of hard-driving, results-oriented men and women. As a group, they can be very disinterested in the "soft" skills, and are much more comfortable with task-specific skill building.

I have had the opportunity to report to this woman and can speak firsthand about the environment she creates and the behaviors she models and elicits from her team. It has been a long dry spell between this caliber of leader and the average leaders we follow for most of our careers. But the quality and quantity of energy I feel her foster within the environment is unprecedented in my corporate career. Stories like these impart such hope for this organization, given the heart that has emerged throughout the entire leadership curriculum. The impact has already been noted in the short time since the training has been introduced. The streamlining of heart and power through information sharing are just two examples of a multitude of efforts in this organization's journey towards transformation.

These stories of transformative leaders demonstrate a creative approach to living and teaching. Each leader has beckoned the soul of their client to awaken—to elicit meaning, richness, and color through events and experiences. They have transformed this raw energy into productive, effective, and innovative techniques, to achieve the organizations' goals and exceed clients' expectations. The globally competitive environment requires such creativity and innovation; corporations will continuously need to make room for a little more soul within their walls.

Conclusion

In the dream, the old man had a message. His message was to view our lives from a larger context, to embrace a world view, to reframe our petty complaints within a larger and more important world context. I hope his message will help us to step outside our selfishness and consider Self in relationship to others, to shift from a fear-based culture to a culture of authentically empowered and vital people. His message for all of us is to drill deep within ourselves so we may release the pressure and pain of past wounds, giving room to the soul's fire below—expanding our access to Self. Only then, with this newfound capacity, can we transform our organizations and sustain a peaceful and empowering existence.

Colleen Burke (left) first entered the Kingdom of Business in 1968 when, fresh out of Vassar College, she became one of the first women MBA's at Harvard. She was the first woman to integrate the university dorms and to storm the all-male fortress of the Harvard Clubs. Burke has been an award winning professor of business and was published by Harvard in *Educating for Judgment: The Artistry of Discussion Leadership*. She has written for the *World Business Academy Perspectives* and was profiled in the book *Merchants of Vision*. A writer, entrepreneur, professor and consultant, she has woven multiple careers around the single parenting of her son. Currently her time is dedicated to facilitating Arthur Andersen & Co. in visioning it's future and to pursuing the study of mythology at Pacifica Graduate Institute.

Lois Sekerak Hogan (right) has had a lifelong interest in soul and spirituality. She is strongly influenced by the ideas of Carl Jung, working with the inner world of dreams and images. For her, the creative processes of art, poetry, and music offer significant opportunities for enhancing individual and organizational wholeness. Professionally a management consultant, she specializes in helping organizations enhance communications and build relationships. Her vision is to weave the practical concerns of business with the principles of depth psychology. This synthesis is the focus of her current doctoral studies in human and organizational development at Fielding Institute. She keeps soul alive in her life by being receptive to serendipitous moments of depth and beauty.

10

Soul Loss in the Kingdom of Great Busyness

Colleen Burke and Lois Hogan

When geometric diagrams and digits
Are no longer the keys to living things,
When people who go about singing or kissing
Know deeper things than the great scholars,
When society is returned once more
To unimprisoned life, and to the universe,
And when light and darkness mate
Once more and make something entirely transparent,
And people see in poems and fairy tales
The true history of the world,
Then our entire twisted nature will turn
And run when a single secret word is spoken.

—Novalis
(Translated by Robert Bly)

nce upon a time, in a kingdom not very far away, there lived an aging king who daily agonized over the peculiar suffering of his people. During his reign and the reign of his fathers before him, the kingdom experienced extraordinary abundance. Yet, the people grumbled from an emptiness they felt and a hunger for even more. Desperate to fill their emptiness, the people produced and consumed, produced and consumed.

There was great busyness in the land.

As time passed, the people's grumbling loudened, the patriarch's body withered, his heart growing ever more frail as the chronic condition of his people worsened. It seemed the king's very body, wracked with consumption, had become the canvas for the ills of the kingdom. As the kingdom lived out its belief in ceaseless growth, the patriarch's frail body surrendered to ravaging cells that, too, believed in ceaseless growth. Knowing his weakness, the dying king called his two eldest sons to his bedside and bade them to go out into the world to seek the cure for the kingdom's malaise.

The eldest sons were eager to be on their way, relieved to escape the fated bedroom of their dying father. Death and dying were never discussed in their kingdom where youthfulness was greatly valued. Death was unproductive, unmanageable, unpredictable, and very unattractive.

Throughout the years that passed, visitors to the court would often bring fragments of stories about the two brothers. It was said they had reached a forest at the edge of the kingdom and, there, had an irreconcilable disagreement about which path to take.

More years passed. Without a cure, the kingdom lay in barren abundance. The people listlessly filled themselves with possessions and obsessions, experiencing one joyless success after another.

Back in the castle, the king's inanimate body lay upon the regal bed surrounded by life support systems. He neared death. Seeing this, the king's youngest son, who had heard his father's orders to his two older brothers as he hid among the dust balls in the shadows of the crown room, reached through the death-defying tubes and gently cradled his father's head. As he did, the king lost consciousness. The youngest son knew it was time to go forth to find his brothers and the kingdom's cure.

Leaving the palace, the young prince walked a long time. Coming to a forest at the edge of the kingdom, he felt lonely and certainly lost. As he wondered aloud why he had ever undertaken this journey, a rag-wrapped old woman appeared as if from nowhere. Startled, the boy realized that the old woman had not just materialized, but her leaf-like wrappings so closely blended with the forest that she seemed to appear and disappear as he tried to focus upon her. At first, he was discomforted by the woman's presence. He knew very little about women. His mother had died at his birth. He had only known his father and his older brothers. He wondered what the old woman was doing here in this forest.

"I could ask you the same question," she crackled with the gentleness of a falling leaf about to nourish the Earth.

"How did you know my question even before I knew it myself?" he asked, thinking maybe she was a witch.

"I am not a witch and don't worry about my seeming to disappear. Old women have been invisible in so many lands for so long that it now requires great attention for you to keep me in your focus. Now, tell me, what are *you* doing wandering in these woods?"

His fear eased; the young prince was comforted by the old woman's companionship and the loving depth of her earth-brown eyes. He began to tell the story of how, in the midst of seemingly unlimited resources and opportunities, the citizens of his father's kingdom had lost their passion for life, some becoming listless and fatigued, numbed by the land's abundance or consumed by its busyness. He told of the ailing patriarch sending his eldest sons forth to find a cure for the kingdom's malaise. He asked if the old woman had heard of his brothers or if she knew of a cure for the ailing kingdom.

The old woman was deep in thought as the young prince told his story. She had walked the forest long enough to know lessons were not easily learned without experience. She knew experience was a strong teacher and should not be cut short. Just how much should she share with the prince? How much was he ready to hear? How much would he have to find out on his own? She knew it was a good omen that he was the king's *third* son. After all, his brothers, had not even seen her when they had passed this very spot.

She knew from the boy's description that his father's

kingdom was surely crippled with chronic soul loss, but wondered if she should share this knowledge with the young prince. The boy might not even know about soul. After a long silence, the old woman's autumn voice crackled to life. "I know much about the fate of your brothers which I can share. First, though, let us talk about the fate of your father's kingdom.

"You come from a realm where opposites have been pushed so far apart there are no longer any common boundaries. There is no meeting ground for the mating of the light and the dark, the inner and the outer. The ancients who live in this forest say that such lands suffer from soul loss."

The prince was both confused and relieved. On the one hand, it seemed this ragged leaf lady might hold the answer to his quest. But, on the other, he did not know of that which his father's kingdom had lost. "What is this thing you call *soul*?" he asked.

"Ah, that is a great mystery! For, the more you know about one aspect of the soul, the less you know about another. The soul is elusive. It does not want to be pinned down. It is very deep. It is like looking into a dark pool of our deepest emotions, our deepest carings. For me the word evokes the passion, the meaning, the purpose, the awe, the wonder—the authenticity of being one's full self. Where there is soul there is wholeness. The fragments come together and dance!"

At the mention of dance, the old lady whirled around in her rags. The young prince began to doubt he would ever fulfill his quest. "If this thing *soul* is as elusive as you say, so unmeasurable, so mysterious, how will I ever find it—much less capture it?"

"Ah," smiled the wrinkled wise one, for this was just the question she had hoped the young boy would ask. "Sometimes it is easier to begin to find something by learning where it isn't. In this wood there are wise ones who know much about your father's kingdom. Let us ask them the ways in which your land has exiled the soul."

"I am ready to listen to anyone who can help," responded the eager prince, "but first please tell me what it is you know about my brothers. Is it true that they have had a bitter argument? Where are they? Why haven't they come home?"

"Many years ago," she answered, "your brothers became lost. The trail they followed forked at the edge of the woods. Your brothers could not agree which path to follow. Your eldest brother chose the path in the sunlight, a path that led back into the Land of Busyness where he has since found financial riches beyond anything ever imagined, even in your father's court. But this path had a very high price. Once he was on it, he could no longer see anything but the bright side of the kingdom. People have criticized his greed and ambition, but, deaf to their words, he walks on with callous insensitivity to anything but the unceasing accumulation of wealth. He sees no shadows.

"Your second brother took the other path, the one in shadow. It was a path just outside the Kingdom of Busyness, taking him to some dark and desolate places. He trod through burned rain forests and along beaches oozing with oil. He walked through mountainous landfills, homeless shelters, and refugee camps. He saw poverty, hunger, disease, riots, and senseless violence. At first he grew sad and then angry. He became an outspoken critic, lecturing about the unmitigated evil of the system. But, like your eldest brother, he too paid a high price for the path he chose.

"Caught in their own polarity, both of your brothers forgot the purpose of their journey. Now, only you can bring back the cure for the kingdom.

"Let us go visit some of the wise ones of the forest, young man. Mother Tongue awaits us. She knows all the languages of all lands. Knowing Mother Tongue is very important for language is more powerful than people recognize. To know the words you speak is to know your kingdom."

other Tongue was radiant. Her voice resonated from a source of such depth it seemed she must be connected to the center of the Earth. As the young prince approached, she bent toward him and asked, "What makes your heart sing today?"

The prince had never heard anyone like her before. Mother Tongue noted his body language and knew by the perplexed tilt of his head and by his tongue-tied silence that he was confused by her question.

"Oh, excuse me sweet one. Let me ask my question in the language of your kingdom. I believe your people might ask, 'What makes you tick?'"

The prince laughed at the familiar words.

"My child, I know you're not a clock and that you don't tick, but did you know there are many words and phrases you use in your Kingdom of Busyness that tell every cell in your body that you think of yourself and of others as machines? You know, much of the language of busyness was manufactured in the industrial revolution.

"It never ceases to amaze me that, in spite of the fact that your word *corporation* sprouted from an organic root *corpus*—body—and your word *organization* has its parentage in the word organ, machine metaphor fills the Kingdom of Busyness where workers are cogs in a very big wheel.

"Clearly machines make ideal employees. Machines don't care about the rhythms of the Earth; they can work anytime, anywhere. Machines don't need sleep, don't dream, don't even know night from day. Machines don't make love, give birth, or stay home with a sick child. Machines don't daydream or giggle or get depressed. Machines don't feel. There is a saying in this forest: *Man made the machine in his own image and the machine returned the favor.*

"If you don't think your kingdom is imprisoned in the paradigm of the machine, when you return to your father's land, listen to your people. They want to get a *jump start* on the next project so they *gear up* for the challenge and even *shift into high gear* when competition mounts. People say they are *getting a little rusty* when they haven't used a particular skill, and they feel p*lugged in* when they know what is going on. People *program* themselves to do the best job possible, but when they have to be retrained into new jobs, they are called *retreads.* When all else fails, your companies bring in consultants who perpetuate the machine metaphor by offering to *retool* the processes or, worse, *reengineer* the whole organization.

"When they drink too much coffee in the morning, they feel *wired* and then they need to get away from the *grind.* When they have their yearly medical checkup, they tell their coworkers they are going for their *annual tune up*—which is especially important to do if they feel they haven't been *running on all eight cylinders.* If they have gotten too *wound up,* the doctor suggests they take a vacation in order to *unwind!* And when they find themselves perpetuating dysfunctional habits, they say they are *playing old tapes!*

"Why do your people think of themselves as clocks that *tick,* get *wound up*, and *run down?* Why do they refer to themselves as cars with gear shifts and cylinders? Why do they talk of themselves as programmable computers? When the stress levels mount beyond tolerance, why do they say they are having a *breakdown?* When they finally run completely out of money, the lifeblood of your system, why do they then say they are *broke?* My son, can you begin to see the underlying belief system that creates these images? Can you begin to see how this relates to soul loss?

"As your kingdom moves from the machine age to the information age, it must be equally careful about the metaphors it adopts, conscious that information *in-forms* the people of your kingdom. It literally creates the *form* of their lives. Just think about how limiting *information highways* are. Highways are dangerous. The cars on highways generate pollutants. The highways themselves assail the land with ribbons of cement and black asphalt.

"And what of your warlike language? Corporations *wage price wars* and create sales *campaigns aimed at target markets.* Companies *entrench, retrench,* and *build war chests.* Some even create strategies in *war rooms* while their people *earn their stripes* by *serving on the front line.* Everyone in the kingdom knows that the *big guns* are at the top of the organization. Sometimes I wonder if, when your people talk of *occupations,* their psyches are not the *occupied lands* in this realm of conquest. The language of war, of dominance and aggression, is not a language that welcomes the soul.

"When you return, listen carefully. You will hear the people of Busyness speak of *capturing* market share by being the *dominant* force. You will hear the militaristic and sexual overtones of their market *penetration* strategies. And you will know this is not the language of the soul. Sometimes I think you should just hang a sign at the entry to your kingdom that announces 'Soul Not Spoken Here'!

"If you listen closely, it is indeed a corporate *body* that has been brought together to do the work of the kingdom. But in the hallways, people mumble that the organization is *heartless* after a downsizing has *cut the fat out of the middle.* In the body corporate, the only part of the anatomy given respect is, of course, the *head.* No one wants to descend into the *bowels* of the organization for God knows what lurks in the darkness there.

"The soul is not exclusively enamored with the head and it does not think of the heart as a mechanical pump! The soul knows that, without the bowels, the head is quite worthless. The very word your kingdom uses to define its economic philosophy is a word of the head—*capitalism* from *capita,* meaning head. Yours is an economic ideology of the head—not of the soul. Getting *ahead* is everything.

"By now you surely recognize that your language is filled with clues. Let me share just a few more that may be helpful when you return to your kingdom. Remember child, that a job without meaning is de-meaning, a worker without passion is a-pathetic. A workplace without spirit is dis-spirited. And a kingdom without soul is desolate. But, enough. It is time for you to visit Father Time who can better explain why there is hardly a moment for soul in your father's kingdom."

Thus the young prince and the ragged leaf woman left Mother Tongue and arrived at a clearing where sat Father Time— an old, old man, robust and greatly bearded.

ather Time spoke. "Welcome, my son, welcome indeed. Come sit near my sundial so you can see the shadows that dance on its face and bring us the treasure of time.

"When I first began to observe the people in your kingdom, I thought your people loved—even worshipped— time. They even wear time strapped to their wrists! Ticking clocks hold the place of honor in every classroom, kitchen, office, and at every bedside in the kingdom.

"Yet, I soon discovered your people were both foolish and fearful about time. Fearful it will run out, they dedicate them- selves to making every second count. Can you imagine what would happen if your kingdom worried about making every second *feel* instead of making every second *count?* Your kingdom focuses so hard on the quantification of time that its quality, its essence, is often lost.

"In your land, time is money. Time is twisted and contorted to serve the end of productivity. Yet, the soul appreciates natural cycles intimately related to Earth's seasons, the phases of the moon, the rising and setting of the sun. The work cycles of your kingdom ignore natural rhythms and impose artificial order.

"Electric lights give license to hold back the dark, prolonging the work day from before dawn to well after dusk. Longer work days are the expectation at many of your organizations. The people who work the longest hours are highly valued. Those who sacrifice their evenings, weekends, holidays, and vacations are heroic. For a while it appeared that your kingdom had changed from the cruel drudgery of its sweatshops, but today, in fact, work consumes as many hours as ever. The soul knows there are times for rest and times for busyness. But the people of your kingdom often don't know how to become unbusy. They are human doings—no longer human beings.

"Workaholism is one of the few addictions that is still revered. The people of your land have a Calvinist hangover—a work ethic taken to an unhealthy extreme. Only the hardest workers shall be among God's chosen. Long hours and high stress are symbols of success. The heart attack is the hero's death.

"The people of the Kingdom of Busyness measure self-worth and importance by how busy they are. If their calendars are completely filled, if there is no time for one more meeting, one more trip, one more conference call, they feel satisfied and important. If someone does have time available to meet on short notice, clearly they are less valuable. People in the kingdom keep detailed time management calendars, believing that a full calendar somehow relates to a full life—while fulfillment itself remains elusive.

"The drive to perform, to make every minute count in productivity, is extraordinary. Business Plans ignore the need for respite or renewal, though in nature, fallow periods must exist if there is to be future fertility. A constant drive for more and more earnings does not afford the organization a chance to catch its collective breath. Now, new super-quick technologies make financial performance figures available in real-time and create the pressure to achieve not quarterly, but monthly earnings! Annual profit must always surpass the previous year. There is no room for renewal as organizations seek perpetual growth.

"Nor is there time for mothers and fathers to build parenthood into the work cycle. Some of your companies have attempted to accommodate families with on-site day care centers and even breast milk extraction lounges—with the result that no one needs to stop work for anything and natural rhythms are, again, lost. Your people even deny the passage of time as gray hairs are dyed and faces are lifted. But the soul lives in the deep rhythms of life and in the poetic movements of the Earth. When these are lost, the soul is lost.

"Time, as you know it, is a human construct, born in the same rhythms it now denies. The Earth's revolutions created your years; her rotations created your days. Your kingdom has reduced time to such infinitely tiny parts that any sense of the whole, of the original rhythm, has been lost. There is little poetry in a digital watch reading 4:17:33.

"Of course, technology has brought extraordinary advances to your kingdom. In many instances, it has bought greater longevity to each of your human lives. The latest instant communication technologies, while creating the potential for interconnectedness beyond anything previously imagined, have also brought busyness into all your times and spaces. The people of your kingdom now must be more available, more responsive. Car phones allow the commuter to begin work before arriving at the office; lap top computers turn vacations into work opportunities; fax machines and E-mail receive messages all night long in your very home. You awake to a new pile of information to sort and process. You don't even stop to sleep as your red-eye airplane flights allow you to keep right on working after you land in someone else's morning. Instead of more time, you have no time.

"We watch in disbelief as your kingdom adopts trends such as cycle time reduction which only exacerbate the chronic condition of the realm. Time and motion studies look for where seconds can be shaved to gain even more efficiency. Watching the people of your kingdom work is like watching the characters in a speeded-up film. Your people have become perpetual motion machines.

"For efficiency's sake, the people even choose to exercise on machines while artificial stimulants like caffeine and sugar leave them unaware of how fatigued they are. It makes us very sad to watch, for they are so preoccupied by their occupations they leave little time for their souls to be fed by being in nature, listening to music, gardening, hiking, painting—or whatever refreshes and restores.

"The people in your kingdom work like Sisyphus—cursed by the gods to roll a stone up hill only to have it fall down again, and then to roll it up again only to have it fall down again, and on and on eternally. In the same way, the work of your kingdom is never complete. Deadline follows deadline and one day you cross that "dead"-line; you literally run out of time and you die—only to discover that with all this productivity, you have not been *making a living* but rather *making a dying.*

"I should send you on your way. But, before you leave, stop for a moment and speak to my wife for she is very wise in the ways of your kingdom. We have lived together so long that we are inseparable—some now see us as a continuum of each other. I think in terms of time; she observes in terms of space.

"Oh, yes. Lest I forget, when you are out in our garden, do take time to smell the roses!"

n the garden was a woman taking up a wonderfully large space in a voluminous caftan of the richest midnight blue. Silver stars and golden crescent moons sparkled from within the garment's great folds.

The Keeper of Space was even more compelling than her robes. Never had the prince seen one so perfectly comfortable in her own body. Even more extraordinary was her garden. Somehow this magical woman of space had switched the foreground and the background of the landscape, giving value to what is seldom seen in the Kingdom of Busyness—the space between things.

"Welcome, my child. Have you survived the old man's ramblings? I have to listen to him all the time!

"As he has undoubtedly told you, I tend to space like others tend to things. Allow me to give you a tour of my space. In some kingdoms, people value the space between objects just as it is possible to value the stillness between activities. Even in some contemporary kingdoms to the east, there is an understanding that it is the space between objects that holds the meaning. The space between the notes turns noise to music; the pause in verse creates the poetry; the space between objects creates design. Like time, space is not necessarily something empty that must be filled.

"There is a woman of the forest who tells me that in ancient Egypt, the meaning of the hieroglyph for *art* literally deciphers as *the space between two people!* In your kingdom, think how many people in relationships cry out that they *need some space!*

"There is spatial polarization in your kingdom, separating the outside from the inside, the up from the down. Your people devalue the inner world, while they deify the measurable, tangible outer world. They create artificial boundaries and maps to classify and organize space. At whim they create globes that empower the developed Kingdom of Busyness by placing it *on top of the world,* while the *underdeveloped* lands (often the lands where there is still open space) are cast into a disempowered global underworld. But there is no up or down in space. There is only space in space.

"Your people see space as empty and they want to fill it. Fill it they do, as your cities sprawl forth across the land into endless suburbs and strip malls. Your kingdom does not seem to recognize that it is the space, the emptiness, that makes the function possible. There is a very ancient Taoist sage here in the forest who reminds us that *we shape clay into a pot, but it is the emptiness inside that holds whatever we want. We hammer wood for a house but it is the inner space that makes it livable.*

"You can tell the story of a kingdom in its landscape and its cityscape. You can quickly learn the values of a culture and what is important to its people by the structures and spaces. Let's look together at the corporate towers, the high-rises and skyscrapers you have built in your land of great busyness, and let us read their story. We watch in amazement as these sharp-edged erections shoot heavenward. Where once the church and the government dominated the landscape, now the structures of busyness rule.

"Anorexic high-rises distance themselves from the bodily reality of the Earth—separating those on high not only from the slums, the traffic jams, the poverty and the random violence below but also from the Earth—its soil, its rhythms, its fertility. These exalted towers symbolize your people's desperate attempt to place themselves *above it all.*

"The people of the Kingdom of Busyness must begin to recognize the systemic nature of the community and its interconnected role. Your kingdom cannot continue to separate itself and its actions from all surrounding lands.

"While your towers defy gravity with their needle-thin height, their skin speaks to us as well. Glistening polarized surfaces deny entry—like permanent giant sunglasses blocking admission. Your architectural bodies, like your corporate bodies and your personal bodies, strive to be lean, mean machines.

"Inside these towers, artificial air, artificial light, and now even artificial white noise create a completely controlled environment where workers are kept busy as bees in honey comb cubicles. Windowless, right angled, cookie-cutter space—efficient, productive, and dead. Depersonalized, dehumanized, the soul of space sacrificed to efficiency.

"Places and spaces can have souls. The qualities of individuality and authenticity are almost tangible. There is an honest interplay among landscape, history, and people. The place has personality, a seeming consciousness, a soul.

"I can see you're a bit spaced out by all my talk so I will shortly send you on your way. But first, let me ask one favor. When you get back to your kingdom, stop for a moment and look at those glimmering corporate towers, those identical malls with their identical stores with their identical merchandise, and those identical fast-food restaurants spreading everywhere along strip roadways in every city of your realm, and ask yourself 'whom do these serve?'"

eparting the spacious garden, the ragged leaf lady knew there was one more wise one the prince should meet before returning to his father's kingdom.

"I want you to meet the forest story teller who understands the economy and the currency of your land. Don't be surprised to find that this one does not choose human form. Indeed, this one is the Mother Creek, known by us in the forest as *Asequia Madre*, whose life giving current runs through the center of our forest and out into your kingdom. She is the grand *Cantadora* of the land for, running from the highest places to the lowest, she receives all and shares all. She knows much about the starvation of soul, soul famine, *hambre del alma*."

With these words of introduction, the crackling voice of the leaf lady gave way to the rippling, pulsing, gurgling, surging energy of *Asequia Madre*, Mother Creek. "Some say I babble and I'll admit that my thoughts do, now and then, meander. Please do stop me if I run on. I am not, and never have been, linear and I am proud of that—for I have shaped some extraordinary landscapes.

I consider myself a real liquid asset and I am overflowing with excitement about the opportunity to share my thoughts about soul loss with you. Over the years, between cash flows, income streams, and bridge financings, I have learned much about the currency of your land. Come, walk by my side and I'll just let my stream of consciousness flow!

"First, my sweet child, do not be discouraged by all you are hearing about how the constructs of your kingdom have exiled the soul. *The essential thing to remember is the soul can never be lost—never, never, never. It can be scorched. It can be bruised. But, it can never, never be lost. It is self-revivifying. It is self-healing. It may be momentarily tortured or astriated or even stabbed but it heals immediately.* So let us help you find ways to invite the exiled one back into the kingdom so that the healing begins.

"Mother Tongue has told you much about the use of metaphors in your land, but the real language of the Kingdom of Busyness is accounting. At its conception, accounting understood the importance of balance, rooted in its most essential document, the balance sheet. But somehow the application of the concept split the balance into an either/or world of assets and liabilities—a world in which people are seen as costs to be controlled and cut—not invested in, grown, and nurtured. Liabilities and equity are the birthing place of assets. The soul knows that you must have both and that you cannot think of one side as good and one as bad.

"What you account for, what you measure and how you measure it, truly creates your kingdom's reality. After all, your people refer to things of value as the things that *count*. As long as you measure your kingdom's success in short-term profits, gross national product and consumer spending, you will perpetuate the chronic conditions you have described. As long as your accounting remains in denial of any costs associated with finite resource depletion and land desecration, your economy will continue to turn away from its own shadow, away from wholeness, and balance.

"Though once your kingdom valued thrift, it now values consuming as a patriotic act. Consumption, it is thought, creates jobs, keeps people employed, and keeps the kingdom strong. Armies of patriotic consuming consumers march out to your malls every day to protect and defend the economy of their kingdom. Everywhere you turn there is a store, an ATM machine, and an advertisement creating a need which must be filled immediately by a purchase.

"But there is a shadow side to all this consumption. Imprisoning credit levels. Non-renewable resources consumed. Landfills. People working to achieve poverty-level wages. Let us remember my fellow rivers, brooks, and streams who have died in the name of consumption.

"Your kingdom commits economic suicide as its continual downsizings eliminate the ability of consumers to consume! Consumption is not sustainable. It is not an ideology of soul.

"So many of the people of your kingdom believe that money is happiness. Your kingdom has learned to fear the darker emotions of sorrow or sadness or depression—the dark nights of the soul. Your people must stay busy, making more and more money, in order to hold on to the hope of finding that happiness.

"The cycle is addictive: More money. More consumption. More things. More money. More consumption. More things.

"Buy something to scare away depression. Buy food. Buy clothes. Buy a house. A car. A coke. A boat. Buy one more thing and you'll be happy. The people of the kingdom have lost the ability to distinguish authentic nourishment. Happiness remains always just out of reach, like Tantalus' grapes just beyond his grasp.

"Of course, there are a few who do not hold money as happiness. They have taken the opposite path, espousing money to be the root of all evil. We have seen your brothers slip into this polarity. Your kingdom needs to discover what money really is before it can create a soul-friendly economy.

"Your kingdom maintains both over-stimulated nervous systems and economies to keep depression at bay. There is no time for rest. No time for soul work. Yet, the forest ancients know that depression is part of the natural and restorative cycle. No one in your kingdom wants to admit depression into the psyche or the economy. Those who seek to find wholeness through psychological therapies find that organizations consider them to be at risk, not trustworthy, borderline. In your kingdom it is considered weak to seek healing for one's psyche.

"Yours is an economy of denial. It ignores its poor. Ignores its pain. Ignores its hunger. Ignores its shadow. But the repressed shadow eventually arises and demands attention through forced stagnation and illness—both personal and economic—which necessitate a period of respite, a recess or recession from the whirlwind of busyness.

"In your kingdom, people value themselves by how much money they have accumulated and how much money they make. They measure the value of their life as their net worth—not their self-worth. But the soul is welcomed in the realm of the unmeasurable, and so the soul is lost to a kingdom that does not consider the unmeasurable to be real.

"In their jobs, the people of your kingdom exchange a certain amount of their life energy for a pay check. Thus, when money is used to purchase things, life energy is being traded. If the job doesn't replenish the life-force with meaning, passion, and community, the force is used up. But, when you love what you do, the soul is fed. By allowing their life energies to be used in work that does not fulfill them, many people are hollow victims of a vampire-like system that steals their lifeblood.

"The concept of money in your kingdom has become an abstraction—the currency of the land disassociated from the soulful things of nature. There was a time when people expressed their economic worth in the number of cows owned, in the acres of land tilled, the number of sheep grazed. The ancient Latin word for money, *pecunia,* quite literally meant "sheep." The coin was worth a certain number of sheep. Then a subtle switch occurred in which the sheep became worth a certain amount of coins—rather than the coin representing the sheep. The value was placed on the coin and removed from the cow, the sheep, the cord of wood, the acre of soil. Yet even in this movement toward abstraction, the currency was still grounded in the Earth, first backed by Earth's golden metal and then her silver. But now your currency floats free of any silver, free of any tether to earthly reality. And the abstracting has accelerated—first to the paper check and the plastic credit card and now to electronic exchanges removing the last traces of tangibility.

"In a similar way, the Industrial Age abstracted the daily life in the kingdom, taking your people off the land and further from the source of their food and shelter, further from the rhythms and the soul nourishment of their Mother Earth. The Industrial Age took you away from the soulful psychology of the craftsman. No longer is there that deep integrity and alignment between the people and the craft of their hands. In your kingdom Anglo-Saxon surnames once held meaning of the family craft. The Smiths as blacksmiths, the Coopers as barrel makers, the Wheelwrights as wheel makers, the Fishers, the Farmers, the Bakers and...whoops, there I go running on!

"My point is there was identity in work. There was pride in work. The craftsperson could experience the whole, not just the part. The stonemason knew he was building a cathedral. The soul frolics in such meaning, such wholeness. Your people do not necessarily need to return to the farm or to build cathedrals; they only need to love what they do. There is a very wise old one in the forest who has said:

> Let the beauty of what you love be what you do.
> There are a thousand ways to kneel and kiss the
> ground.

hey had walked a long way next to the babbling creek. The ragged leaf lady knew they would soon reach the forest edge but she still had much she wanted to share. It was time for the prince to return to his kingdom.

"When we began our exploration of soul, I said that, rather than search for some soul to capture and bring home, it might be more fruitful to look at reasons for soul's absence. Now that we have heard so many reasons for its absence, I do not want you to leave the forest in despair. There are signs of the soul awakening in your kingdom. Like the fragile first buds of spring, we are hearing whispers about new initiatives to empower people, to embrace diversity, to broadly define stakeholders, to honor systemic inter-relatedness, to quest for vision, to build community and even to recognize responsibility for the stewardship of our Earth. The soul finds home in even the most hesitant of these harbingers of wholeness.

"You should know that to approach this wholeness in which the soul finds such welcome, your kingdom must recognize the dynamic interdependence of the opposites. This is an enormous challenge in a kingdom that long has lived with oppositional thinking and a deeply embedded belief in dualism. You push opposites to the polar ends of linear spectrums, separating black from white, good from bad, light from dark, night from day, east from west, rich from poor.

"But the soul lives in the overlap of opposites, in the overlap of the inner and the outer, the dark and the light, the masculine and the feminine. It is when the opposites dance and embrace that a new kingdom can be born.

"I know you have heard much and it is time for you to return, but I must give you one last gift before you leave—the gift of the feminine principle. Your father's kingdom suffers greatly from the absence of the feminine. The kingdom's renewal of soul, the anima, depends on the re-union of the feminine with the masculine.

"You might ask, 'What does this old leaf lady know about the masculine and the feminine principles?' I know much for I came to this forest many, many years ago when the people began to banish the qualities of the feminine. I brought that wisdom with me here to the deep forest to keep it safe so that one day I could share it with those who would come seeking.

"Know, my son, that when I speak of the masculine and the feminine principles, I do not speak of gender. For the women of your kingdom, like the men, have been so encultured in busyness that they too have exiled the feminine. I am talking about qualities—ways of doing, ways of being—that are associated with the polar opposites, the anima and the animus, the yin and the yang.

"When you return home, notice how your father's kingdom has pushed away the intuitive, the receptive, the reflective, the passive, the dark, the non-linear. These are not the qualities for success taught in your schools of busyness. But an organization without the feminine principle, though it may generate a multitude of ideas, provides no dark place for their gestation, no soil for the seed, no vessel for the vision.

"Mother Creek spoke to you of how the consumptive model supports your kingdom's materialistic culture. But look within the word materialism and see the word *mater,* mother, matter. We here in the forest sometimes wonder if, when your people hunger for material things, they are not in fact seeking the mother that their ancient memories associate with matter. The kingdom's rampant *mater*ialism may be misplaced and distorted, craving for the love, the comfort, the *mater,* the great mother, the feminine principle of which I speak here.

"I know, from long, long ago, that soul is truly awakened when both the masculine and the feminine qualities are present creating the potential for wholeness. With both present there can be insemination, procreation, innovation.

"As the people of your kingdom begin to remember these truths, do not let the pendulum swing from honoring only the masculine principle to honoring only the feminine. Neither the masculine nor the feminine is better than the other. They are interdependent equals, the negative and positive poles of the wholeness. As with the batteries that run the gadgets of your land, both the masculine and feminine poles are necessary for the awakening of energy.

"As you prepare to return, recall the fate of your brothers. You will only repeat their mistake if you turn away from either the brightness or the shadow. In seeking wholeness, the paths need to come together—not go further apart. And also, beware of peddlers who may come offering quick soul fixes for sale. The soul is not a strategic tool to be purchased from without. When these peddlers come, as surely they will, remember the soul is not the next busyness fad. Know that the soul comes from a different place. It cannot be purchased. It can only be received."

The young prince, knowing it was time, reached out to embrace his precious new friend who somehow seemed more visible to him than at any time since their meeting. Following the banks of life-renewing Mother Creek, he returned to his kingdom, where the ending of the story would be written and in that ending would be the beginning.

Part Three

Rediscovering Our Souls through Work

11
Reflections on a Spirituality of Work
Matthew Fox

12
Business and the Journey of the Soul
Mark Youngblood

13
The System Versus the Soul
Dorothy E. Fischer

14
Soul Dusting™
Kathleen M. Redmond and Juli Ann Reynolds

15
The Human Heart and Soul at Work
Joel Levey

Another best-selling author, Matthew Fox, leads off this segment which directly addresses the need for soulful enterprise in the human being. It addresses how the soul has been systematically and gradually squeezed out of modern workers since the advent of the Industrial Age.

The authors in this section examine the revolution of the human spirit as it begins to demand the return of its soul. No longer are people who work willing to leave their hearts and souls at home when they leave for their jobs. Fewer and fewer people are willing to "sell their souls" for the positions, titles, incomes, or images that have traditionally been the bribery for compromising their values.

This segment was written for your soul.

Matthew Fox is a postmodern theologian. He has been an ordained priest since 1967. He holds masters degrees in philosophy and theology from Aquinas Institute and a doctorate in spirituality, *summa cum laude,* from the Institut catholique de Paris.

He is the founder of the Institute in Culture and Creation Spirituality (ICCS) at Holy Names College in Oakland, California; the editor-in-chief of *Creation Spirituality* magazine; and the author of fifteen well-known books, including the best-selling *Original Blessing: A Primer in Creation Spirituality; Creation Spirituality: Liberating Gifts for the Peoples of the Earth;* and *The Reinvention of Work.*

In addition to his work as a writer and teacher in the San Francisco Bay Area, Matthew Fox is in great demand as a lecturer and has traveled throughout the United States and Canada, as well as the United Kingdom, Ireland, Germany, Switzerland, the Netherlands, Belgium, Australia and New Zealand, bringing his message of ecological and social justice, mysticism and blessing to an eager and ever-growing audience. His essay was originally published in *Creation Spirituality* and is reprinted with permission of the publisher.

Reflections on a Spirituality of Work

Matthew Fox

Today there are close to one billion human beings out of work. In the United States alone there are more unemployed people now than at any time since the Great Depression. At the same time, in the industrial world, there are a great number of persons who are overworked, who are, in Meister Eckhart's phrase, "worked" instead of working, giving rise to a new addiction: workaholism. Of those who are employed, some are in jobs that are inimical to the health of our species and the planet; for example, tearing down rainforests or killing endangered animals or selling drugs or making armaments.

Some politicians, looking for a quick fix shout that we need "jobs, jobs, jobs" (as former President Bush put it). But such simplistic slogans simply do not cut deeply enough. They avoid the questions that must be asked of work at this critical juncture in human and planetary history when, as Lester Brown concludes in his State of the World Report, the planet has only 16 years remaining unless and until human beings change their ways.

And changing our ways includes changing the way we look at work, define it, compensate for it, create it, and the way we let go of work and learn to confuse it and fuse it with play and ritual. We should not allow ourselves to be deceived that today's crisis in jobs is just about more "jobs, jobs, jobs"—it is not. It is about our relationship to work and the challenge put to our species today to reinvent work. The issue is at bottom an issue in spirituality, which is always about "all our relations" as the Lakota people pray.

Work is clearly a deep partner in our relationships: the middle class prepares itself for work by getting an education, working, recovering from work, and trying to raise children who can successfully enter the work world. Clearly work is at the center of adult living. This is one reason that unemployed persons can so readily succumb to self-hatred and despair: not having a vehicle to express one's blessing in the basic meaning of work renders one mute and blocked up inside. The artist within, the *imago Dei,* never gets a chance to express itself.

The fact that communism has collapsed only exacerbates the issue at stake when we talk about work. This is not only because communism had a definite (and often appealing) philosophy about work which raised such important issues as "alienation of the worker," "exploitation of the worker," and "work for everyone," but also because communism's demise leaves capitalism standing naked for everyone to observe. What are its values vis-à-vis the worker? The unemployed? The uninsured? The addicted worker? The gap between workers' salaries and top management's salaries? The relationship of top management and owners of industry (including the media industry and the defense industry) to government decision-making, legislative law-making, and the political decision-making and candidate-anointing in the civic process? What is capitalism's attitude toward minority hiring and training? Toward work in ghettos where there are no jobs? To the educational agendas in schools that in turn create the marketplace of workers? In retraining persons who are being expelled from the war industry to other industries? What about the relationship between crime, violence, a burgeoning youthful prison population, and no work? The money that money makes versus the money that workers make? In other words, capitalism itself is now in the limelight once again, as it was in the Great Depression. The lessons of the get-rich-quick artistry of Ivan Boessky, Michael Milken, and Thomas Keating must not be lost when we reflect critically on work in our world today.

Ecological

Another dimension in our consideration of work today must be the environment. All work depends on healthy soil, water, air, bodies, minds, spirits. In short, work is subject to the laws of interdependence that operate throughout Nature. Humans are Nature, humans are in Nature, Nature is in humans, and work is Nature. When humans work it is Nature at work. Indeed, Hildegard of Bingen said in the twelfth century that "when humans do good work they make the cosmic wheel go around." In other words, work has a cosmic dimension to it. But evil work—that which interferes with the intentions and plans of Nature—also has a cosmic dimension to it: The powers and principalities come unleashed as a result of misbegotten and evil work. All injustice is that sort of work; this is why the Scriptures say that "when the widow and orphan are dishonored all the pillars of the Earth are shattered." A cosmic rupture occurs when humans do bad work.

The environmental crisis tells us much about our crisis in work today. Lester Brown and the Worldwatch Institute point out that industrial countries have declined in their work output the world over as a result of diminishing natural resources over the past few decades. For example, in the United States alone, our GNP has effectively declined since 1979 when it reached its peak. So, too, has the health of our soil, water, forests, and therefore, food and bodies. In other countries the reality is even more stark. In the Philippines, for example, and Ethiopia and Peru. There can be no question that good work presumes good health—not only human health but the health of the environment that gifts the worker with everything from food to clothes, from moments of beauty and grace to hope in bringing new children into the world.

The environmental crisis, then, furnishes us with an opportunity and a responsibility to ask deeper questions of work: To ask how a spirituality of work might assist us in redefining how, why, and for whom we do our work. It also clearly opens the door for creating new kinds of work that will invent and install sustainable energy and sustainable agriculture and sustainable minds (i.e., education) and spirits (i.e., worship). A time like ours is a time for whole new forms of work to emerge. The decline of the "defense" industry, understood as warmaking, can make way for the emergence of a defense industry understood as defending the hopes and spirits of our children, as defending the Earth: tree planting; soil preservation; water purifying; air cleaning; recovery of streams in cities and recycling of wastes as well as the creating of new rituals. All these constitute potentially new "industries" albeit small and people-owned.

Spiritual

The spiritual results of a lack of work are devastating. When people lack work they lack pride; they lack an opportunity to return their unique gifts to the community; they also lack the means to provide the taxes that make services possible in the greater community. Welfare ought never to be a replacement for work. When the despair that unemployment creates sets into a community or neighborhood the results can be seen everywhere: Increased crime, drugs (the only work available), a bloating of the prison population, racism, resentment. As Thomas Aquinas observed, "Despair is the most dangerous of all sins," for when despair takes over "all kinds of wickedness follow."

All these considerations point to how the issues raised by the crisis in work around the world today are spiritual issues. They demand a radical critique of the way we have been defining work during the modern era, an era that is rapidly disappearing.

Work versus Job

First, we must speak of the difference between a job and work. A job may be helping at a fast-food place for $4.25 per hour in order to pay one's bills or make some spending money as a youth: But work is something else. Work comes from inside out; it is the expression of one's soul, one's inner being. Work is unique to the individual. Work is creative. It is an expression of the Spirit acting in the world through us. Work is that which puts us in touch with others—not at the level of personal interaction so much as at the level of service in the community.

Work is not just about getting paid. Much work in our culture is not paid for at all; for example, raising children, cooking meals at home, organizing youth activities, singing in the church choir, listening to a neighbor or friend who has undergone trauma, tending a garden. And yet, in a fuller critique of work, these questions need to be asked: How is it possible that these examples of good work might be rewarded in some way so that they get counted in our understanding of "gross national product"?

In pointing out the distinction between "job" and "work" we don't want to create an unresolvable dualism. Given a deep spirituality even a job may be turned into work. That is a worthy task that a person needs inner work to develop.

Work as Vocation:
Intimations of Resurrection in Work

Meister Eckhart says that when he returns to the Godhead from which he came, no one will ask him what he has been doing because no one will have missed him there where unity is so perfect. We will not be judged on our work so much as on our being. "Think more about who you are and less about what you do," he counsels. "For if you are just, your ways will be just." The invitation to move from doing to being is one of the powerful contributions of a spirituality of work. To begin a discussion of work from the point of view of our being not only resets our entire dialogue about work, but gives us the imaginative freedom to start over in our assessment of work and non-work. We will see work differently. What does our work do to our being, to other peoples' and other species' beings? What demands are our beings making on our work—what are rainforests and whales and birds asking of us today about our work?

A Heart-Call

Here we face the theme of vocation or calling. Somehow the universe, the Maker of the universe, calls us to be participants, at the level of our being, in the work of the universe. This is a heart-call; it must be listened to with an open heart. Many are letting go of their work (as well as their jobs) to find themselves a work in the New Creation. This act of obedience—this listening with an open heart and responding responsibly—is an eschatological sign; a promise of the future which has already begun. It is a sacrament in the literal sense. Our work is a sacrament; our vocation is a sacrament; changing our vocations under the influence of the Holy Spirit is a sacrament. For it's a silent mystery that calls us from some deep and uncontrollable place to take risks, to let go, perhaps to change lifestyles. Why? Because of the future, or better, the jeopardy to the future: the real possibility of there being no future.

A Future

The eschatological is our response to the future. The Earth crisis today suggests to many observers that there is no future for our species on this planet and no future for the planet so long as our species refuses to change its ways. But this is where vocation enters—a voice from the future calling persons to believe in a future. A voice from the young and the yet-to-be-born asking adults to change their ways and therefore start living as if there were a future. Belief is not primarily about dogmas but about action. If we believe in a future we will act like it; and included in this activity may well be a whole new way of working in our world.

Work is about eschatology, then, both because it is about death or the "last things," and because it is about life, or what we believe about life in the future and after we are gone. From this point of view, work is indeed about what we leave behind: whether it is a gift or not.

Those without work are seldom invited into the eschatological romp with the greater community. This very sad state of affairs leads to self-hatred and violence, for there swims in all human souls intimations of gift-giving as well as intimations of the finiteness of our presence on this Earth. In short, we all dream dreams of work. Good work. When the eschatological is allowed no space in which to expand, no heart-place in which vocation can be attended to, then violence can readily set in. For violence bears signs of being eschatological—of being something greater than ourselves—as indeed it is. It includes the cosmic forces known as Powers and Principalities. Violence qualifies as a pseudoeschatology. That is why its presence is exaggerated in an historical period like ours when hope is so rare and pessimism reigns.

Eschatology is not only about death. It is also about play. For in reality none of us knows what the future holds and so we can choose to image it either as totally apocalyptic and nihilistic (if we do this all work stops), or as a playground of possibilities for our species and our loved ones. If we do this, creativity can begin anew and with it unpredictable discoveries of work and work-making. Indeed, when fantasy and playfulness return to our sense of eschatology—and therefore our sense of work—the Spirit returns, who is the gift of the Transcendent in our time. The Spirit of surprise. "Praise," says Oyne Onyemichi, "takes all of you. Give it all away. Hold nothing back." When we do that our work returns. It returns as spirit, as strength, as comforter, as hope.

When we understand this we understand the connection between work and Resurrection. Work can be an ascetic spiritual discipline, a "sweat of the brow" experience, an incursion into the *Via Negativa,* and a hint of the shadows that accompany death itself. But it can also be a *Via Creativa*—indeed all cosmic work is of this kind—and then work becomes an eschatological story of hope and new life.

Play, surprise, the Spirit: these are eschatological elements of work. Work without them at their base is not truly human work nor true work in the universe. Who could have predicted the making of the eye by the universe? The invention of water on this planet when it was only rock? The emergence of life? The work of the universe is permeated by surprise. Our work must be of the same kind. It will be to the extent that we truly live in the universe, that is, in God's temple, and not just in the human-made worlds of what Eckhart called the "merchant mentality," or in the vestibule of the Temple where Jesus found the merchants selling their wares instead of honoring the mystery.

If God is, as Aquinas puts it, "Life, per se Life," then those who want to respond to God have no choice but to choose life. "I put before you these two: Death and Life. Choose Life." But to choose life is to opt for a future for our planet, for our children and theirs, for the species that render this planet so amazing and so beautiful. It is an eschatological choice, an act of hope. It is a response to the call or vocation to choose life from the One who is "Life, per se Life." Any work that operates out of a source other than a life-source is less than divine; it is not the cosmos' work. It is the way of pessimism, not of New Creation. It expresses a belief in death, not in the power of Resurrection.

Mark Youngblood is president of Quay Alliance, Inc., a training and professional services organization dedicated to empowering personal and organizational transformation. He has nearly twenty years of experience in business performance improvement, information technology and change management. His book, *Eating the Chocolate Elephant: Take Charge of Change Through Total Process Management,* explains how to implement organizational change to achieve significant, sustainable performance improvements. Total Process Management is unique and holistic—providing a synthesis of the leading approaches for managing organizational change. He provides workshops and facilitation on the topic of organizational change to businesses nationally, and has lectured on the topic to audiences around the world.

Quay Alliance's clients include Army & Air Force Exchange Service (AAFES), ADVO, Inc., F.W. Woolworth, Micrografx, Mitchell International, Mobil Oil, Nations Bank, Paul Ray Berndtson, and USAA.

12

Business and the Journey of the Soul

Mark Youngblood

Business has become today's religion. Somehow, we have come to confuse the means with the ends and treat business success and the accumulation of wealth as our life's purpose. We spend most of our waking hours in service to the god of business, where "prophet" is replaced with "profit." We wreck our health and personal relationships in this pursuit. We do violence to our neighbors, to the earth, and, ultimately, to ourselves. We measure our personal worth based on our income, the jobs that we hold, how much power we wield, and the prestige and social acclaim that we receive. Our heroes are chief executive officers, entrepreneurs, salespersons, and entertainers who command enormous incomes and who accumulate vast wealth.

In establishing material pursuits as our highest ideal, we have forsaken our true nature. Humans are spiritual beings having a material experience, and not the opposite, as we have come to believe. In not recognizing our spiritual essence, we have created a mostly lifeless, soulless business world. The opening scene of "Joe vs. the Volcano," one of Tom Hanks' lesser known movies, provides a vivid illustration of just such an environment.

We are shown a parking lot with people threading their way through the cars toward their workplace: a metal, windowless, single-story building surrounded by tall,

*forbidding fences. Employees in drab clothes plod list-
lessly through gates flanked by guard towers and
armed attendants. Heads hang down and no one speaks
to anyone else. A single yellow flower, standing bravely
amid the mud and water puddles, is crushed under the
boot of an unfeeling, unseeing human robot. The interior of the building is stark, gray, undecorated, and lit
by harsh neon lights that sputter and buzz. A vulture-
like supervisor descends on the arriving employees
and begins the daily ritual of domination and antagonism. The supervisor removes the one vestige of humanity that Hanks claims—a desk lamp with a scene
of a tropical island on it—for no reason other than to
enforce unblinking compliance and capitulation to authority.*

Our wish would be that this experience be limited to the
realm of movie fiction. Sadly, it isn't. In my experience, finding
companies that are vibrant and full of life is the exception rather
than the rule. Businesses, as they are conceived today, operate
outside of the fabric of life. People are expected to deny their
humanity, conduct themselves as emotionless automatons, and
dedicate themselves to the "noble" pursuit of unlimited wealth.
Each year, people are working longer hours, juggling more
responsibilities, and struggling under increasing demands for
improved productivity. Constantly, we labor in fear and anxiety
as our friends and co-workers lose their jobs through layoffs and
"right-sizing." There is little joy or meaning in what we do; we feel
isolated and cutoff from our emotions and from each other, and
we are forced into inhumane actions that offend our higher
sensibilities.

The modern business world struggles under a paradigm that
is outdated and destructive. Paradigms are powerful conceptual
filters through which humans shape their understanding of the
world. Paradigms are mental models which are so fundamental to
how we think that rarely are we aware of their existence or of
their influence on how we interpret the world. Paradigms shape
what we are able to perceive, literally acting to filter information and limiting our ability to learn and to change. Our mental
models make it difficult to perceive information that is counter to
our beliefs and expectations. In some cases we ignore such data, in
others we distort it to meet our expectations, and in extreme cases

we are literally unable to perceive it. This makes it extremely difficult to change deeply rooted paradigms, and our modern business paradigm is no exception.

Today's business paradigm holds that companies exist for profit, that this profit is earned through competition, and that employees exist to serve the interests of the company. Businesses are viewed as machines with profit the product and humans just another mechanical piece. The ultimate aim of business is to grow endlessly and at an extraordinary pace. Little regard, beyond that required by law, is afforded the environment, community, or concerns of employees. Given this view of business, there should be no surprise that we find little evidence of soul in business. Machines don't have souls.

A Dawning Awareness

I became aware of the need to reintegrate soul into the world of business through my first work experience. My indoctrination into corporate life came in the service of a giant oil company. During this time, oil companies were experiencing unprecedented growth, and profits were so extreme that the U.S. Congress enacted the Windfall Profits Tax. The employees were reaping their share of the profits through accelerated performance review schedules and double-digit pay raises. You would imagine that if money could create the joy and vibrancy that you would expect to find in a soulful business, surely this would be the place. It wasn't. The employees were miserable.

I worked in a skyscraper where the walls, the carpet, the furniture, *everything* was gray. Personal decorations were allowed only to the extent that they conformed to corporate standards (and almost none did). The company operated under a rigid command-and-control management style and internal politics dictated who had power and received the prestigious jobs. Work was something you were paid to do, not something you were expected to enjoy. As you might imagine in an environment like this, most people lived in fear for their jobs and careers. After six years I was sick at heart. It took all my strength to drag myself to work.

I was making more money than I ever imagined, I held a position with ample power and prestige, and had a bright future ahead of me. But something was deeply, profoundly wrong. I felt that some important part of me was starving to death. It made little difference that I had material prosperity, so long as I lived in spiritual poverty.

I discussed this feeling with my boss. I explained to her how unfulfilled I felt despite the material comforts and prestige. Her advice was both startling and disheartening. She said that most people in the company felt much the same way, and that they had come to accept work as just a way to make money. She advised me to find something *outside of my job,* such as a hobby, charity, or church activity, that would give me the meaning for which I was looking. I was thunderstruck. It seemed unthinkable that I should have to live the majority of my waking life in a dreary, meaningless existence—only to find respite a few hours each week squeezed in between work and the normal demands of living. In the hopes of finding fulfillment through economic freedom, I left to start my own business.

The Turning Point

On the morning of June 6, 1985, I died. Not a physical death, but a psychological death; what Dr. Stan Grof calls an "ego-death." I had just spent the past year trying to start my own company, spending my entire savings, going deep into debt, and exhausting myself in the process. On that morning, I finally admitted what had been obvious for a while—my company was going to fail. With it went everything that defined who I was to the world. I could no longer say that I "was" my job, because I had none. I couldn't rely on my wealth to create a sense of worth and identity, for I had no money and loads of debt. I could not look to social standing, for a failed entrepreneur has no social standing. And the failure of my love relationship a month earlier ensured that I could not find myself through the love of another. I had nothing, therefore I was nothing. And I died.

The failure of my business proved to be the pivotal point in my life. Up to that point, I had defined myself through my income, job status, relationships, and other external material concerns— all the things that my business indoctrination had taught me to value. When these were stripped away, I was left with nothing. I was in abject despair. I couldn't eat. I couldn't feel. I couldn't think. I wanted to cry but had forgotten how. In final desperation, I closed my eyes and withdrew deep inside to find a place of safety. Down, down into a place of deep, dark, soothing coolness I went. Then I let go of myself and simply fell away.

In that instant something marvelous happened. I experienced a flash of brilliant light and was instantaneously bathed in all-encompassing, unconditional love. Although this experience was ineffable, you can imagine the experience if you recall the most intense feeling of unconditional love you have ever experienced, and then multiply it by a million. In that moment, I was reborn. I opened my eyes to a new sense of joy in just being alive. I felt mesmerized by the wonder of life and its mysteries. Since my own experience, I have come to look at the world with different eyes. I have remembered the real purpose of life—to provide a vehicle for the spiritual journey. I have realized that external circumstance has nothing to do with who we really are: marvelous, infinite souls on a journey of self-discovery and spiritual evolution.

The business environment, which had been my entire world for so long, suddenly seemed completely inhospitable, even toxic. It simply didn't seem to have any relationship to my spiritual purpose. I realized that business is an integral part of life, but it doesn't operate in that way. Business has a life of its own—it serves its own purposes, not those of spirit, and it operates by its own rules. As spiritual beings, we are on an inevitable journey to ever higher levels of consciousness. We crave meaning and a worthwhile purpose in our lives. As Chester Barnard, past CEO of New Jersey Bell Telephone, said, "People want to feel bound to some cause bigger than they, commanding, yet worthy of them, summoning them to significance in living." Businesses are mostly emotionless, amoral machines. There is little hope in such environments for finding fulfilling work.

The disparity between our experience of business and our need for soul fulfillment is the source of much misery. We reach out for something—anything—to fill the resulting emptiness. Ironically, our pursuit of material wealth and pleasure is, in large measure, due to the lack of fulfillment that such pursuits create. Instead of seeing this vicious circle for what it is, we simply intensify our efforts, convinced that if we can only earn enough money, buy enough things, have enough social prestige, we will be happy. And of course we never are.

No person whom I have ever met believes that people are born into this world solely to earn a living. And yet, that is exactly the way in which we have constructed our societies. Think about your own life over the course of the past year. Where have you spent the majority of your time and what do you spend most of your time thinking about? Dr. Juliet B. Schor, writing in her book, *The Overworked American: The Unexpected Decline of the Leisure*, notes that the average American now works the equivalent of a whole month more per year than did his or her counterpart in 1970. In fact, people are working longer hours than at any time in history other than the Industrial Revolution— spending more time on the job than did medieval serfs! We have created an insidious cycle of "work and spend" that keeps us tethered to an economic treadmill. The time has come to end this destructive cycle and rediscover the art of living.

A New Model for Business

There is much irony in knowing that we, the creators of our paradigms, have come to be enslaved by them. This is also the source of much hope, since anything that we have made we also have the power to change. Our present business practices are leading us on a perilous course of self-destruction—destruction of our social framework, destruction of our health, and destruction of the Earth. In order to avert this fate, we must conceive differently three key elements of our business paradigm. These are the beliefs that the ultimate purpose of business is to create material wealth, that employees exist to serve the interest of the company, and that successful business is characterized by rapid and endless growth.

For purposes of illustration, we can consider the metaphor of business as a vehicle. Clearly, money is required to run our businesses. Under our current business paradigm, businesses exist to create wealth for the owners. Restating this in the language of our metaphor, the *vehicle exists to consume fuel.* Gasoline powers our vehicles. Without fuel our vehicles are out of service. The destination for our vehicle is no further than the next source of fuel, and our largest concern is that we take on enough gas to get us to our next fill-up. So, we wander aimlessly from fuel source to fuel source, getting nowhere at all. The journey is virtually irrelevant so long as our vehicle consumes as much fuel as possible; and the bigger the vehicle the more fuel it can consume. In reality, we are quite reckless in our travels, leaving a trail of destruction and suffering behind us. These vehicles are machines in which mechanical parts and the human passengers are treated equally. Both are components to be consumed and discarded at will, without regard and without remorse. After all, parts are parts.

There is, however, another way of conceptualizing business. We can recognize that our destination is spiritual living, and that the journey is the evolution of the soul. If we reorient our model and say instead that the vehicle's purpose is the journey—to deliver people to a destination—then business comes to serve employees and we have another use for money, which is to fuel the journey. Clearly, we must always have enough gasoline to keep the vehicle moving, but we don't need an excess. Nor is our purpose to use gasoline. In fact, we would hope to use as little as possible. The size of our vehicle would be relevant only in that it be big enough to make the journey. The quality of the journey becomes as important as achieving the destination, and only those vehicles that can deliver us to our destination with suitable quality are acceptable.

We will never achieve truly soulful businesses until we redefine the basic tenets of the current business paradigm. We can achieve increasingly humane workplaces, but that is not the same thing as a soulful business. In fact, quite a few of the current business practices are creating a better workplace for employees. Worker empowerment, self-directed work teams, the quality movement, cultural diversity—all are allowing more soul to shine through into the business world. But these concessions are weighed against their contribution to profit and shareholder value, and rarely because they are important to human development and self-expression. In an August 1, 1994, *Business Week* magazine article titled "Managing By Values," Levi's CEO, Robert Haas states that "We are not doing this because it feels good....We are doing this because we believe in the interconnection between liberating the talents of our people and business success."

Characteristics of the Soulful Business

In many ways, a soulful business looks much like any other business. These businesses are fully committed to generating revenue and making a profit, operating effectively and efficiently, and hiring and retaining the best people available. They may "right-size" and have layoffs. They survive through product innovation and effective competition in their markets. And they insist on dedicated, purposeful effort from employees. Becoming a soulful business takes less a change in operations than a fundamental shift in the psychology of how we think about business. Out of that shift flows the basic changes in behavior and decision making that characterize a soulful company.

Soulful businesses are committed exclusively to worthy causes. They strive for a positive influence on community and nature. The quality of the employee work experience is a high priority. Corporate values are centered around selflessness, service, personal growth and learning, truthfulness, openness, and equity. The entire range of human emotions is accepted. Hugging and other modest shows of affection between consenting people are common, and love is an acceptable word. Balance is encouraged between work and personal time. People are not expected to hide or suppress events in their personal lives. Authentic human reactions are valued over "polite" behavior. Individuality and independent thought are revered. People shape the business rather than the business shaping the people. Every employee takes personal responsibility for the welfare of the company, which is easy because the corporate purpose is aligned with their personal journey.

Soulful businesses have a distinct feel to them. They have a robust, vibrant energy. People are excited about their work. There is a bustle of activity, but it is not the frantic activity of the profit-driven, cost-minimizing company. People seem to know and enjoy each other. There is a strong feeling of community. Employees walk with a spring in their step. The environment is radiant with human energy and expression. In companies like this, you feel uplifted after visiting them.

Soulful Business Requires Soulful Employees

If you were to wander through most large charitable organizations, you would see the same lifeless, automaton existence that you find in for-profit corporations. So, it is evident that orienting the business around a noble cause is not enough. It requires each individual entering into his or her unique journey. The company can promote a positive environment for people to express their full potential, but it still takes people who are committed to fully realizing their potential. This requires releasing our illusions, having the willingness to change, and dedicating ourselves to self-reflection and inner exploration.

Joseph Campbell, the renowned historian and mythologist, calls this the "hero's journey"—a prerequisite for "finding your bliss." Your "bliss" is in finding the work that you were uniquely called to do. When you find your true work, the feeling is unmistakable. Your work is effortless and has a timeless quality about it. You are fully engaged and feel energized by doing the work. Robert Henri, writing in *The Art of Spirit,* describes this phenomenon:

> When the artist is alive in any person, whatever his kind of work may be, he becomes an inventive, searching, daring, and self-expressive creature. He becomes interesting to other people. He disturbs, upsets, enlightens, and opens ways for a better understanding....Where those who are not artists are trying to close the book, he opens it and shows that there are still more pages possible.

Being on a personal journey of self-realization does not imply saintliness. It is about unfolding. It is about becoming truly, completely, authentically who we are and evolving to ever higher levels of consciousness, of spiritual being. But we are still human. Being soulful is being *completely* human. There will always be dark and light, shadow along with beauty, and we need to see reality for what it is—to overcome our illusions and self-deceptions. So, if we think about businesses and individuals aligned around their spiritual journeys, you will not find some Utopia. You will find humanity—good and evil, joy and despair. You will also find passion, vibrancy, and the sheer joy and wonder of being alive.

Businesses with Soul

Fortunately, there are companies which have been able to conduct business profitably while simultaneously demonstrating a robust spirit and soulful environment. The consulting firm where I presently work is an excellent example of a company centered around creating a soulful business environment. Over a decade ago, the two founding partners, Dr. Kareen Strickler and Dr. Don Brush, shared a vision of a business where they could live out their values and pursue their spiritual growth in a business context. Kareen determined early in life, through her father's example, that she would not spend her time doing things that were not meaningful and that did not bring value to the world. While working with the Institute of Cultural Affairs, she internalized their credo that "anything worth doing cannot be completed in your lifetime." This led Kareen and Don to conceive of a "mighty cause" for their business, one that was bigger than both of them. They wanted to have an impact that would make the business world different, that would help give people a sense of purposefulness. Their journey, and mine, is the revitalization of the workplace where people will have a sense of meaning and renewed joy in living. Remaining true to their vision has not come at the cost of personal financial sacrifice—in fact both have enjoyed top incomes for most of the years the firm has been in business.

Most of the companies that I encounter which are able to sustain a soulful environment are relatively small. Perhaps smaller organizations find it easier to create a soulful environment. If so, there is hope, since most of the new jobs in the United States in the past decade have come from small companies. Tom Peters, noted business author and consultant, predicts that companies in the future will break into smaller and smaller components, until they attain a level of no more than one hundred employees. Smaller business units may foster the feeling of small, closely knit communities of people working toward a shared vision. Developments such as these may portend a more fertile environment for the emergence of soul in business than we ever before have known.

Conclusion

People today are in greater transition than ever before in history. The rapid and profound changes in our lives are forcing increasing numbers of people to reevaluate their values and to assess what is truly important to them. As more and more top people drop out of the traditional job market and seek more fulfilling work, we will see a profound shift in the working world as we know it.

Businesses are in a position to have a profound effect on human consciousness. Campbell notes in *The Power of Myth* that humans have always placed at the center of society the institutions which had the most importance. Initially, churches were the largest buildings and were located at the center of the society. Later, political buildings were the most prominent as governments and politicians gained supremacy in power and influence. Today, the buildings of industry are unparalleled in size and importance. We spend a huge amount of our time at work. Much of our behavior is shaped by our work environment. I believe that it is here that the spiritual transformation of our society will take root.

As we approach this exciting new time for our world, we will find our paradigms shifting. As they do, we will lose whatever security we may have known as we leap to an uncertain future with nothing more than hope and faith to guide us. Perhaps we can gain some comfort from the words of the French poet Guillaume Apollinaire, who wrote:

> *Come to the edge.*
> *No, we will fall.*
>
> *Come to the edge.*
> *No, we will fall.*
>
> *They came to the edge.*
> *He pushed them, and they flew.*

Dorothy E. Fischer, MBA, founded InnerAwareness in 1990 to help individuals and corporations create positive change and achieve greater success. A dynamic and inspiring speaker, she has appeared on numerous radio and television shows in the Dallas and New York City markets.

Fischer earned her MBA from the University of Michigan, specializing in organizational behavior. She also holds a BA in economics and mathematics from Lawrence University in Appleton, WI. Originally from Cedar Falls, Iowa, she moved to Dallas, Texas in 1979. Starting as a strategic planner for a Fortune 100 company, she then spent four years as manager of financial analysis for a subdivision of Standard Oil. For the next five years, Fischer was an independent consultant, creating customized corporate programs to improve quality, customer service, and the human factor in business.

13

The System Versus the Soul

Dorothy E. Fischer

"The end justifies the means," said Niccolo Machiavelli, Florentine statesman and writer, in 1513. These five words have come to represent an entire rationale for corruption and the abuse of power, leadership, and authority. Canonized by our English language, the author's own name has become an adjective. Webster's acknowledges Machiavellian behavior as "characterized by political principles and methods of expediency, craftiness, and duplicity." These values, outlined almost five hundred years ago, still serve as a working definition of what I call the "System."

It is this System which robs the business world of its soul. It is this System which each one of us must confront in our own hearts and minds. It is this System which forms the temptation of greed, ego, and control. It is this System to which we either succumb as sycophants, servants, and slaves, or transcend as soul-filled individuals with integrity, ideals, and conscience.

I believe the business world of the 1990s is at a crossroads. The Politics of Greed have had their turn, and we are not particularly pleased with the fruits they have borne. Cynicism is at an all time high. Special interest groups, insider trading scandals, savings and loan crises, and "Me Generation" values all have left a bitter taste. It is now time for a renaissance of deeper values, ethics, and principles. In short, it is time to bring back the true soul of business. In so doing, we heal ourselves and our world.

I have had my go-arounds with the System. My experiences have defined my life and propelled me into a career to help people and companies reclaim their ideals, visions, sense of purpose, values, and their souls.

One of my first teachers in the lessons of the System versus the Soul was Josef Patik, whom I met at the impressionable age of eleven. Due to my father's business, our family spent the summer of 1968 in Yugoslavia. It was there we met Josef, a Czechoslovakian political refugee marked for death because he disagreed with the System. Josef's crime was that he had written pro-Democracy editorials in the Prague student newspaper and criticized Communism, exercising what we call "First Amendment Rights." After Russia invaded Czechoslovakia in August that year, Josef was on the KGB hit list. They had already killed most of his friends who had also been active in the student-based freedom movement. Josef temporarily escaped to Yugoslavia, but was within days of being forced to return to Czechoslovakia to face certain death, when my father met him by happenstance.

It is one thing to hear about abusive systems. It is a whole different experience to sit across the dinner table from a twenty-one year old man whose life hangs in the balance, telling us his life story, as we all await word on whether he can successfully escape to freedom in North America or not.

I remember Josef clearly. He was soft-spoken, medium height, slim, and had very dark hair and fair skin which had a slight bluish cast where his closely shaven thick beard wanted to grow back. He wore a dark suit, white shirt, dark thin tie and black dress shoes which were worn down but brightly shined. It took him a while to overcome his shyness as he spoke in self-conscious English, but there was a quiet confidence about him that belied the uncertainty of the circumstances in which he found himself. As he spoke of his leadership role in the freedom movement his eyes shone with pride. He evidenced no regrets. Even though he did not want to become a KGB statistic, he clearly had known all along that he was taking such a risk by having his name published with the editorials he had written. He very simply and without swagger said he had already decided that the principles of freedom and democracy were, if necessary, worth dying for. To an American eleven-year-old, he was Patrick

Henry come to life. With my father's intervention, Josef was able to escape to Canada where he continues to have a productive and fulfilling life. To me, Josef stands out as a pure example of soul transcending the System.

My turn came when I was not much older than Josef. At the age of 22, as a new MBA hire for a Fortune 100 company, I experienced the tyranny of another form of the System. Looking back from this vantage point 15 years later, I see the surprising parallels of the abuses of the totalitarian government which Josef escaped and the company for which I went to work.

Ego, territory, power, and unkept promises were the cornerstones of both. Fairness and opportunity were words easily expressed, but rarely experienced except for the privileged few who knew how to work the System. Both systems brought out the worst in people who operated from a survival mode, paralyzed with fear and intimidation from continued abuse of power and authority. I don't mean to diminish Josef's actual life or death dilemma by comparison to mine, but I can say that I *felt* like I was dealing with a life or death struggle at the time. I had completely lost my own direction and given way to the overwhelming stress of 90- to 100-hour work weeks, political knives in my back, needless competition from supposed teammates, continually having to "prove myself" (especially as a female MBA in 1979) and continuous erosion of my personal integrity. In a matter of months, I had managed to slip into the dysfunctional patterns of the System that abused me. Unlike Josef, I had lost my soul. In my case, the "KGB" had won.

Before my first job experience, I thought the American corporate business world could do no wrong. The free enterprise system represented the shining example of democracy in action, the quintessence of those principles to which Josef Patik had dedicated himself and for which he would have died. Inspired by his example, I entered the workplace with the zeal of a freedom fighter, ready to "win one for the Gipper." Two parts Rebecca of Sunnybrook Farm and three parts Pollyanna, I was about as far from Machiavelli as you could get. I had no survival skills for what lay before me other than the family motto which had always worked for me in the academic world: "When in doubt, just work harder." Slowly but surely I began to realize that I was in the worst shark's nest I could ever have found. But I was still too naive to realize that I could not beat the System by just working harder. Caught-up in my own blind spot of survival, eroding self-esteem, and the need to make a success of my first real job, I did not even know enough to leave the System for something healthier. I was fired after a year and a half. The System finally won.

Not many 23-year-olds get to experience a full blown soul-searching midlife crisis. My values and belief system were totally shaken from top to bottom, and I faced the challenging task of rediscovering my true soul.

The surprisingly painful awareness I had to face came from realizing that my idealistic beliefs about the corporate business world were more the issue. Why had I so stubbornly refused to see reality? The answer lay with the eleven-year-old girl inside me who still wanted to think that Freedom = Democracy = Capitalism = American Free Enterprise System = Fortune 500. I did not want to admit that my cherished beliefs in the pureness of American business could be wrong, and that there was such a dysfunctional side to it. It was at some level easier to believe that I had failed the system than the System had failed me. After all, if the blame were all mine, then I had power over the situation and could find a way to correct the problem. If the System itself were flawed, what then?

There is no greater example in our entire cultural and literary heritage for the redemption of the soul in both an individual and a company than our old friend, Ebenezer Scrooge. Using Charles Dickens' classic *A Christmas Carol* (first published in 1843) as a case history familiar to us all, let me point out nine key aspects related to bringing back our souls.

1. Denial of the Problem is the Biggest Obstacle. Scrooge consistently refused to see that there was anything inappropriate in his behavior. That blind spot was enough to keep the System alive and well at the firm Scrooge and Marley. Like most executives who have been entrenched in the System long enough, Ebenezer was quick to defend the status quo, and determined not to change. Most of the entire *Christmas Carol* storyline is dedicated to breaking up Scrooge's denial process, one spirit at a time. When first faced by the ghost of his former business partner Jacob Marley, Scrooge refuses to think the apparition is anything but a figment of his imagination. When Marley confronts this denial, Scrooge replies,

"A slight disorder of the stomach makes [my senses] cheat. You may be an undigested bit of beef, a blot of mustard, a crumb of cheese, a fragment of an underdone potato. There's more of gravy than of grave about you, whatever you are!"

Our limiting belief systems make deniers of us all. We simply subconsciously screen out all information which is not consistent with the operating program that is running our human software. Since we are not conscious that we are doing this, we never know what we don't know! This inevitable catch-22 is still the biggest single factor stopping positive growth and change on the individual level and therefore on the aggregate corporate level. What limiting belief systems might be blocking you or your company right now? If your denial system is intact, you will not have a clear answer to that question. Ignorance is not bliss. We must continuously search ourselves to uncover our hidden denials if we are to lead fulfilling lives.

2. Getting Out of Denial and Developing Soul Requires Pain. The truth hurts, which is why we run from it. We must be willing to experience the temporary pain, shame, embarrassment, and hurt which comes from seeing behind the denials. Ebenezer faced one painful reality after another as the spirits showed him the impact of both the negative choices he did make (commission) and the positive choices he did not make (omission). I have always been struck by the image of the charwoman stealing the bed linens off Scrooge's not yet cold corpse and feeling no remorse, knowing she was treating him the way he had treated her. As painful as this must have been for Scrooge to witness, anything less dramatic might have not done the job of blasting through his tough denial system.

This soul-birthing process requires emotional labor which takes courage and determination. But as most mothers would tell you, the labor pain is worth it for the results produced. During labor, it may seem like the painful part of the process will last forever, but it does not. Once completed, the pain generally fades from memory and is quickly replaced by tremendous joy. Which brings us to the next point.

3. Great Joy Comes from Rediscovering the Soul. Few scenes in the history of drama are guaranteed to bring tears of joy to the audience the way Dickens does when Scrooge returns from the future and finds out that he has not missed Christmas Day. But even after the initial giddiness has worn off, Ebenezer is still a profoundly happy and deeply satisfied man.

"He went to church, and walked about the streets, and

watched the people hurrying to and fro, and patted the children on the head, and questioned beggars, and looked down into the kitchens of houses, and up to the windows, and found that everything could yield him pleasure. He had never dreamed that any walk—that anything—could give him so much happiness."

The true reward of living a soulful life and creating soul in business comes not from the big victories. The everyday satisfactions and continuous love for life itself will far outweigh, in the end, any specific celebrations. Of course, the good news is that we don't have to choose between these alternatives—we can enjoy them both.

4. Having Soul in Business Can Improve Profitability. The difficulty comes in having to prove and justify this in short-term "bean counter" terminology. Intangibles are hard to measure, and I know of no accounting reports which reflect the opportunity cost of the loss of human spirit in a company. But the loss is very real, nonetheless. Would any of us have liked to work at the firm of Scrooge and Marley prior to Ebenezer's transformation?

The new Scrooge immediately increased Bob Cratchit's wages and used more coal to heat the frigid counting-house. In the short term, that may have imposed a negative impact on the bottom line. But what about the long-term impact? Scrooge & Marley's productivity surely improved greatly once the clerk's fingers weren't stiff with cold and Cratchit was no longer distracted with worry and grief about Tiny Tim or how to feed his family.

The fact that the soul of a business cannot necessarily be measured in numbers doesn't mean that it is not a positive contributing factor to the bottom line. Business has overreacted to the anti-establishment days of the 1960s and must now get over its defensive posture. "Love, peace, and happiness" are not the enemy of "profits, earnings per share, and dividends." In a healthy balanced system it is possible to have the best of both worlds.

The remarkable success of Southwest Airlines, led by founder and chairman Herb Kelleher, is a clear demonstration of the blend of hard-core Yankee business smarts and forces of the human spirit. Now the most financially successful airline in America, a key competitive advantage Southwest relies on, and Wall Street acknowledges, comes from the spirit of the employees. A 1992

Harvard Business School case study of Southwest concludes that the airline's success comes from "differentiating itself through its focus on service, operations, cost control, marketing, its people, and its corporate culture." This culture did not happen by accident. Kelleher told *Fortune* magazine (May 2, 1994, cover story), "What we are looking for, first and foremost, is a sense of humor. Then we are looking for people who have to excel to satisfy themselves and who work well in a collegial environment. We don't care that much about education and expertise, because we can train people to do whatever they have to do. We hire attitudes." In other words, Kelleher looks for people with soul to build a company with soul.

Those attitudes go straight to the bottom line. "Southwest employees are willing to pitch in wherever they are needed, to walk—or fly—the extra mile," *Fortune* reports. "Pilots might man the boarding gate if things are running slow; ticket agents might find themselves schlepping luggage." Not a common picture of a labor union work force. As a result, Southwest planes are turned around at the gate twice as fast as competitors, and have more time to focus on the more profitable pursuits of transporting passengers.

5. To Develop Soul Is to Risk Being Laughed At. The good news is, the results are so wonderful, you won't care about others' skepticism. Both Charles Dickens and *Fortune* magazine can validate this. Dickens writes,

> Some people laughed to see the alteration in
> [Scrooge], but he let them laugh, and little
> heeded them, for he was wise enough to know
> that nothing ever happened on this globe, for
> good, at which some people did not have their
> fill of laughter in the outset; and knowing that
> such as these would be blind anyway, he
> thought it quite as well that they should wrinkle
> up their eyes in grins, and have the malady in
> less attractive forms. His own heart laughed,
> and that was quite enough for him.

Fortune reports,

> There is much talk about the Southwest 'family'
> around the airline's headquarters, the sort of
> talk that makes the corporate cynics snicker.

But the halls are littered with converts to the cause. Says David Ridley, who arrived at Southwest six years ago to direct marketing and sales after working at two more traditional Fortune 500 companies: 'I was pretty dubious at first, having been at places where everyone but two or three top people were considered commodities. But I have come to appreciate a place where kindness and the human spirit are nurtured.'

Surely the loyalty and employee satisfaction engendered by such a culture creates even further contributions to profitability from low employee turnover. Who wants to leave an environment filled with kindness and nurturing of spirit to go back to being treated like a commodity? Let the cynics laugh. I suspect we know who is getting the last laugh.

6. Dysfunction Breeds Dysfunction. Dysfunctional systems are self-perpetuating; specific action must be taken to break the cycles. "I'll do unto you like they did unto me" becomes the operating mode. This happens automatically and subconsciously. Abused children do not purposely grow up to be abusive adults. Some of them do escape the cycle. But every abusive adult was once abused by someone or some system. Even the villainous Ebenezer Scrooge is quickly unmasked by the Spirit of Christmas Past as simply the adult version of the neglected, unloved boy deserted at boarding school during the Christmas holidays. Small wonder he later developed a "Bah! Humbug!" attitude toward Christmas and did not know how to accept the loving invitation from his nephew to share the holiday with family.

The dysfunctional habits we have buried deep within us will invariably show up in our business life. How can they not? We are holistic beings and are unable, despite our best efforts, to sequester the unhealed aspects of our personalities. This generally takes us back to square one—denial of the problem. Which in turn forms the breeding ground for the negativity within us to grow unchecked. Self projection is our last defense, and it is relatively easy in this complex world to find someone or something else to blame. Witness again Scrooge's response to his nephew's suggestion that he not be so cross.

"What else can I be...when I live in such a world of fools as this?...If I could work my will...every idiot who goes around with

'Merry Christmas' on his lips should be boiled with his own pudding, and buried with a stake of holly through his heart."

Unfortunately, blaming others does nothing to heal the hurt within.

Dysfunctional family systems clearly contribute to dysfunctional business systems, since we humans are the carriers. But this equation works both ways. Few can maintain as kindly and forgiving a nature as Bob Cratchit did. Mrs. Cratchit gives us a more accurate portrayal of the emotional pressures in their family resulting from Scrooge's demeanor. "I wish I had him here. I'd give him a piece of my mind to feast upon, and I hope he'd have a good appetite for it."

Had fortune not intervened to rescue the Cratchits from this downward negative spiral, no telling what might have happened. Unable to cope with the grief of Tiny Tim's death, Bob might have stayed chronically depressed, turned to drink to drown his sorrows, had an extra-marital affair to soothe his mid-life crisis, become surly and emotionally abusive to his family members, or simply lost himself in continued workaholism. These and many other choices await those who lose their souls to businesses. And so the cycle continues, unless we realize the next major point.

7. There are No Victims, Only Volunteers. The Bob Cratchits of the world actually perpetuate the System by succumbing to it. I am reminded of the story of the woman who complained and complained about her various health problems, all brought on by the high stress from her job. Her friend, tired of the litany, finally said, "why don't you just get another job?" "What!?" exclaimed the woman indignantly, "and give up my company's health plan?"

Whether the dysfunctional system be in business, government, religion, education, or any other aspect of society, those who get caught up in it are either seduced by the power of being the abuser or stuck feeling powerless, helpless, and hopeless. Our responsibility as individuals is to be true to our own souls and NOT sell out to the System. If we cannot help heal the System we are in, then we must leave the System and find a better opportunity, even if we have to create our own system to do it. I know this is not easy. I didn't know how to do this in my first job. I had to be spit out of the belly of the whale. Josef Patik tried to impact the System he was in for the better, and when that did not work, he had to flee. But he had made his mark. Others like him persisted; twenty years later the Iron Curtain came falling down throughout all of Eastern Europe.

As devastating as my first job was, I did not have to face Russian tanks, watch my friends die, or leave my homeland. In this country, the systems most of us face can be dealt with more easily than Josef's. None of us need be victims for long. There are healthy opportunities and choices available, if we can just over-come our denial and pain long enough to find them. If you have trouble assessing the soul of the business you are in, or one you might want to join, try using the twenty questions I created to help my clients address this subject (see Illustration 1). And remember, you don't have to work through your difficulties all by yourself. Josef needed my father's help. I have needed others' help. Many people have needed my help. Don't hesitate to seek out competent help in healing yourself from unhealthy systems. It is the easiest and most nurturing way to succeed.

8. Business Leaders Bear the Greatest Responsibility for Developing the Soul in a Business. We can do our best to rectify and heal the System, or leave it for another, but it is the business leader who sets the tone for the business soul. Scrooge was reminded of this when he revisited the firm where he once held a Cratchit-like job as apprentice and clerk. His old boss, Fezziwig, was a kindly man who eagerly led one and all in great celebration, stopping early on Christmas Eve and transforming the warehouse into a snug warm ballroom with musicians, food, and family members. The Fezziwigs themselves led the dancing, making it safe for all to join in.

The Ghost of Christmas Past chided Scrooge, "A small matter, to make these silly folks so full of gratitude....He has spent but a few pounds of your mortal money: three or four, perhaps. Is that so much that he deserves this praise?" Scrooge replied uncharacteristically,

"It isn't that, Spirit. He has the power to render us happy or unhappy, to make our service light or burdensome, a pleasure or a toil. Say that his power lies in words and looks, in things so light and insignificant that it is impossible to add and count 'em up; what then? The happiness he gives is quite as great as if it cost a fortune."

There you have it. The greatest possible acknowledgment of the intangible yet priceless value of the leadership role which creates the soul in business, direct from the mouth of none other than Ebenezer Scrooge, himself.

Illustration 1

Twenty Questions Used to Measure the System vs. the Soul in a Business

1. Are managers more concerned with their own career paths and advancements than the company's profitability and welfare?

2. Is the business focused on providing needed products and services and serving the customer, or strictly concerned with profits?

3. Are promises kept, both to employees and customers?

4. Is more time spent in "CYA" (cover-up) activities than actually producing? Are mistakes punished publicly?

5. Is more time spent discussing politics (e.g., how do we get this past another department) than product?

6. Are people always trying to assess the mood of the manager? Are secretaries used as buffers to assess moods, protect people, pass along back-door information?

7. Is workaholism encouraged? Do people brag about how long they work? Is this a "badge of courage?" (e.g., "I was here till midnight last night!") Are people afraid to leave on time?

8. Is blame always passed down the ranks?

9. Are there continual power struggles between departments?

10. Does the company train people, or is there just "baptism by fire?"

11. Does the company value the individual? (e.g., Do people take their vacations? When they want to?)

12. Are accomplishments recognized on a regular basis (not just birthdays and retirements)? Are successes celebrated? Is success shared, or does the boss take all the glory?

13. Do employees have a healthy sense of humor, or does cynicism rule?

14. Does the manager listen? Can employees comfortably ask for help?

15. Are managers taught human relations skills (proper communication, delegation, follow-up, etc.)?

16. Are people afraid to state the obvious (the emperor has no clothes)? Can a person ask, "Why are we doing this project?"

17. Can people question the system comfortably, without fear of reprisal?

18. Do people exist in a survival mentality, reduced to thinking in terms of how to maintain their jobs?

19. Does the system rely on fear or intimidation to get results? Does top management create "crises" to get higher productivity?

20. Do people find the longer they work in the company the more their self-esteem, personal power, healthy ego declines?

There are many good examples of leaders who understand and practice these principles. In a major hospital known worldwide for its heart surgery, a sixty-year-old janitor who cleans the messy post-surgery operating theaters, broke into a toothy grin when asked what he thought of his job. "Me and the Doctor help fix people's hearts." The Doctor—a famous household name—clearly shared his victories with everyone on the team, right down to the cleaning staff.

Alan S. Boyd, retired Chairman of Airbus North America and an acknowledged expert on the airline industry, says, "At other places, managers say that people are their most important resource, but nobody acts on it. At Southwest, they have never lost sight of the fact."

A Wall Street securities analyst who has observed Kelleher since Southwest started flying in 1971, says, "He is the sort of manager who will stay out with a mechanic in some bar until four o'clock in the morning to find out what is going on. And then he will fix whatever is wrong." Kelleher knows what it is to be the apprentice, having worked six summers on the factory floor at a Campbell Soup Co. plant.

In 1913, Mr. J.C. Penney adopted into company policy "The Penney Idea," principles he had personally written which to this day are maintained as the soul of his retail company. Today's businesses would do well to emulate his leadership and policy (see Illustration 2). Rotary International, a service organization comprised of business leaders around the world, asks its members to put all decisions to "The 4-Way Test: (1) Is it the TRUTH? (2) Is it FAIR to All Concerned? (3) Will it build GOODWILL and Better Friendships? (4) Will it be BENEFICIAL to all concerned?"

Unfortunately, it is all too easy to give lip service to such guidelines. If you are a business leader, go back to the questions in Illustration 1 and see how well your company, department, division, or group fares. Then remember the next point.

9. There are Ways to Rediscover the Soul in Business. Rediscovering the soul in business is a job that requires every one of us. Although I place greater responsibility on the leaders to do so, the process is the same no matter where we are in the System. First we must get out of denial of the dysfunctional aspects of the System, both externally and within ourselves. By telling the truth, we may begin the process of healing the shame of having been corrupted by the System in the first place. This

---

Illustration 2

The Penney Idea

The Penney Idea as stated below was written by J.C. Penney and adopted as the operating business principles of his retail company in 1913.

- To serve the public as nearly as we can to its complete satisfaction.

- To expect for the service we render a fair remuneration, and not all the profit the traffic will bear.

- To do all in our power to pack the customer's dollar full of value, quality and satisfaction.

- To continue to train ourselves and our associates so the service we give will be more and more intelligently performed.

- To improve constantly the human factor in our business.

- To reward the men and women in our organization through participation in what the business produces.

- To test our every policy, method and act in this wise: "Does it square with what is right and just?"

---

opens the door to great joy, and the rediscovery of deeper values which can join up with the healthy side of free enterprise to create a successful system for all.

This renaissance will likely require changing policies, behaviors, reward systems, evaluation methods, hiring systems, and power structures. It requires a deep commitment to achieving a higher path—especially in the face of opposition when vestiges of the old System inevitably try to reassert themselves. It may mean we are laughed at and misunderstood by others. It may require deep introspection to confront and heal the hidden wounds of childhood which leave us vulnerable to perpetuating abusive systems. But the rewards are many and vast, both in potential improvement to the tangible bottom-line, as well as the quality of life which numbers can never capture. *I know this can be done.*

We no longer have an excuse for the dismal status quo of the System. I challenge American businesses to commit to the ideals upon which this nation was founded. I challenge our current and future MBAs and executives to search themselves for a purpose, passion, and mission to contribute to the world, and no longer sanction greed as a suitable motivation. I challenge the abused employees of the System to break their chains of misery and seek higher ground. I challenge our business leaders to create a nation that will light the lamp of freedom for the Josef Patiks of the world. I challenge the leadership of our nation's businesses to come forth and develop the soul in our companies and in ourselves.

Kathleen M. Redmond (left) is president of Cardinal Concepts which provides marketing advisory services to corporations and individuals. For corporations, the firm specializes in the development of marketing strategies, brochures, advertisements, presentation materials, direct mail and marketing letters.

Prior to founding Cardinal Concepts in 1993, Redmond had 22 years of experience in marketing and sales, most recently as executive vice president at a major Boston-based investment firm. She holds a BA from Marymount College.

Juli Ann Reynolds (right) is a principal at Korn/Ferry International, a major executive search firm. She is a leader in providing executive search and human resources consulting services to the technology and health care industries in the United States and Canada.

Prior to joining Korn/Ferry, Reynolds was a vice president of a Boston-based international executive search firm. She has 17 years of experience in organizational development and HR management consulting. She holds an MA from the University of Georgia and is a member of the Advisory Board of Cardinal Concepts.

14

Soul Dusting™

Kathleen M. Redmond
and Juli Ann Reynolds

American business is in crisis and the current volatility of the stock market reflects it. Business is wary and watching the bottom line, and the American worker feels anxious. Too many have been laid off, too many can't find jobs, too many hate the jobs they have, and too many are fooling themselves when they measure their satisfaction by their sizable salaries and large corporate offices. Reality is far from the American dream of a secure, satisfying, well-paying job. The future in the land of opportunity seems to hold fewer promises. Ever since the end of the Second World War, we have been lulled into a false sense of security, becoming dependent on a very paternalistic attitude in both government and business. The economy was generally thriving and companies could afford to maintain large payrolls and pension benefits. And we came to expect them. Those days are over. Even many of our safe government jobs are a thing of the past. In today's global economy, competition is stiff and companies have to take strong measures to succeed. Stream-lined staffs and budgets are here to stay.

But let's be serious. Those golden days may look good now, but they weren't really all that great. Since society valued the long-term continuous career, many who chose change suffered losses in seniority, advancement, and peer respect. Although the economy was prospering, there were many bored executives just hanging in until retirement. And women and minorities were struggling to get a foothold on the corporate ladder. There was something soulless about all of it. In retrospect, it's easy to see that the price of that American dream was the individual soul.

The world is undergoing a major transformation and we are smack in the middle of it. The American dream is changing, but into what? It feels like a nightmare because we don't know what the future holds. There is no clarity when you look into the crystal ball. We are in unfamiliar territory and since there is no new dream, there is no visible road to take us there. We are at a crossroads and the only roads clearly marked are the old ones which will just take us back to where we started. We need a significant vision of the future—a new positive American dream. A dream in which we as individuals are independent not dependent. A dream in which individuals are empowered to create new avenues and approaches to their future. A dream in which a career now has options. A dream in which we live inside-out, not outside-in. A dream in which we are defined by our internal soul gifts and not by external expectations.

Management consultants are asking us to move from reengineering the corporation to rediscovering soul in business. The search for soul in business? Is this the new solution? We aren't being asked to forfeit our quality initiatives, our customer satisfaction guidelines, or our purpose, vision, and mission statements. They are still very important, but they aren't enough. We are being challenged to go deeper and discover what is called the soul of our company. Soul is being offered as the latest in elusive answers to the malaise of American business. If you can identify the soul of your corporation, you will not only survive, but thrive.

Soul on Madison Avenue

It would be easy to dismiss this "soul in business" theory as something on the fringe, something that only socially responsible companies, the "goody-two-shoes" of the corporate world, are interested in. But there must be something to it because, overnight, Madison Avenue has discovered soul. Soul is showing up in advertisements in print and television. According to the media, all sorts of products have soul. Cars have soul, that's what Audi claims. Shopping centers have soul; the Prudential Center in

Boston's new slogan: "The heart of the city now has a soul." Permasoft hair products declare, "Change is good for the soul but murder on the hair." Aveda Esthetiques claims, "For Body and Soul. Pure Plant Skin Care." Anita Roddick states in her American Express ad copy, "Stories are the soul of The Body Shop." And, right before Easter, Serenade Chocolates were marketed as "food for the soul." Eat chocolate and save your soul?

So what's going on? It appears that Madison Avenue has tapped into something. Is it the consumers' unconscious search for soul? Has business sincerely adopted a new search for meaning? Or is this just the latest twist in the old strategy of selling our soul for profits?

What is the significance of what's happening on Madison Avenue? By endowing inanimate objects with soul, our most valuable asset, the agencies have taken something precious and turned it into something common, into a commodity. The soul scholar Thomas Moore states in *Care of the Soul* that objects can have a soul. We disagree. We believe that objects do not possess souls. However, we also believe that any object or work of art carefully created, crafted, cared for, and loved reflects the soul of the person or persons who did the creating, crafting, caring, and loving. Those objects may be soulful, but that is very different from having a soul. Some readers might feel that we are overreacting to marketing hype or playing word games. We don't think so.

Marketing trends are a recognition of the mass need. Clearly there is a need for soul, but if we project soul into everything that surrounds us, including business, then the chances are we will continue to project our uniqueness onto the external world. It is, of course, a lot easier to have an intellectual alliance with a commodity, without ever doing any soul search-ing. But this is exactly what is desperately needed—a journey to the interior—an introduction to our own unique souls.

Entrepreneurs Tom Chappell and Anita Roddick have both written books about the search for soul in their business. Although the titles might hint otherwise, Chappell's and Roddick's books suggest that it is the individual's soul that must be discovered. In *The Soul of a Business*, Tom Chappell states very plainly that his first step was to find his own soul. And in *Body and Soul*, Roddick states, "What I have learned is that people become motivated when you guide them to the source of their own power and when you make heroes out of employees who best personify what you want to see in the organization." Entrepreneurs and founders of their own companies are in an enviable position. They have the power to create the company they want. And what they both want is a company that is profitable, retains its core values, and provides an environment in which each employee is encouraged to discover his or her own soul and to flourish.

Lois Lindauer, founder of The Diet Workshop tells this story: "I was a fat child and understood the pain and humiliation of not having control over your body." In building her company, Lindauer's commitment to herself and others to have "control in their lives" was founded on a pervasive and powerful vulnerability. Her soul purpose guided the creating of programs that nurtured first herself, then her employees, and together, her clients. "When leaders use their own passion as a driving force in building their organizations, it stimulates every one's sense of passion. There is a flurry of ideas going at all times. It's exciting; people want to work for a company that is spirited with meaning, that becomes the whole, and is greater than a part." Lindauer is an inspiring lecturer who speaks from the inside out, passionate about taking the creative responsibility for looking at life from different perspectives. "There is a certain bliss, an energy force that radiates through the decisions that are your purpose in life. It is gratifying. Every moment is complete in itself."

Yet another business frontiersman, Alan Lewis, chairman and chief executive officer of Grand Circle Travel, developed a vision statement for himself, his employees, and his customers that has driven revenues to $130 million annually. "We will strive to be a great company, providing a workplace that is stimulating, fulfilling, and meaningful to our associates (employees); an environment where associates connect to their passions and to each other as we achieve professional and personal goals. All associates will be given the opportunity to maximize their potential in an organization that is supportive of Body, Mind, and Heart." Lewis defines Body as "recognizing our dynamic and stressful environment, we will provide opportunities for associates to strengthen, develop and maintain their physical selves." On Mind, he states, "We will maintain a commitment to growth and expansion of our intellectual selves through experiential learning, training and the sharing of experience with other companies." And with Heart: "We will continue to be a diverse, compassionate organization that supports associates' balance between professional and family lives, with caring and empathy for all."

And there are more stories.

The leaders are using a new language that begs for innovation, responsiveness, courage, vulnerability, and a rigorous transformation of visions from pyramid to concentric circles where everyone leads themselves with soul purpose. There are no footpaths where the leaders of these companies chose to go. "We learn to build this company everyday. We learn together as partners to help one another," stated John Meyer, vice president, Human Resources, ChipCom Corporation, a company whose revenues have reached the $180 million mark. Members of the executive team are clear that they are each other's customers. "We are creating new ways of building as we go. It has brought us honesty with each other, a vulnerability that is full of rich wisdom and a dynamism that we respect. We see it as living from the inside out."

These men and women, visionary leaders, are fortunate and so are the people who work with them. Having connected with their own souls, they clearly understand their responsibility to provide an environment of challenging growth for their employees. However, many others in the business world are still entrenched in organizations which are solidly standing still in the old paradigm. Their challenge is to engage their own souls, create their own visions. But how do they do that? Where do they start?

Our Search for Meaning

Our search for answers came to us on a bitter winter day. We, Kathleen and Juli Ann, had been meeting regularly for a few months, getting together to discuss many topics, explore various ideas; but generally, we focused on career issues and business trends. We recognized that we were on a search, but the object of that search remained illusory. Time and again however, we kept coming back to one subject: the widespread disillusionment in business. Juli Ann was seeing it as she interviewed candidates and companies in her work as a principal at Korn/Ferry International, a major executive recruiting firm. She reported that she was increasingly aware that many whom she interviewed were anxious and often unimpressive. They looked fabulous on paper but, in a face-to-face interview, they presented career histories that sounded empty. She was astounded that a great percentage of these candidates, extremely qualified and highly recommended, were passive and lackluster, as though they had expended all of their energy. They were exhausted. They apparently had lost the connection to anything that could rekindle that energy. Many had no idea that this was the image they projected. Others, those who sought out Juli Ann's counsel and wisdom, were the executives who knew they were in trouble, who knew they needed to do something. But the question was always what? And if they could answer that question, the next big one was how?

The circumstances surrounding Kathleen's recent resignation as executive vice president of a large financial institution had left her disenchanted with the corporate world. As Kathleen tried to get her career back on track, she did the required networking and informational interviews. She was overwhelmed by the lack of enthusiasm, the absence of passion in these executives. Most of them were just playing the game and hanging on until their children were out of college, or some other similar future scenario, when financial responsibilities were decreased. They were bored and tired, or worn down by constant reorganizations that offered solutions that never materialized. Some of them were resigned to their careers and lifestyle and dismissed any real concerns with a shrug of the shoulders. They didn't see any alternative and refused to acknowledge any real problem, choosing to stay anchored in what they saw as their safe harbor. They wore their mantle of responsibility visibly and any exploration of new personal waters would have to wait. These successful businessmen and women looked at Kathleen with a combination of fear and envy, reflecting back to her her own confused emotions about the meaning of "life" in the corporate world.

In this process, Kathleen also interviewed with two rising stars who didn't fit the profile of the disillusioned executive. However, they didn't strike Kathleen as positive role models either. One in particular was quite taken with his executive office with the oriental rugs and antique desk and credenza. He certainly didn't admit to any ennui, since he was fairly new in his position as executive vice president of a major regional bank. But when Kathleen asked him what his vision was, why he joined the bank, and what he hoped to accomplish, she received standard, run of the mill answers, when he chose to answer. The only added value in that office that she could see was the antiques.

In sharing these experiences we realized that we were both

encountering the same phenomena. We weren't surprised, since there has been a lot of publicity, books, and articles surrounding burnout and midlife crisis. But it did seem as though the numbers were increasing. And we had both been exposed to individuals who really identified with the power of their position and sometimes abused that power. Another fascinating dimension to this was the number of women who had reached senior management levels and were leaving corporate America, having suffered from meaningless bureaucracy. What was happening? Was this the same old story or was this indicative of a new trend, another facet to the search for satisfaction, the pursuit of happiness in the corporate world?

At this point in our conversation Juli Ann said, "So what is it? What's going on? What's happening? It's like an epidemic of disillusionment or boredom. What's causing it? These people are intelligent, creative business people. It's like some science fiction movie where aliens from space have sucked out their life blood, and returned them to their lives as robots. It's as though they have stolen their souls." Soul! We looked at each other. We knew that with that one word—soul—we were on track. These people have lost touch with their souls.

What did that mean? Was it true? What can be done about it? If our souls are buried under the debris of layers of cultural expectations, how can we discover/uncover them? The idea that they needed to be dusted off and recognized felt right. We see the search for soul in business as a process for individuals, a personal journey in a corporate environment.

Soul Dusting™

We named the process Soul Dusting™. But what exactly is it? Is it the same for everyone? What are the similarities? Was it possible to assist people in the process effectively? How could we concretize a spiritual quest? And in the clear light of day we would critically ask ourselves, "Is there really a connection between soul and careers, or have we gone around the bend with this?" Searching for those answers, we proceeded with our discussions and research. It was through this stage of our work that we began to see more clearly the various stages and steps in the soul searching process. And as it evolved, we began to use it in our work and test our findings.

Soul Dusting™, the search for soul, is the process of stripping away the superficial, the shedding of unsuitable roles. It is learning to recognize our souls when they speak and to listen to what they tell us. We developed the Soul Dusting™ process by documenting our own stories and those of other business executives. These stories reflected the risk and reward of the personal search for soul. Many of us have emerged on the other side of our midlife crises with new and happier lives and fulfilling careers. From this we concluded that midlife crisis is most likely your soul screaming for some attention after being ignored for so long. But the search for soul doesn't need to wait until midlife, nor does it necessitate a crisis. What we do need is widespread recognition that soul exists and that each of us has a soul purpose. And we need to be taught an approach to discovering our soul and our purpose. Heeding Joseph Campbell's mandate to "follow your bliss," just isn't enough for most people.

As a result of our research and development, we encourage our clients to look at the soul searching process. It moves from the internal to the external. People who are living purposefully live from the inside out. It is critical to understand this layered approach: that what happens on the inside is reflected on the outside. Soul, bliss, and purpose are the interior components. We define soul as our essence, our being, our spirit. Bliss/passion is our personal soul gift that we bring to the world. Our purpose is simply stated as "to share our soul gift with the world."

The exterior components are your own personal story, résumé, and career. Your story is the creative way in which you compose your own career, life, and soul's journey. Your résumé is, of course, the accepted business format for telling your story. Your career can be defined as the manner in which you share your soul gift with the world.

Both parts of the process, interior and exterior, are influenced by the physical body which houses the soul. We must learn to develop a sensitivity to hear its internal messages to us. Equally important is to be aware of the external messages we send to others through our physical presence, style, and composure.

The process begins by filling in your own specific definitions, in order to clarify your unknowns. For example, Mary, a participant in one of our seminars, shared her story. She had recently relocated to Boston with her husband when he was transferred. As most people do, she began by describing her professional background. Mary told her story chronologically and sincerely, focusing on her career in health care administration. Her résumé was a simple recitation of her health care history. She spoke in an easy manner and admitted that she enjoyed the work but had some concerns about the future of health care. She had been on several interviews. As the conversation continued and she could see how her story was developing, she blurted out, as if embarrassed, "Well, you know what I really want to do is have my own catering business. I had started one some years ago but my husband talked me out of it because it was such demanding work."

Mary was a great cook and loved the art of food preparation and event planning. She became very animated and excited thinking about the possibilities. She understood then that she had been living from the outside-in, having chosen the expected and safe career route over her passion. For Mary, determining her bliss was fairly easy. She knew what it was; she had just been listening to others, rather than to her soul. Once she defined bliss as a passion for cooking and catering, she needed to rewrite her story from that perspective, and develop strategies for turning her bliss into a career.

It is important to note here that it is the process that is important, not necessarily the end result. Mary might find that catering is not for her, but if so, she will look at other alternatives—perhaps writing a cookbook or opening a gourmet food store. Or perhaps taking the soul path will introduce her to something new and unfamiliar that will excite her and become her bliss. It isn't written anywhere that we are only gifted with one passion.

For others, it is more difficult because they have lived all of their lives meeting the expectations of families, teachers, bosses, etc. And not everyone is ready to accept the risk involved in living purposefully in today's world. Bob, another client of ours, has had a successful career in sales and marketing in high-technology services. Bob, who was in his late forties, confessed that he hadn't been happy with his situation for the last few years, but didn't see himself making a change until his son graduated from college, which was in five years.

The last of his career successes had been a promotion to sales manager, which proved to be his downfall. As a salesperson he was first rate; as a manager he was unable to translate his personal success to his team. He knew that he wasn't satisfied with his performance and, when he spoke to us, he had just learned that his senior management was not satisfied either. He was to be replaced. He had the option of looking within the company for another situation and they were giving him plenty of time to make his decision. Bob is one of those individuals for whom the concept of bliss and passion is foreign. Intellectually he understands it, but for him it is not an option. He will continue to postpone finding his soul until his son graduates. In our conversations, he wasn't even willing to entertain the idea of living and working from his soul. He has found a position in sales and marketing in another division of his company.

In Kathleen's own experience, she remembers vividly her first introduction to Joseph Campbell many years ago. She was unaware of him until she read an article in a decorating magazine. It was about a woman who had turned her hobby of antiques into a profession. She had left her frantic New York City job, bought a farmhouse in the country and opened an antiques store. The title of the article was "Follow Your Bliss." It was intriguing but depressing. Following your bliss sounded wonderful and easy. But she didn't have a hobby that she could turn into a paying profession. And who on earth would pay her to sit on the beach and read? Joseph Campbell's ideas were alternately fascinating and frustrating. The appeal of living a life that was filled with challenge, passion, energy and fun was, of course, enticing. But it was impossible for her to align the reality of her life with anything close to being called bliss. It was with a great deal of sadness that she admitted defeat as she had apparently hit a dead end. Today she looks back and knows that if she had reflected on what she found blissful, she would have benefited a great deal. She was correct in assuming that she probably would have been unable to make a career out of sitting on the beach and reading, but what she didn't understand was that her bliss was related to a deep love of the sea and of words. She now lives and works on the Boston waterfront, spends as much time as possible sailing, and in her marketing communications and consulting firm she is actively involved with the spoken and written word. She is also convinced that even though subconsciously she wasn't aware of it, her soul played a central role in her career decisions.

Living from the soul is not easy in today's world. Our culture does not respect the inner life but idolizes consumption, money, and power. Those of us who choose to live from our souls must first learn to face our own vulnerability and to embrace it. For in our vulnerability is the seed of a new kind of power, the power of the soul.

It is up to each of us—leaders, entrepreneurs, managers, administrators, trainees, and students—to clarify a significant vision of the future for ourselves. It is time for individuals to reconnect with their soul gifts and transform their dreams into economic reality. It is time for all of us to take responsibility for ourselves, to rediscover our soul and our purpose. And as we find them, we will bring them to work and business will thrive.

Joel Levey, PhD, is co-founder with his wife Michelle of Seattle-based InnerWork Technologies, Inc., a firm that specializes in building and renewing organizational cultures in which team spirit, community, creative intelligence, and authentic leadership can thrive. His pioneering work has inspired leaders and teams in more than 150 major organizations including AT&T Bell Labs, Du Pont, Weyerhaeuser, Hewlett-Packard, Travelers Insurance, Imperial Oil, and NASA. Dr. Levey has also served as director of Biofeedback & Stress Management for the Group Health Cooperative HMO; founding member of SportMind, Inc.; director of Biocybernautic Training for the U.S. Army Green Berets' Ultimate Warrior Program; and as core faculty for International Center for Organization Design, the Performance Edge, and Antioch University. With Michelle he has co-authored *Quality of Mind: Tools for Self Mastery & Enhanced Performance* and Nightingale Conant's best-selling business audio program *The Focused Mindstate*. He has also contributed to several books as a contributing author, including *Learning Organizations* and *Community Building: Renewing Spirit & Learning in Business.*

15

The Human Heart and Soul at Work

Joel Levey

In all of my experience,
I've never seen lasting solutions to problems,
lasting happiness and success,
that came from the outside in.

—Stephen Covey

The crimson sunrise over the Canadian Rockies sets the maple trees ablaze in a glory of autumn colors. Silently we sit together—leaders, change champions, mostly engineers. All are members of the Change Strategy teams from six leading companies: four major oil companies, one large utility corporation, an international construction company, and a university hospital. We are linked by many shared concerns, aspirations, and challenges.

We are the crew for a "Corporate Learning Expedition"—a retreat organized by the International Center for Organization Design. Our mission is to support each other in designing the most sustainable and successful organization for each company to meet the challenges of the next ten years. Over the course of the next year, we will meet together for four retreats to share our knowledge and experience, and to support each team in formulating its most viable and sustainable organization design to meet the challenges of the decade ahead.

At the end of the previous evening's opening session, a leader from one of the four oil companies suggested that we set a time and place for some "focusing and centering" at the beginning of our intense and busy days. "Let's get together in the Glacier Vista Lounge at 7:00 a.m.," he said to the fifty expedition members. "Everyone is welcome and I've asked Joel and Michelle to help us get focused with some coaching tips from their personal mastery training for the Green Berets, Olympic athletes, and other businesses like ours. I don't know about you, but I can use all the help I can get to keep my energy high on these long days where the stakes are high and the pressure is on. If you are interested, set your clock and join us in the morning."

As 7:00 a.m. approached I walked across the campus of the Banff Center toward the lounge. Walking through the autumn leaves, I dodged the grazing elk. Around a corner I overheard a couple of engineers as they walked ahead of me. "I've read about this personal mastery stuff, but I've never really done anything like this before," said one. His buddy nodded and replied, "Yeah, me neither. But look, if they did this kind of work with guys in Special Forces and with Olympic athletes, it can't be too 'new age.' You know me, if it works, I'll use it. Who knows, maybe I'll pick up a few ideas to improve my golf game."

We settled into the room just as the first rays of dawn ignited the maple tree outside into a blaze of autumn colors. As the time arrived, nearly a third of the whole team had arrived. Most of them had never done anything like this before, especially at work. The air was charged with a sense of curiosity and self-consciousness.

At the request of the group, Michelle and I offered a few simple suggestions to help people focus their attention in preparation for the work to come. We explained that we'd take a three-phase approach: first a few minutes to create context, then some brief instruction followed by fifteen minutes of practice, and finally some time to share insights or ask questions before breakfast.

To create context we pointed out the value of doing the inner work necessary to improve the quality of our outer work. We introduced the notion that "control follows awareness" and explained that we can only manage what we are mindful of. We discussed the performance advantages of being mindful by contrasting it with "mindlessness." When we are mindless, we noted, we lapse into reactivity, habit rules and it is impossible to be creative. Third, we explained how our capacity for complex and creative systems-thinking is directly proportional to our development of the quiet mind skills which determine the quality of our attention.

"If you are like most people, you have already mastered mindlessness and distraction," I began. "This morning we would like to introduce you to some new skills and challenge you to learn how to be wholeheartedly present or mindful, focused here and now in the present moment. Upon reflection you will notice that this moment has two important characteristics. First, it is the only place that you have any leverage to create change in your life or work. Second, it is elusive, fleeting, and constantly changing. Recognizing this, you will understand that mindfulness represents a flow or continuity of attention. Our challenge is to build this continuity of mindfulness by learning how to catch the wave-form of awareness and ride it without falling off into mindlessness or distraction.

"With this in mind, let's learn how develop our mindfulness," I continued. Having created some context for *why* to train, we offered a few guidelines for *how* to train. We suggested that people begin by focusing their intention or motivation. We explained that one of the first steps in focusing the mind is to be clear on intention. Knowing what is important to us can help to stabilize and focus the mind. To do this, we invited everyone to bring to mind the circle of "stakeholders" who would be influenced by their decisions—their co-workers and loved ones supporting them back home, their suppliers and customers spread all over the globe, the members of their local and regional communities who would be influenced by their work—and the generations to come who would live with the impact of their decisions.

Building on the clarity of intention, we invited people to begin to build the power of their mindfulness by focusing their attention on the natural flow of their breath. "As you inhale, simply know that you are breathing in," we reminded them. "As you exhale...simply know that you are breathing out. As you breathe, begin to collect all your wandering thoughts or gather your loose ends, and begin to arrive fully focused right here and now. As you use your breathing to help you get focused, stay relaxed. Avoid taking yourself too seriously. If you have a tendency to try too hard, hold a sort of half smile in your mind as you enjoy your breathing. Use some discipline to keep your mind on what you are doing, so that when the time comes, you'll be better able to keep your mind on your work. As you are mindful of your breathing, be attentive to the emergence of distracting thoughts. If or when your attention wanders off, notice if it is drawn to a fantasy of the future or to a memory of the past. Make a mental note of the distraction and, then as you inhale, simply draw your attention back to focus mindfully on what you are doing. Be mindful of your breathing."

To help the people who were particularly distracted by the chatter of their internal dialogue, we suggested that they experiment with synchronizing their breathing with the quiet mental repetition of two words. We explained that since the mind is busy thinking or talking to itself most of the time, using a quiet mental recitation is an effective strategy to harness and focus mental activity in a more intentional and productive way. With each inhalation we suggested making a brief mental note, "Arriving..." and breathing out the mental note, "Home...." "Arriving....Home....Arriving....Home...." As an alternative we suggested that people could also experiment with, "Here....Now....Here....Now...." if they preferred.

Having created some context and offered some simple instruction, we suggested that people simply stay with this mindful breathing for about ten minutes to quiet, calm, and focus their minds.

Then I suggested that each person think deeply and clearly about the work and strategic challenges of the day. Again we suggested that if the mind wandered to unrelated thoughts, that people be mindful of the distraction, and use discipline to return the focus of their thoughts to the subject they had chosen. At the end of these quiet minutes, we invited the group to debrief and to discus their insights and inspirations about how their inner work had informed their outer work.

One member of the group—an engineer in charge of a new refinery—commented, "I've done this kind of mental fitness training on my own for years, but never with a group of people that I work with. I've always wondered how it would be to work with a group of people who knew how to work in a more focused mind state together."

The foreman of a new drilling site commented, "I never knew that my mind could get so clear and quiet in such a short time. This is like learning how to push the "clear" button on my mental calculator. I never realized how learning to clear the slate could help me to think more deeply and clearly. Thanks coach!"

One of the senior vice presidents said, "You know, I think my greatest learning from this morning is that other people that I work with are interested in this inner work too!" People nodded. Looking around, his gaze met the eyes of people who he worked with on a daily basis and people he had known for years from the other oil companies.

A plant manager for another drilling operation and a director of human resources for another company echoed these sentiments.

"My doctor's been telling me I've got to learn how to relax and let go of my stress or I'm going to have another heart attack," said another man. "I always thought this stuff was kind of strange, but you know this mindfulness of my breathing gives me a sense of my self like what I touch when I'm out fishing on a warm spring day. If I work at it, I bet I could tap into this sense of presence, clarity, and calm whenever I want. Wait till I tell my doc. Will he ever be surprised." At that point someone laughed and chimed in, "OK, its time to break this huddle and get to work. We've got forty-five minutes before the whole team circles up. Who's ready for a cup of coffee and some breakfast?"

For the days that followed we continued to meet in the mornings before breakfast. Each day the circle grew as more of the team joined us. Some of the others who preferred to run, walk, or sleep in made a point to join us for breakfast where the conversation tended to focus on how the quality of mind is related to the quality of life and work. Questions about finding more balance between personal and professional life and on how to improve one's golf game were common. For some, these quiet morning sessions provided a deep sense of communion and connection with themselves, their team, their natural surroundings, and what was most essential or sacred in their lives.

After one of the strategic planning meetings with the staff, some of the leaders who hadn't been attending the morning sessions invited me to lunch. They started talking about how the energy level and performance of the whole team had bumped up a notch since the morning focusing sessions had begun. As one of the senior VPs put it, "You know, the members of our team who've been attended your morning sessions have really made some significant contributions to the breakthrough that our team has had. I'm not sure what you've been doing in your morning sessions, but we'd like to encourage you to keep up the good work! We need all the inspiration and clear thinking we can get on our team if we're going to meet our goals, and this inner work seems to be making a real difference."

Over the months to come, this momentum continued and took different forms among the different company teams. When Michelle and I flew in to Calgary to do some strategic work with one of the teams a month later the director of operations gave me a call at the hotel. "Welcome back!" He said. "I forgot to tell you two to plan on showing up forty-five minutes before our meetings start while you are here. Some of us have taken over the boardroom in the mornings to do some focusing before work. Not everyone comes, but for those of us who do, it has made a difference. Some of us have some questions and want to see if we can bump our personal mastery work up a notch while you are in town. Will you come and join us?" I smiled at Michelle and said to him, "You've got a deal. We'll meet you at your office at 6:55 A.M."

The next morning we sat quietly in the boardroom on the 27th floor. In the predawn light the ghostly pillars of steam rise in a gray sky above the silent skyscrapers in this tiny corner of the frozen Alberta plains. For a moment, I am back in jeans at Glacier Vista with the maple tree ablaze in the crisp crimson dawn. Arriving....Home....Here....Now....As I sit here quietly with these friends and fellow explorers, something inside shatters, opens, dissolves and sets loose a flood of joy, wonder, and laughter inside my quiet mind. Astonished, I ask myself, "Could it be that in some holonomic way, this moment contains every moment, or that each moment contains all moments?"

> *When you eventually see through the veils to*
> *how things really are,*
> *you will keep saying again and again, 'This is*
> *certainly not like we thought it was!'*
>
> —Rumi

The Spirited Leader

In our work with leaders and change champions in corporate America we are continually inspired by the people who invite us to work with their teams. They are often the idealists who still have a sparkle in their eye who care deeply for others.

These people often live with deep questions catalyzed by major breakdowns or breakthroughs in their life. Some have suffered heartbreaks, heart attacks, or near-death experiences. Many have fought for their health, for peace, for justice, for sobriety, and are willing to take a strong stand to help others. Often they are people who might say that they have a spiritual orientation though they wouldn't necessary call themselves religious. Their faith and determination are forged in the fire of the personal epiphanies that opened their hearts and souls to find grace and to commune with the sacred presence at the heart of humanity. Having hit the wall and broken through, these people are willing to fight fiercely to create opportunities to improve the quality of life and work for people in their organizations or communities. They are willing to take risks in order to help others learn to live and work in wiser ways that respect their health, dignity, and wholeness.

Suzanne, the VP in Information Systems for one of America's oldest and largest financial institutions, is an inspiring example of such a leader. Shortly after she returned to work after experiencing a life threatening illness, the president of her information systems division launched a new Vision and Mission Statement calling for a radically different approach to achieving world-class information technology by developing a culture of high-performance teamwork, effective change management, and continuous learning. As the president said to his team of three thousand five hundred people, the challenge would require "each and every one of you to become a bit of a visionary to make this Vision a reality."

In her search for a way to help her team meet this challenge, she was given an article on our work and she called to talk with us about how we might support her team. We learned about Suzanne's struggle to regain her health, and her concern that others might face similar threats to their own health. She wanted to offer a program to help them to take better care of themselves and support each other more effectively at work.

We designed a pilot program for her teams—one that emphasized a synergy of personal, team, and organizational development. When she excitedly approached the internal HR staff with the idea of bringing in outside consultants she encountered some resistance. She stood her ground saying, "Sure, there are lots of local consultants doing team development, but I want more than that for my people. These people have an impressive record of success. But more importantly, they bring love to their work and that's what I want for my people. I'm committed to making this happen!" In the end, Suzanne's fierce commitment won and the success of the project quickly ignited interest for programs in many other departments throughout the organization.

Bill, a former Catholic priest on Suzanne's team, offered the following explanation for the success of the program: "The principles we are applying, when understood and taken together, give us a picture of a new way we can live and work. It's an inside-out approach to change. If managers ask: 'How do we get our work done more efficiently, with a better end product?' I'd tell them that, along with improving the work process, go out and build trust, communicate honestly, support each team member, and find ways to drive out the fear and relearn the idea that it's important for everyone to seek balance and wholeness in and through our work. When this catches fire, an epidemic of sanity— even love—can spread."

"We've made some big strides towards making the Vision a reality in this year," said Suzanne. "But our people know this is really a journey of self-discovery that we are on, and that it never really ends. Our work here is to learn about constantly renewing ourselves, our team, and renewing our organization—one day at a time."

The Spirit of Total Quality

Though Total Quality Management has helped focus the collective attention of thousands of organizations and millions of people worldwide, the tools of total quality are seldom turned around 180 degrees and applied to improving the quality of our own lives. Over the years, we have often been invited to address this theme at conferences or in businesses open to an inquiry regarding what *total* quality could really mean at work. On one occasion we were invited to offer a special program entitled "Where Quality Begins: Personal Paradigms for Continuous Improvement" at the GOAL/QPC conference in Boston. Though there were nine other workshops running concurrently, our workshop drew nearly 30% of the total audience.

The room was filled to overflowing. As Joe Colletti introduced us, I scanned the room hoping that the hundreds of people standing in the aisles or sitting on the floor would be comfortable. "Why do *you* think there are so many people at this workshop?"

I asked as we began. A Navy admiral spoke up explaining that though they had all the technical systems and procedures in place, they still had difficulty motivating people to stay focused on improving the quality of their work. The director of manufacturing for a large manufacturing plant added that he wanted to learn more about how personal values and organizational values could be brought more in line to help people. Next a human resource director from another corporation shared her desire to have a business show more concern for the quality of worklife and for the health—physical, mental, emotional, and family—of their employees. My eyes met Michelle's with a twinkle. Nodding to each other we shared a spark of excitement that this audience was primed to take this presentation to heart.

The presentation that followed walked the participants through a series of questions, case studies, and inquiry exercises that illustrated how and why the human dimensions of total quality could be addressed in a business setting. For many people, the presentation affirmed what they already believed in. It offered useful data, anecdotes, and terminology to help integrate this theme into their work. Others left with an expanded sense of what a Total Quality initiative could look like in a large organization. After our presentation we lingered and talked at length with people who were inspired and enthused by the new possibilities they were seeing. As we were packing up our notes, we were approached by a distinguished older businessman with a broad friendly smile.

"You have it, " he said excitedly in English strongly flavored by a Brazilian Portuguese French accent. "You have the piece that we've been waiting for. I'm convinced that no one is going to get their Total Quality programs to succeed unless they listen to wisdom in the message you have shared. Come, let's have supper together and talk more about this." His enthusiasm and noble dignity were inspiring and we were happy to accept his invitation. And so we went off to have our supper with Andre and his protégé Eduardo.

Over supper we learned that Andre had introduced Total Quality Management to the industries in Brazil many years ago. He was a respected elder in his field and was often referred to as the "guru" in his company. He knew from experience how challenging it was to balance business objectives with the needs and values of the people who do the work. "You can give people all of the measurement tools in the world," he said, "and give them all of the new concepts and words to get their minds focused in on the right things, but unless you capture people's imagination, their values, and their passion you will not be successful. You only have a small fraction of a whole person at work unless their spirit is engaged. If people are to focus a high quality of attention on their work, we need to build an organization and equip our people to be really committed to quality in every dimension of their life. To do this, we must re-examine how we reward people and we must equip them with skills for staying focused and managing and renewing their energy in more effective ways. In this way the inner and outer problems that we waste so much time with would disappear and our creative spirit would be set free in service of building a better organization and better world."

"Andre," I said, "you're so passionate about these ideas. Tell me, how have you come to value this inner work and its role in business?" Andre looked both deep into himself and to us. "My father was a rancher and I grew up in the country. As a young boy I lived very close to the earth," he said. "When I was young, I was a cowboy and would often be off with the herds for long periods of time. Being alone, living simply and close to nature, under that night sky, I learned a lot about my mind, body and spirit. I still carry much of that sense of wonder and aliveness with me. Nature taught me how to listen deeply, to pay careful attention to my world, and how to focus my mind. It showed me that there's much that's hidden from the eye that's important, and it can only be known with the heart and soul.

"If we can carry more of that deep respect, wonder, and quality of attention into our work, then we could be enormously successful. For many years I've dreamed of doing what you're doing within my company. Discovering you and the work you are doing renews my hope that it can be done." Raising his glass, he said, "A toast to new beginnings and to the potentials for our work together!" We were deeply touched by his excitement and sincerity. He talked as though he'd lived with a dream for many years and was finally on the threshold of seeing it manifest. Looking at this wise elder businessman, there was a vitality and sparkle in his eye and the glint of a few tears of joy. Deeply touched by his passionate spirit, and his sincerity, we raised our glasses to join his toast and I remembered the words of a great man who once said, "You know when you're close to the truth when you have tears in your eyes."

You Are More Than You Think

Lasting improvement does not take place
by pronouncements or official programs.
Change takes place slowly inside each of us
and by the choices we think through
in quiet wakeful moments lying in bed
just before dawn.

—Peter Block

Research shows that we think more than sixteen thousand thoughts each day. What's more—we had ninety percent of them yesterday as well! Can you imagine who you would find yourself to be if you pushed the pause button on the prerecorded story you keep telling yourself about who you are? As the great physicist Werner Heisenberg reminded us, "The theory determines the result."

If you take these thoughts to heart you may discover that you are more than the story you've been telling yourself. Much more. Your thoughts are the creative display of your deeper reality. Don't mistake the story for the truth. The reality of your soulfulness is here at work or play in every moment: It is here as the silence amidst sounds and as the stillness within ceaseless motion; as the clarity within confusion and the knowingness here at the heart of your unknowing. Each day the tides of hope and fear, beauty and pain, breakthroughs and breakdowns of life and work break our hearts and minds open and help us to wake up and to remember who we really are.

In our work we are often called to help discover, renew, or revitalize the spirit of leaders, teams, and large organizations. It seems that the dizzying complexity and breakneck pace of our modern lives has exiled us from the vitality of our true nature. We have lost sight of what our ancestors saw as essential—the importance of family, creative expression, and a deep, spiritual connectedness with our world and the living creatures who share it with us. There is a gaping hole in many people's lives, and a gnawing feeling that something vital has been lost, yet we don't even remember what it was. For some it feels like something essential in our lives is calling us home, though they don't even know what to call it.

I find it helpful to keep in mind that the polls say that sixty percent of the population feels a deep yearning for spiritual growth. A third of us—your friends, family, and co-workers—have had a profound or life-altering religious or mystical experience. In reality, soul or spirit is as close to us as water is to waves. Even if we don't talk about it, or have the right words to describe it, there have been moments in most of our lives when we realize that we are both particle *and* wave, wave *and* ocean. As Saul demonstrated on the road to Damascus, and as countless others have experienced playing sports, giving birth, or simply walking down the street, we are utterly unable to protect ourselves from spontaneous moments of grace. For millennia, the world's great wisdom traditions have empirically tested and refined a myriad of effective inner technologies that consistently increase the incidence of close encounters with the sacred—if you practice them.

Research on high-level human performance shows that people who have cultivated a greater sense of their wholeness are more change and stress resilient, creative, and productive. No organization can afford to waste the vitality, productivity, passion, or creative spirit of its people. These rare and precious human resources are as necessary for sustained business success as they are for personal well-being.

As the Corporate Learning Expedition was concluding in the Canadian Rockies, the pre-breakfast group of our Change Strategy team reviewed our work over the time we were together. It was our last morning at the Banff Center. The engineer who originally had proposed the early-morning sessions offered the following poem as a reminder of our learnings. It is by the Persian poet Rumi and it seems a fitting way to conclude this essay.

> The breeze at dawn has secrets to tell.
> *Don't go back to sleep.*
> You have to ask for what you really want.
> *Don't go back to sleep.*
> You know, there are those who go back and forth
> Over the threshold where the two worlds meet,
> And the door it's always open and it's round.
> *Don't go back to sleep.*

Part Four

The Organizational Perspective

16
The Sixth Need of Business:
"Wisdom From an Oarsman"
Charles Handy

17
Organizational Transformation:
A Return to Soul
Jayme Rolls

18
Soul Work:
A Corporate Challenge
Jacqueline Haessly

19
The Commonwealth Organization:
Healing the World's Ailing Soul
Robert Leaver

Best-selling British author Charles Handy leads off this section, which focuses on the organizational perspective of soulful work. The four authors contributing to this part have each offered original writings with the corporation or organization in mind. As we have learned, individuals can change, recover their souls, and achieve all kinds of incredible personal transformations—but getting organizations to change is an entirely different matter.

These authors address the organization—the environment in which individuals work—examining how the workplace culture, climate, and atmosphere can work against or toward personal change. The transformation of our work organizations is one of the biggest challenges of this generation and these authors provide significant enlightenment on how to proceed.

Charles Handy is an independent author, teacher, and broadcaster, focusing on the changing shape of work, organizations and the future of capitalism, with its impact on every aspect of our lives. He is the author of *The Age of Unreason* and *The Age of Paradox* (titled *The Empty Raincoat* in the UK—a British bestseller). In total, his books have now sold over one million copies around the world.

He has been an oil executive in Southeast Asia, an economist, professor of management development at the London Business School, the Warden of St. George's House in Windsor Castle, and chairman of the Royal Society of Arts in London. He now describes himself as a social philosopher. Handy was born in Dublin, Ireland, and now lives in London, Tuscany and Norfolk with Elizabeth, his wife and business partner.

The Sixth Need of Business: "Wisdom from an Oarsman"

Charles Handy

Instrumentalism and reductionism have been the besetting sins of business in modern times. Between them, they have turned the organization into a prison for the human spirit. By strange good fortune, we now have a chance to set that spirit free and, in so doing, to see it infect the organization and, perhaps, the whole of our modern-day society. Unfortunately, the odds are that we shall pass up the chance and see the old devils of instrumentalism and reductionism resume their steady march. That would be sad, because it would be an admission that the organs of capitalism see man and, increasingly, woman, as things made for the organization, not the other way around.

Instrumentalism

Instrumentalism is the underlying premise of capitalism, at least in its Anglo-American version. The business is the instrument of its owners and the individual the instrument of the business. Unless its owners are interestingly quixotic, the purpose of the business has to be to increase their investment, preferably in as short a time as possible. When the management is the agent of the owners, they have little excuse to do anything else, especially when the owners are largely anonymous investors, unseen, often unknown and seldom met. The average mutual fund, I am told, turns over 80% of its investments every year. Under these circumstances, there can be little interest in anything other than short-term returns.

Given that background, it is only reasonable to apply the same instrumental philosophy to the people who work the assets of the business. They are there to add many times more value than they cost. Should they fail to do so, their cost must be cut or they must go, unless they and their work can be "re-engineered" in some way to produce more.

The formula of $\frac{1}{2} \times 2 \times 3 = P$ sums up all too accurately the intentions of any business or, indeed, of an organization in any sector which aspires to be "business-like." The formula suggests that the route to productivity (P) is to have half as many people, paid twice as well on average (because you keep the best half), producing three times as much. The only argument, then, is about how many months or years it will take to get there and how best to get rid of the unwanted half.

The formula has a seductive simplicity. I met one chief executive who was so enraptured by it that she had it posted up above the door to every office. It had energized the place remarkably, she said. They were all enraptured by it. Or fearful of it, I suggested, because there is no guarantee that one will be in the better half. Life outside the organization can be fun and freeing for some, but it can be awfully precarious for others who have to pile one part-time job on another in order to make ends meet. To be a discarded instrument is not pleasant. Yet, already, over one third of America's workforce is outside, if you add together the self-employed, the part-timers and the unemployed. In Europe, it is over 40% and growing. The formula is biting into our society.

If one is fortunate enough to be retained as part of the "better half," it isn't all good news, either. The "3" in the formula can turn out to mean three times as hard and as long in order to achieve three times the added value. Traditionally, a lifetime job has meant 100,000 hours of work, which is roughly 40 hours a week for 50 weeks and 50 years. It still is 100,000 hours but now compressed into 30 years, from early twenties to early fifties. That implies 68-hour weeks and a life dedicated, inevitably, to the organization. Deny the dedication and your job is on the line. The reward is money, and excitement if you are lucky, but no time or energy for anything outside the organization, and the prospect of 25 years beyond the job, a period which no sensible person could call retirement.

For many it is a Faustian bargain—the sale of one's life for money, as when Faust sold his soul to the devil. There has to be more to our lives than that.

Reductionism

Instrumentalism is compounded by reductionism, the urge to reduce everything to its component parts in the hope that you can then understand and control it better. When I first sought employment in the new Business School in London thirty years ago, I was asked what I thought that I could teach would-be managers. "Why, management," I said, fresh from ten years of managing difficult businesses in the Far East. "I'm afraid that 'management' is not a subject," I was told. "It has to be marketing, or production, or strategy, or human relations, or one of the other component parts of management." The hope was, and still is, that if you know all the bits, they will add up to the whole. They don't, as often as not, any more than knowing the techniques of lovemaking guarantees a great lover. The whole is nearly always both greater than, and different from, the sum of its parts.

Although we all instinctively recognize the truth of this, organizations persist in breaking things down into their component parts. F.W. Taylor made a management philosophy out of the practice and was able to demonstrate that, by so doing, the efficiency of relatively unskilled workers could be greatly enhanced, their training times reduced, and the measurement of their results made much easier. We all repudiate the cruder aspects of Taylorism today, but the philosophy of specialization continues. Organizations divide themselves into specialties and then combine them to achieve their desired result. Efficiency and control can often improve but the individual is, more obviously than ever, only one cog in a complicated process.

So complex and interdependent are some of the processes, in fact, that it can be counterproductive to try to improve the working of your particular cog because that might throw the whole system out of alignment. This applies most obviously to the old-fashioned assembly line, but it also happens in today's corporations where an unplanned expansion in sales, for example, can increase total costs and reduce profits because extra capacity has to be found at an excessive price. It is best and safest to keep to the budget, do what you are supposed to do, and seek not to make a difference.

In one such reductionist organization, I found that the door to my office had a bronze plate on the outside. Stamped in the bronze was the name and number of my department. Below it was a slit where a plastic slip had been placed with my name on it. I suddenly realized what a "temporary role occupant" really meant: a necessary cog in someone else's machine. I found that even the memos went from that department—MKR/32—to other numbers like FIN/51, not from person to person because, at that level anyway, the name of the temporary role occupant was irrelevant. It may have been efficient, but it was certainly soul-destroying. It may, in fact, not even have been efficient. The only way I could make my presence felt was by activating my negative power, by blocking things instead of passing them on. I am ashamed to say that my frustration with anonymity was such that I occasionally succumbed.

The New Reality

Instrumentalism and reductionism will not work so well in our organizations as we face up to the implications of the workplace of the future. It is now a cliché that knowledge and applied intelligence are the keys to added value. They are the new property, the new bases of wealth. Land, the old basis of wealth, is no guarantee any longer of future prosperity, as property developers are slowly learning. Physical assets of any sort don't count for much. The market value of any decent business is nowadays at least four or five times the value of its fixed assets. The gap is the market's estimate of the difference which the intangible assets of knowledge and intelligence of all sorts can make to the profits. The fact that accountants have not yet figured out a way to measure this broad kind of intellectual property does not mean that it does not exist. The chairman of Boeing has remarked on the strange fact that his neighbor in Seattle, Microsoft, should be worth so much more as a company than his when all its physical assets could fit into one of his parking lots, but he only speaks the truth and heralds the future.

We may know all this, because it is the conventional wisdom of our time, but not many have taken the full implications on board. Karl Marx saw his dream come true. The "means of production," as he called the wealth-producing assets, now truly belong to the workers, as he wanted, but not in the way he foresaw. They belong to the workers because they are in the heads and the fingers of the workers. When that is so, it no longer makes moral or practical sense to think of the financiers as owners of the assets. It does not make moral sense because no man should "own" another man, any more than a husband can own his wife. It does not make practical sense because the ownership cannot be enforced. There is nothing to stop the new human assets from walking away.

One consequence will be an equity market even more like a casino than ever. To buy shares in Microsoft is to bet on Bill Gates' ability to continue to draw out the creativity of his young people, to keep them as long as they are creative and to replace them, in due course, with equally creative people. Investing is like betting on the continued productivity of assets who can't be measured, can't be sold, and can't be disposed of without cost. Such a risky bet needs quick returns to justify it. The pressures for short-term rewards will grow. In response, the corporations will want to shield themselves from such demanding investors. They will seek to reduce the powers of their financiers and to increase the rights of their new assets, their job-holders. They will rely more on loans and retained earnings to finance their futures, thus giving them more control over their own destinies. They will, in short, think of themselves more as self-controlling communities than as the properties of their investors.

In order to keep the interest and enthusiasm of their people, corporations will have to give their people more control over their destiny. Holism will once again be virtuous, as it was in the early days of the Catholic Church. In those days, it was held, and believed, that every priest was "Pope in his patch," that every parish was a microcosm of the Church as a whole, that each parish was independent but also part of something bigger and necessarily dependent on that bigger something for its own strength. In business, we shall see more autonomous, self-contained business units, independent but intertwined. Twin citizenship, one of the key principles of Catholicism and of federalism, will be key. The idea that one can and should belong to more than one group, to the small and local, as well as the big and global, will become more accepted.

The Sixth Need

The example of the Catholic Church is not coincidental. At its best, the Church holds together because of its shared beliefs.

No system of controls, or planning, or resource allocation, not even the power of patronage, could stop it disintegrating if it loses a shared conviction in its purpose and its methods. We may yet live to see such a disintegration.

It will be no different in any organization. The only thing which will, ultimately, hold any organization together will be a shared conviction in its purpose and its methods. It could, of course, be that the purpose is to make as much money as possible as cheaply as possible, but that will only hold the organization together if the money is made for the people who work in the organization. No one is going to jump out of bed in the morning to make some unknown financier seriously rich. Such a common purpose will, therefore, only unite quite small organizations where all the workers are also co-owners, with loans as the main source of outside finance. At the moment, we see this sort of financial driving purpose in the small family enterprises of Southeast China and Hong Kong, in new entrepreneurial partnership businesses, and in some concerns where money is the matter of the business, as in financial dealing.

Even then, in my experience, the money-making focus ultimately becomes subordinated to some further purpose. The money becomes a means and not an end. What is the point of being rich in the graveyard? Businesses, it seems, also follow Maslow's suggestion of a "hierarchy of needs": When their physical and economic survival is assured, they look for identity, recognition, and self-fulfillment. But Maslow, at the end of his life, sensed that self-fulfillment was too self-centered to give us a justification for our existence, even if it included a feel-good factor. Maybe there was a sixth need, he said, which we might call idealization, or the search for a purpose beyond oneself.

It is this sense of a purpose beyond oneself which, I believe, separates humans from animals. It is to this sense which most religions appeal, and on which they draw. It is what lifts any person, any family, any organization, to go beyond the limits. It is the loss of this sense that turns us back into self-centered creatures, interested only in our own survival, no matter what.

I once devised a different sort of course for my part-time MBA students, and ran it for a period of years. Instead of lectures and case studies, I asked them to divide into groups of seven or eight. I made sure that each of these groups had representatives of two or three not-for-profit organizations, charities, schools, or hospitals. I then asked them to spend a day in each of the other organizations and to report back on what each organization could learn from the others. The reaction of the students from the business sector was always the same. They were amazed at the commitment and dedication of the people in the other sectors, often in spite of bad conditions, lousy management, and poor pay. They had encountered the power of a purpose beyond oneself, of a cause, which should never excuse poor management, but so often manages to rise above it.

It is this sense of a purpose beyond oneself which, alone, will hold together the new organizations of contract and consent, organizations which will increasingly replace the old organizations of command and control. The new organizations will be built on contracts; formal contracts between the organization and the individual, and informal between individuals in and between their groups. But if the organization is going to be anything more than a "box of contracts," it will need a sense of common cause and of shared commitment.

I got a glimpse of what this might mean, once, when I jokingly described a typical business team as being like a rowing crew on the river—"eight men going backwards as hard as they could without talking to each other, steered by the one person who couldn't row." I thought it quite witty, but I was put straight by an Olympic oarsman who was in the room. "You are quite wrong," he said. "How do you think we can go backwards so fast without talking, unless we had total trust in each other's ability and a shared commitment to a common goal? It is a recipe for an ideal team." He was right, of course, and I knew how much time and effort goes into building up that trust and shared commitment, both on and off the river.

I have wondered since if a great rowing crew could be said to have a "soul." Perhaps the term is too grandiose. But "personality" or "culture" are not enough to describe the sense of contained capacity that such groups have; a sense of going places, of leaving something of themselves behind for others to feed from, of a whole that is greater than its parts, of an essence which infects and inspires. Whatever the word, it is the necessary ingredient in great teams and, increasingly, in all organizations. To glimpse it, however, requires leaders with qualities beyond normal: the power to set goals beyond oneself and make them the norm, to set high standards, to keep a straight course despite the currents, to select the right people and discard the wrong, to coach and cajole, to build trust over time so that we can rely on those we do not see or hear from.

I asked my oarsman to tell me who he thought was the leader in a rowing crew. "It's a good question," he replied, pondering. "You could say that it's the little one who can't row because when we are racing he's in charge and steering, but there's also the stroke who sets the pace, whom we must all follow. And then there's the captain who, on the river, is just a member of the crew, but who is responsible for the selection, the team-building and the morale of us all. And, lastly, there's the coach who trains and mentors us. They all lead, in their way, but we call no one of them *the* leader—and none the 'manager' of course." I sense that his description of a shared leadership is the right one for the organizations of the future, if we could only give up our ingrained sense of hierarchy.

I am not optimistic. Old ways and habits have to die before they change. Organizations will persevere with their attempts to command and control, to see themselves as the instruments of their owners and their people as the instruments of their purposes. They will overwork, and often overpay, the best of those instruments, wearing them out before their time. They will discard the ones they do not need in the interest of efficiency and leave it to "the market" to take care of them. But the market does not care and, anyway, now reaches beyond national boundaries to countries far away. Society will get even more divided between rich and poor, forcing people to take care, first and only, of themselves and their own, and the devil take the rest. Some of us will be rich in the desert, but it won't feel good, even for us. The rest will, in time, revolt. It won't be nice.

But there is another way. I have tried to etch its outlines here in this essay. A business could and should be more than a wealth-creating instrument for its owners. It could and should be a community with a purpose beyond itself, because, if we are honest with ourselves, it is only that sort of purpose that can justify our existence. Business is, in the end, a moral matter.

Jayme Rolls, PhD, is president of Rolls & Company, Inc., a Santa Monica, California-based organizational transformation consultancy utilizing new models of transformation that build and support new corporate culture. The firm is working with organizations Ernst & Young, John Hancock Mutual Life Insurance, *The New York Times,* Digital Equipment Corporation, Bank of Boston, Lotus Development, and Southern California Edison.

Rolls is a psychologist and holds a PhD in organizational transformation. Formerly she was founder and president of a multimillion dollar, award-winning communications agency, a Fortune 500 communications manager, and professor of mass communications.

She is a contributing author of the book *Learning Organizations: Developing Cultures for Tomorrow's Workplace.*

17

Organizational Transformation: A Return to Soul

Jayme Rolls

The 21st Century is being called the Age of Choice. The shift from authoritarian to libertarian values is dramatic and evident globally: in politics, in religion, and in corporations. People are no longer willing to accept a belief unless it is of their own experience. Self-determination is a dominant trend and organizations are being widely impacted.

The Move to Soul

People are making the choices that create richer, more meaningful lives. People have begun consciously caring for soulful needs. The new values are resulting in lifestyle downscaling, the rising value of home life over workplace, deeper relationships, workplace democracy, flex firms responding to employees who want to adjust and shrink worklives around other needs, and home offices that offer improved quality of worklife and increased freedom.

The work environment provided by corporations needs to be meaning-rich to acknowledge the values of an increasingly soul-conscious workforce—and not just out of altruism. What motivates employees has changed from receiving a paycheck to opportunity for fulfillment. Identifying and fostering soul in business is likely to result in some very big wins for corporations.

For example, a very fundamental tenet of soul is that it

seeks relationship. According to Margaret Wheatley, author of bestselling leadership books, power in organizations is generated by *relationships,* and what is important is how an organization organizes its relationships, not its tasks, functions or hierarchies. Power is energy and needs to flow *through* an organization. What gives power its "charge"—negative or positive—is the quality of its relationships.

Today's organizations are in transformation. *Transformation is about changing relationships.* Transforming corporate cultures is about changing relationships—with the customer, with the employee, with the manager, with the work, and with each other. Rethinking work to allow for the emergence of the soul may well provide an impetus for transformation.

The self-directed work team is a natural outgrowth of the soul's needs for relationship, connection, and empowerment. Teams of all descriptions are changing the social context and landscape of the workplace—from individual contributor roles to collaborative, joint ownership, and shared responsibility.

During the management of projects, teams are building consensus and engaging in mutual exploration and discovery. Their perspectives and experience are broadened. It serves corporate interests as their work creates integrated, synergistic solutions and secures the buy-in and commitment of all constituencies. Soul's expression is in just such exploration; the soul thrives on communication and connecting with others and their ideas. It seeks the creative, complex, and information-rich. It enjoys individuality, self-expression, and eccentricities.

With the requirement for a redefinition of boundaries in the workplace, an acknowledgment of the soul's need for attachment, community, and meaning could help to accomplish the various forms of new partnerships. These include cross-functional, cross-unit teams; leaders and followers alternating roles; peer assessment and mentoring; shared leadership positions; short-lived, outcome-based alliances with competitors, suppliers, et. al., in virtual corporations; and more.

Making the Shift

Business can unwittingly starve the soul and taste the consequences or celebrate it and profit from it. When the soul is neglected, it doesn't just go away. The neglect can appear symptomatically in emptiness; meaninglessness; vague depression;

lack of connection to the company and its purpose; lackluster, just-enough performance; absenteeism; poor morale; drug abuse; and lack of fulfillment.

Distress seems widespread today and may be responsible for the movement we are witnessing in people's search for meaning. Because we have lost touch with our souls, we can measure its neglect only as problems manifest. Interestingly, examining the characteristics of the new paradigm in American business and comparing them to the individual expressions of the soul, suggests an almost seamless alignment, as outlined below.

A True Harmony of Interests

Needs of Business to Remain Competitive	Employees' Soul Needs
learning	learning, exploration
change agile	experimentation
creativity, innovation	creativity, innovation
partnering	relationship
continuous training	discovery
teaming	connection
dialogue	dialogue, expression
participation	engagement
risk-taking	space to make mistakes
proactive	empowerment
peer assessment/mentoring	reaching out, friendship, closeness
vision	meaning
large context	complexity, depth
alternating roles	experience
invention	possibilities
imagination	imagination, reflection
communication	communication
integration, end of silos	wholeness
broadening of boundaries	expansiveness
employee growth	growth
communal sense of self	attachment
community	community, neighborhood
stewardship	family

The Dimensions of the Soul

If the soul's capacity for creativity is not honored it will wreak havoc. The soul doesn't hold a compartmentalized view; it is full and encompassing. It isn't soulful to have truncated work experiences. Reengineering efforts often strive to eliminate micro jobs, done in countless unproductive handoffs with the oversupervision and the auditing that leaves a job soulless. The result is increased productivity, leaving the wholeness, passion, and rich experience in the work as it exercises the potential of each employee.

Soul helps us to solve problems. We need to engage in dialogue to get at all the nuances, to access deeper wisdom, to imagine. Answers and choices lie in the subtleties.

The soul is eager to explore new forms of community, and community building is a key component of the new paradigm. Soul seeks self-expression and, in communications, it is important to amplify the voice of the employee. Soul all but disappears with purely technical approaches to learning. It craves firsthand, rich, and complex experiences.

As Thomas Moore tells us:

> The juxtaposition of retreat and engagement is necessary for soul to satisfy its need for reflection and wonder. The soul does not thrive in a fast-paced life, because savoring and feeling how new experiences integrate takes time. Non-doing is essential nourishment to the soul.

How Management Contributes

Organizational transformation deals with the deep issues of personal growth, vision, trust, creativity, purpose, and leadership. Today the leader responsible for helping to transform corporations is charged with fostering growth, with leading cultural change.

These new leaders need sound values, reverence for each individual, and a stewardship concept of his/her role. They stay in the background and allow workers to have their own soulful, rich, whole experiences at work. They let employees teach themselves. Workers want to say "come join me but don't tell me how." Human mistakes and failures are part of the soul's experience, and it needs permission to make mistakes in its exploration. Corporations need to take risks to stay competitive, and underlying risk-taking is the opportunity to stretch, to reach, to experiment, to fail. It is a much more soulful experience for the managers, too, to lead their people in this way, embracing risk, relationship and deep connection.

The move toward whole self-integration—the end of separate selves for work and personal lives—is another manifestation of soul. The new leader supports an environment of nurturance and acceptance that fosters a disclosing of true selves.

Soul Expressed in Technology

The rapid colonization of cyberspace—the population of Internet grows at 15 percent per month—is in service of interconnection to one another. The newness of cyberspace is a social experiment and we can observe how people are acting, what they want, and what draws them.

The creation of virtual communities responds to the soul's craving for interrelatedness. The computer allows us to contact people formerly out of reach, create connections of all descriptions, engage in new kinds of social relationships. This dramatically demonstrates the strong need for people to connect and communicate with one another.

Communicating in egalitarian cyberspace provides a very different access to other people. Connections are established with people who share values and interests without regard to their race, gender, age, and other barriers that prevent people from connecting with each other. Rather than what has been traditionally a small number of people controlling the information that a large number of people have access to, now a large number of people have access to a large number of people. Communication is flowing in all directions. It is unpredictable, chaotic, and messy.

Soul is emerging in technological developments. As PCs are networked, more ways to create relationship are possible. Groupware connects us and builds relationships. It is the end of "information float," when we all have direct relationship and immediate ability to participate. Futurist and author John Naisbitt observes that we create "electronic tribes" that make us more tribal at the same time as the capability globalizes us. The soul seeks experimentation and complexity, and the greater the capacity of computers to handle life's complexities, the freer the individual is to think of creative ways to exploit them.

How Soul is Manifested Today in Business

The soul is gaining greater expression in today's changing corporate cultures, as is evidenced by teams with their mutual exploration and discovery, transformational leadership, groupware, systems thinking, integration and the elimination of silos, egalitarian and libertarian values, extensive use of dialogue, welcoming diversity of opinion, risk taking, using stories and metaphors to talk with employees about meaning, and much more.

There are many other ways that soul manifests itself: marketing-as-relationship; customers expressing their desire for "just for me" service and attention; intolerance for external locus of control and authority; an insistence on co-design, co-creation, and co-ownership of what is developed; focus on interconnectedness and people; managers being asked to move from a command and control function to become counselors, mentors, coaches, facilitators; and the new levels of honesty, sensitivity, and trust. Soul is driving the new communications with its greater emphasis on listening rather than telling, on individuality, communication from inside out, hearing the internal and external customer, partnering and, most of all, relationship.

What Tomorrow Might Look Like: Acknowledging Soul in a Corporation

As paying attention to soul pays off and the mutual interests of employees and corporations are met, we may see:

- New ways to create and understand attachment in virtual communities whether technology-linked, shamrock-configured, etc.;
- Identifying more avenues for service, both internally and externally;
- Task forces to explore new ways to enhance meaning in companies;
- Employee-selected training and new models of experience training;
- Expanded notion of teams who come together driven not by task but to explore what emerges;
- Increased use of teams as the primary unit for organizing work;
- Designed-in mechanisms and places where friendship can occur;
- Employees designing their "corporate neighborhood";
- End of "need to know" and beginning of "want to know";

- Exploring the soul of a product, soul of a job, soul of a team, soul of an individual, soul of a company—the soul in every component of the whole;
- Expanded sense of community where all constituencies and stakeholders connect directly and frequently;
- More self-empowered, employee-owned communications;
- New accepted means of connection through contiguous community with those who have been severed from the organization;
- Dedicated time for reflection and integration of experiences;
- The advent of periodic retreats for the nourishment of the soul;
- Managers who are given time, whose jobs are re-envisioned to give weight to creating the conditions for soul to emerge;
- Legitimization of non-doing time and acceptance of "imagining" time;
- A heightened appreciation of paradox where all choices can be opted for, no dualism, "both and" rather than "either or";
- New approaches to heal the wounds of community when it is split apart, as in downsizing.

Examples of Innovative New Practices with Soul

Search Conferences: A common issue is addressed in a free-form style with little structure and extensive use of inter-relationship.

Conference Model: Work redesign involves employees from all levels and departments as well as customers and suppliers in a series of conferences: visioning conference, customer conference, technical conference, organizational design conference, and implementation conference.

Discovery Teams: Members represent all levels of management and employees from different departments and processes. The discovery team's mission is to determine if the organization needs to change and, if so, what specifically needs to change.

It has been said that creating meaning may be the true managerial task of the future. Virtually all institutions and disciplines are moving in more soul-satisfying directions. This is a result of the sociocultural shift to wanting more meaning in our lives and to empowerment, which enables people to build soul-centered worklives for themselves.

As organizations align with their own souls, they become more inhabitable. We need to be innovative, to use imagination, to create practices and ways of conducting business that will allow the collective and individual soul to emerge and thrive, to create meaning in the workplace that will serve both the corporation and the employee.

Jacqueline Haessly is the founder of Peacemaking Associates, a for-profit educational and consulting company. She is the author of *Learning to Live Together*, co-author of *The New Entrepreneurs: Business Visionaries for the 21st Century* and *When the Canary Stops Singing: Women's Perspectives on Transforming Business,* which was named one of the top ten management books for 1993 by *Industry Week* magazine.

Haessly has been named to more than twenty Who's Who international biographies, including Business and Professional Women, Women of the Americas, Authors and Writers, and International Leaders for her extensive work in the field of peace and global awareness education.

She offers consultation, lectures, workshops, and retreats to local and national business, educational, and community organizations. She is currently pursuing doctoral studies at the Union Institute in Cincinnati, Ohio.

18

Soul Work:
A Corporate Challenge

Jacqueline Haessly

Corporate leaders, like most in our society, see the world around us hurting, crying out in anguish for relief. Today, a growing number of business leaders recognize that the afflictions to people or the earth are the direct or indirect result of social, economic, or political policies and practices of government and corporate leaders. Too often, these policies are for the benefit of corporations rather than the communities in which they reside. We know that some corporate and government leaders engage in hiring and promotion practices which limit employment, deny education and health services for the needy, refuse access to capital for home or business needs, promote use of arable land for cash crops rather than for family need, reap large profits from world-wide arms sales, or destroy our fragile ecosystem through the plunder and pollution of the resources of the earth. We witness the results of these decisions in the pain-filled eyes of children and families on our evening news. In one way or another, we want to stop the pain and bring an end to the suffering.

But what, we might ask, does any of this pain have to do with corporate leadership? How does soul find expression today in our life and in our world in a way that reflects a corporate culture committed to social responsibility? Whatever our professional role in this world, we are first of all, people who share a common humanity on a small planet. The decisions we make in the workplace influence for good or for ill the quality of life of individuals, families, communities, states, nation, and our planet. Thus, corporate leaders with soul, who see the sacredness and connectedness of all of life, have the capacity to help heal our hurting world.

In this essay I identify ten characteristics of a corporate culture which reflect soul in a business. I follow this with a description of a methodology which business leaders can use to develop and express soul in their own business. Lastly, I identify several ways that some business leaders manifest soul in their corporate culture. Companies who take steps to express soul in their own business environments are helping to both heal the pain that exists and create a more just and peace-filled world for all.

Creating a Corporate Culture with Soul

Below are ten characteristics essential to the development of a corporate culture based on spiritual values or soul. How well these are manifested in your corporation determines your own company's "Soul Quotient" (or SQ).

1. **Contemplation.** If our life and our work are to have meaning we must plan time in our day and our work for contemplation. We need time for personal reflection on our experiences, our work, and the impact these have on ourselves and on our family. We also need time to reflect on the impact these have on the lives of others who share space with us in our global society. Lastly, we need time to contemplate our connection with each other and a spiritual being or higher power who gives life meaning.

How we answer the quality of life questions implicit and explicit in our corporate decision-making is determined by the quality of our "soul work," our contemplation. In some companies, prayer and meditation groups meet regularly before the beginning of the work day. A growing number of corporations provide for moments for reflection, for meditation, or for centering before beginning important business meetings. Others provide quiet meditation rooms where staff can go for moments of reflection. Some plan retreats where spiritual and emotional needs of staff as well as financial, development, and marketing needs of the company are addressed.

2. **Care.** As individuals and as corporate leaders, we need to develop an ethic of care which is based on respect for ourselves, for others, for the organization, for the community in which it resides, and for the environment. An ethic of care manifests itself in attentiveness to our own and others' needs, including those of workers, customers, investors, and other stakeholders. An ethic of care in the workplace is reflected in a variety of policies and practices, including those that lead toward (1) a just return to investors for the use of their capital and workers for the use of their labor, (2) the development of quality products and services, (3) inclusiveness in hiring and promotion policies, (4) care for the legitimate needs of the community in which a business is located, and (5) tender care of the ecosystem in the production of products and the disposal of waste.

3. **Compassion.** We are compassionate people to the degree that we show sensitivity to the physical, emotional, and spiritual needs of others. Corporate leaders immersed in a corporate culture of compassion acknowledge that both women *and* men have families whose members give birth, have children and other family members who become ill, and whose loved ones die. Women and men have children who need dental care and who desire parental attendance at school plays and soccer games. A corporate culture of compassion reflects this reality in family and people friendly policies and practices. Such policies are evident in flexible work hours, job sharing options, family leave for child care, elder care, personal care, and other family needs for *all* workers. Further, the corporate culture itself must support family need choices in ways that don't penalize men or women who make these choices in regard to work and promotion opportunities. Compassion extends to the community and the world as corporate leaders make business decisions based on both corporate goals and the common good.

4. **Concern.** Every community consists of some people in need. A corporate culture of concern is reflected in corporate awareness of the social, political, and economic needs of people in the communities in which it does business. Such a culture of concern has led growing numbers of companies to establish corporate sponsorship of literacy, hunger relief, shelter, clothing, education, and recreation programs for special populations within the community and the world. When soul is involved, these expressions of concern are seen as more than "free advertising" or promotion of "good will" for the company. They are seen as an

expression of the very soul of the company, considered by some as a form of tithing. In some companies, workers are encouraged to perform outside community service; for others, such expressions of concern are built into the work hours for all staff. A corporate culture of concern also examines corporate policies in terms of how they contribute to, or alleviate, the suffering of people in need.

5. **Creativity.** Creativity is energy directed toward the outward expression of an inner vision. One must first have space and time for reflection in order to nurture the vision if it is to see fruition. Creative people link unrelated objects in new ways, express common ideas in uncommon ways, and imagine the impossible as possible. Creativity flourishes in a corporate culture that provides time for reflection and rewards the expression of new ideas. This leads to creative thinking and the development and improvement of products and services as well as critical problem solving and the establishment of effective team building and quality relationships within and beyond the corporation.

6. **Cooperation.** Cooperation occurs when women and men work or play together to achieve a common goal. It is based on a model of inclusiveness, equality, and full participation, and leads to a win-win mode of group problem solving. Today, a growing number of companies recognize that competitiveness divides and dissipates individual and corporate energy and dilutes economic and physical resources. These companies are leaders in discouraging competition between individuals within departments, between departments, and even between differing corporations. They are replacing competition with effective team-building processes that promote collaboration, collegiality, and consensus decision making—the ground pins of cooperation. In these corporations, diverse gifts of all the members of the team are acknowledged and leadership tasks are shared.

As we approach the 21st Century, economic partnerships such as the European Economic Community, North American Free Trade Association, and General Agreement on Tariffs and Trade provide an economic framework whereby new forms of cooperation at the global level can evolve. This will require a major paradigm shift, one that replaces a mentality of competitiveness at the global level with a mentality and model based on cooperation and new forms of team building. The EEC, NAFTA, and GATT challenge corporate leaders to consider new possibilities for corporate and community development. For corporate leaders with soul, decisions will be made based on the good of the community as well as the corporation, labor will be paid a just wage, and environmental concerns will be addressed. All will share in the allocation of resources and the economic rewards. Only then will corporate leaders be engaged in working together for the common, and not only the corporate, good.

7. **Celebration.** Play nourishes our soul as food nourishes our body. Happy, contented people play together, have fun together, celebrate together. In many corporations, the attainment of individual, team, and corporate goals are celebrated with food, good cheer, even song and dance. A growing trend in corporate settings provides for creative or structured playtime activities, such as lunch hour volley-ball games, cooperative games festivals, or Friday afternoon "popcorn" parties. A characteristic of these activities is that they involve workers and managers playing together as equals, generating renewed team spirit in the process. This is qualitatively different from earlier patterns where managers sponsored sports teams or provided company picnics or holiday parties *for* workers and their families. Corporate celebrations, where everyone has the opportunity to participate as an equal, foster team spirit and nourish attitudes of care for each other and the community.

The soul of a business also affects celebration in two other important ways: the "how" of celebration and the "what" of celebration. The "how" of celebration determines the products we use for our own celebrations, or the products we produce or sell for others' family, community, or religious celebrations and national holidays. Soul work invites us to examine the quality of these products, as well as to examine the way these products are produced. Soul work invites consideration on a number of questions, including but not limited to the following: (1) Whose labor is used for the production of these products? (2) Is the return for labor just? (3) Do the products reflect quality in work and materials? (4) How do the resources used impact on the environment? Corporate leaders with soul want to assure that products used or produced for celebrations honor the earth and the people who produce or use them.

The "what" of celebration calls for an examination of corporate policies to determine the way company decision makers respect the celebrative occasions significant to different members of their staff, and to the community in which the company resides. The "what" of celebrations addresses such questions as

(1) which religious holidays are celebrated corporately, and why? (2) Is time off allotted for participation in religious events, and if so, for which events, and for whom? (3) How does the company honor the religious traditions of people from cultures different from its own, including respect for sacred land and artifacts? Corporate leaders who are grounded in a sense of spirituality reflect on these questions and address them in ways which honor diverse religious and cultural expressions within both the company and the broader community. Corporate practices which honor opportunity for diverse religious expressions and which also provide opportunity for celebration sustain and nurture each for the journey toward corporate transformation and global wholeness.

8. **Connection.** We live in a globally interdependent world, one where social, economic, political, and environmental concerns cross local, national, and regional borders. As business leaders we are challenged to see the connection between the impact of our decisions on our own businesses and their impact on the rest of planet. Spiritual power draws us into the experience of human suffering, the plight of all of humanity who still live in poverty, suffer political oppression, economic exploitation, or cultural, racial, religious, ethnic, national, gender, ability, or age discrimination. However, our concern with these experiences does not begin at the abstract level, or at the international level; it begins with the everyday experience of ordinary people— ourselves and those we know and love—in the home, the neighborhood, and the workplace. Drawing upon these personal experiences, we are better able to see the linkages between the pain experienced within the sanctuary of the home or the public sector of the workplace, and the pain of those whose stories make up the evening news. Our heightened awareness will lead us to make corporate decisions which respect the needs of others and the environment and which affirm our global interdependence.

9. **Community.** Carter Hayward describes community, as "an inclusive, non-authoritarian body of interdependent members whose lives *literally are bound up one in another* and who share a common commitment to justice....The power of community is sparked among persons who come together and is embodied in mutual engagement," for the common good of all humanity. Riane Eisler suggests that true community can only occur when there is true partnership based on equality and just relationships among all members of the community. She evokes a sense of

urgency about the dilemma facing the planet if new patterns based on ecological balance and planetary justice are not practiced, and she promotes an image of partnership—in human relationships and with environmental systems—as a means to planetary survival. Members of the partnership participate in work team activities that build a spirit of bonding, care for the needs of communities in which business operates, share a commitment to work together for the common good, and celebrate their efforts at community-building.

In this vision of a renewed society there will be respectful openness to the ideas and experiences of others. Relationships will be based on inclusiveness, where participation in decision making that affects one's life is full and equal, and where response-ability is both mutual and life-giving. In this place, the full range of human emotions and human experiences will be honored and treasured. Women, children, and men will celebrate their existence, their struggle, and their vision in song and dance.

10. **Commitment.** Commitment requires a recognition that there is work to be done, a vision of what one wants to accomplish, and a willingness to act to accomplish it. Feminist theologians believe that one cannot have a transformed self unless one also has a transformed society. They are at the forefront to articulate a vision of a world where all people are treated with dignity and respect. They prefer a "circle of equals" to a "ladder of rank." They prefer to widen the circle rather than exclude anyone. They seek to listen as well as to speak. They choose to follow as well as to lead. In the process, they grow in numbers, in strength to take risks, and in a willingness to suffer the consequences of their actions.

Corporate leaders also recognize that current economic and political structures and systems are energy draining and lead to wide spread inequalities in relations, including lack of access to goods and services, inability to participate in decisions that impact on one's life, and a widening gap between the wealthy and the poor of our world. Those with spiritual values share a commitment to the corporate good and to genuine social transformation. Thus, they seek full participation and mutuality in all phases of corporate life. They recognize the need to work with both women and men to create a society where participation in decision making that affects one's life is full and equal, where values of mutuality, response-ability, compassion, consensus, cooperation, inclusion, reciprocity, interdependence, and openness to the ideas and experiences of others, are treasured and where human rights, affirmation for the common good, and full human liberation are espoused and practiced.

Developing a Methodology for Soul Work

How can corporate leaders implement soul in their businesses? We turn now to a methodology which offers the possibility of community building, and which can lead to genuine personal, corporate and social transformation. Such a four-step methodology, often referred to as "feminist," is grounded in experience and is based on principles of inclusion, respect, mutuality, compassion, and cooperation.

Step One roots us in our own personal, family, professional, and community experiences. This is a time to make observations about those experiences and reflect on their influence on our life. What do our own family, work, and personal experiences tell us about life? Who do we know in our family or friendship circles who has suffered from the effects of family illness, loss of a job, loss of a loved one in war? How have environmental pollution or hazardous consumer products affected our own life or the life of someone we know and love? What do I think about, and feel, as I listen to news reports of human suffering? This is the stuff of our observations, reflections, and the stuff we enter into personal diaries and journals.

Step Two connects us to others. When women and men gather together to share stories and personal experiences in a common circle, they recognize the similarities in the patterns of their lives. From these stories we discover a greater awareness of the common threads of our individual and corporate experiences. For honest sharing to occur, it is necessary to provide a safe place and time for the sharing of one's personal story. As trust develops and people gain ease in the sharing, bonding occurs.

In Step Three we analyze our stories, questioning what is, why it is, and what should or can be done to change it. As people share their stories, and learn from each other—at times with great personal risk—they grow in their ability to recognize the common threads, concerns, questions, fears, and hopes across cultures, races, nationalities, religions, and gender. They also deepen their understanding of the interconnectedness between issues. A vision of what can be emerges from their collective stories.

Step Four moves us beyond analysis to strategize ways to bring our vision to reality. The urgent question is "What can we do?" This question reads in two ways. "What can we DO?" addresses the urgency for establishing an effective action plan. "What can WE do?" challenges each of us to be involved in seeking workable solutions to common and not-so-common problems. We are the ones who need to act! We are the ones empowered! We are the ones with the strength, the power, the courage, and the willingness to risk!

In this step we must be as committed to the process of bringing about social change as we are to the strategy. Strategy relates to the "what" of social change and suggests a willingness to focus on any means necessary to achieve a defined goal. For some, unfortunately, strategy takes precedence over relationships in an effort to achieve social change. Process, on the other hand, is rooted in soul, and relates to the "who" of social change. It implies a sensitivity to relationships, mutual respect, and an openness to new insights. Those concerned about process are as concerned about what happens to *all* the people during efforts to bring about social transformation as they are about achieving their goal of social transformation.

Managing With Soul for Profit and the Common Good

How then is soul manifested in our world today? Where are women and men claiming their power, reaching out to share their stories, bonding together, and working together to bring healing and wholeness to a hurting world? Examples, too numerous to detail, abound from every continent. Here I will identify several with an international flavor and several from the United States. In each, women and men are joining hands to weave a new tapestry of relationships with each other and with the earth that gives them sustenance. In each they are also forging new ways of doing business—as Tom Chappell says so powerfully about his own company—"managing for profit and the common good."

Indigenous peoples in India, in Costa Rica, in Brazil, and elsewhere, have seen the destruction of the forests that provide shelter for the animals, plants to nourish the body, shade to refresh the spirit, and fuel to warm the hearth. Clear-cutting of the rain forest for economic gain was creating erosion of soil and contributing to the destruction of the ecosystem through a reduction of the oxygen level of the earth. As people reflected upon their observations, shared their stories, and named their experiences, they began to analyze their options in light of the language of both economic development and human and environmental needs.

As a result of their reflection and analysis, the people in these countries made a decision to act. In India whole villages of people came to the forests to "hug" trees tagged for cutting, replanted trees in clear-cut landings, and petitioned for and received government support for their efforts. "Development" continued, but in ways that were less destructive, and in some cases were helpful, to the ecosystem. In Costa Rica and in Brazil, peasants identified ecologically safe ways to stop the destruction of the rain forest while providing for the economic needs of the community through eco-forestry, a method of using the fruits and other renewable resources of the rain forest while leaving the trees intact. Similar examples are occurring in countries of Africa, Asia, and in Eastern and Western Europe. In all these places women and men, acting with soul, have claimed their power and have given new meaning to the term "economic development."

Examples of companies in the United States who are managing for profit and the common good abound. In the US some of these companies started as nonprofit organizations which added a for-profit component. Neighborhood economic development programs bring together the nonprofit sectors with a for-profit component in a true spirit of entrepreneurialism.

In Washington, DC, the Center for Creative Non-Violence now has a for-profit housing rehabilitation company which provides job training for the homeless and aids in their own economic development as new entrepreneurs. In Los Angeles, Detroit, Trenton, and Philadelphia, for-profit and nonprofit companies have created new job opportunities for former gang members.

In Milwaukee, New Life, Harambee, Esperanzo Unidas, the Lisbon Avenue Neighborhood Development Association (LAND), and SET Ministry (Service, Empowerment and Transformation) are just a few of the several dozen community economic development projects that have emerged. These groups grew out of dialogue with religious leaders and community people living and working in impoverished areas of city. Reflecting on the need for a "preferential option for the poor" in their own communities, they formed development funds, education programs, and empowerment projects aimed at generating a sense of personal self-worth, economic self-sufficiency, political responsibility, and an awareness of the need to act cooperatively in order to create a just society. Out of this commitment there has arisen training programs and entrepreneurial opportunities for childcare, food service, healthcare workers, auto repair, home construction, asbestos removal, and a printing and publishing company. Each program and project provides time for reflection, analysis, and further action based on spiritual values for personal, community, and global wholeness.

Summary

In this essay I have posed ten characteristics necessary for the effective expression of soul in a business and have presented a four-step methodology which could lead to effective and inclusive analysis of situations, empowerment of individuals within the corporation, and the formation of a caring corporate community. I also identified ways that some business and community leaders are already working to bring about the transformation of society.

The world around us is in pain. We can lament the pain and hide in the comfort of our private corporate offices. Or we can acknowledge the pain and, understanding that it is part of the birthing process necessary to bring forth a new way of doing business, we can assist to bring it to birth.

Let us accept this corporate challenge. Let us join other business and community leaders and visionaries, committing our heads, our hearts, and our hands to the work and the process of healing and transforming our hurting world.

Robert Leaver, an eagle scout, is president of Organizational Futures, a consulting firm focusing on strategic visioning and workplace restructuring. Formed in 1982, its clients include businesses, health and educational organizations, economic/community renewal groups, trade associations, artists, and refugees. The firm integrates imagination, poetry, and art with the concrete and practical.

Leaver has delivered hundreds of lectures for groups such as Business for Social Responsibility (for which he was past president of the New England network). He founded the three-year Common Good Collaborative, an assembly of thinkers and doers focusing on bolder ways to serve the common good. Former director of University Without Walls, he is a business partner and adjunct faculty member at Boston College's executive leadership program, "Leaders for the Common Good."

19

The Commonwealth Organization: Healing the World's Ailing Soul

Robert Leaver

We in the industrial world live in sorrowful times—times in which our cultures are undergoing a huge shedding. We feel the angst in the upheaval of all institutions: family, community, government, and places of worship. Our current organizational structures—business, government, and the nonprofits—are bankrupt. Most of what we historically held in common is splitting apart.

Our culture is at a critical juncture. We must learn to live sustainably or we will destroy ourselves. There are no more holes for garbage; governments are in gridlock; complete species have been obliterated. We are not considering the impact of our economic decisions on nature or our children and their children. We are slowly realizing we can no longer transcend the messes we have made by moving on to a "better place." We are facing E.F. Schumacher's first economic principal: There is such thing as enough. With no virgin slate left for us to soil, we must turn and drop into the soul of the world.

Soul lies below; a descent. In the tradition of James Hillman, part of soul is the underworld of pain and sorrow where psyche knows no limits. Soul contains our mistakes and all that is inferior. In soul, all becomes a slow and entangled web of complexity. Soul is moist, dark, and low; the home of poverty; the place of pathology and shadows. Soul is in the earth.

What if we imagined that all existence began in the bowels of the earth instead of heaven? Would not we love the earth as our home? Would we not grant the earth its soul? In the words of Thomas Moore: "Societies have denied soul to that which they wanted to control: We can only treat badly those things or people whose souls we disregard." When we hold regard for everything, all is alive with energy. Granting the world its soul requires that human beings would no longer be the heart of the economy—all things would become part of it. This challenges the dominant view that places humans as the center of economic activity.

If we asked the soul of the world to bare itself, what would it say? "I have been neglected and uncared for; I am grieving. You are sick and in pain because I am sick and in pain. I have complaints. My 'stuff' effects you and your 'stuff' effects me. You have stopped visiting 'out there' where dreams are moving in the mythos. Return me to the world so you will no longer have to carry me on your back. Your continued attempts to carry all of soul keeps you trapped in your ego. How foolish to think you are bigger than me and can hold soul in your frail body. The soul of the world is all pervasive."

The soul of the world demands a new form. Bad form disturbs the soul of the world. Leaders keep trying to transform (note the root of "transform" is "form") the culture with mutant, resistant forms. They impose their crude form onto the soul of the world without listening to its cry. We need a new form that will breathe in and out the vital issues of the commons—one that simultaneously surrenders to the soul and nurtures it.

The Commonwealth Organization:
A New Form to Serve Our Common Wealth

The Commonwealth organization mediates the old and the new, the known and the unknown. It begins with basic questions: What does the soul of the world want? What time bombs are embedded in our communities, our governments and our businesses? What antibodies lay in wait, ready to heal the soul of the world? The Commonwealth organization animates the soul of the world to address tangible social and environmental problems.

The Commonwealth organization builds our commons by simultaneously shaping healthy, productive and vibrant work places, allowing us to live fully in our communities as citizens who care for others, honoring nature and her aliveness by reducing the harmful impact of products; respecting the intelligence of consumers by providing them with "highly informed," reusable products; forging truth and transparency with shareholders and stakeholders; and by making a profit and generating wealth for the common good.

The Commonwealth organizational form will give rise to ideas and energies that can serve our decaying world culture. From government comes the notion of a public trust to uphold. The business form conjures profit and capitalism. The nonprofit form communicates service and philanthropic grants. None of these forms give birth to an image of the soul of the world, protecting the commons, or generating broader, more inclusive wealth. All three are too limited. We must burst the old conceptual boundaries of how to serve the commons.

The Commonwealth organization is a mediating form. It is a larger container that goes beyond business and public-minded organizations to become a synthesis and destruction of these older forms. From business, the Commonwealth takes the principals of profit, markets, and results. From the nonprofit organization comes the principals of a social purpose, credibility, and accountability to others beyond stockholders. The government form lends the concept of civic duty, with each citizen responsible for participating for the good of the whole.

The Commonwealth organization seeds and carries planetary culture. In the words of Joseph Campbell, "the mythic layer collapsed with the industrial revolution" and we are now preparing the myth that "will be about a multicultural society of the planet." The emerging mythology will be shaped one event at a time by "learning how to live life under any circumstances." The Commonwealth organization will restore and sustain the soul of the world—nature, community, workplace and mythology—to a livable and respected state for ourselves and future generations.

Prototypes of the Commonwealth Organization

There are prototypes of the Commonwealth organization. In upstate New York in the late sixties, the Rensselaerville Institute began a bold course of community development with the intent that each community they work with be renewed and that each person own his or her own home. In 1973, the Institute launched this process by literally buying a town—Corbett, New York—from the factory which owned it. Using recoverable investment moneys, the Institute sold the town, piece by piece, to the people then renting their homes. With the Institute as their development partner, the town's citizens used self-help principles to rebuild water lines, create community buildings and refurbish all of the housing stock.

Another prototype of a Commonwealth organization can be found in Chicago: the Shorebank Corporation. This regulated bank holding company most nearly represents the Commonwealth organization. Its confederation of forms—including two subsidiaries and two affiliates—imports and directs economic and human resources to develop the South Shore community of Chicago. The subsidiaries are the South Shore Bank which serves as the primary source of economic resources; and the for-profit City Land Corporation which rehabilitates real estate and buys and sells land. Its affiliates are the Neighborhood Institute, a nonprofit which works with the softer aspects of the project (e.g., mobilizing citizens); and the for-profit Neighborhood Fund which provides equity capital and subordinated loans.

Seeking to accelerate its community renewal objectives, Shorebank chose this confederation of legal forms because the task of system-wide, community development and crafting a power base for citizens required a stronger vehicle than the conventional nonprofit community development corporation. Begun in the 1970s, this bank holding corporation is far from finished with its agenda. If anything, it is just learning the important lessons from its failures. The new agenda is the deep work of community renewal.

Core Processes of the
Commonwealth Organization

Uses a Confederation of Legal Forms to Move Money

As is the case with the Rensselaerville Institute and the Shorebank Corporation, the Commonwealth organization is a confederation of legal forms directed toward furthering the well-being of the commons. This confederation is a generative form, a new synthesis of resource-rich organizations directed to the common wealth. As a confederation, the Commonwealth organization would blend multiple legal forms and work flows like a land trust, manufacturer, service business, a philanthropic foundation, a bank/loan fund, retreat or space for reflection, elder and child care services, social service supports or a community development corporation—whatever is required to serve the commons in that locality. It goes beyond both for-profit and not-for-profit organizations to hold equal relationships with business, earth, people, and mythology.

Dances With Images and Puts Its Feet on the Ground

The Commonwealth organization is designed to move the psyche of our culture. To achieve this end requires Michael Meade's three realms of learning: concrete, psychological, and mythological. Concrete learning is a singular process; data is absorbed one item at a time. This is the realm of facts and human touch. It is the realm of the practical and all that is linear. Nature and our senses are rooted in the concrete world.

Psychological learning occurs when two things come together. Here you have the potential of two truths colliding and tension resulting. Learning psychologically is relational; this and that. Mythological learning occurs when two things come together and many other things arise out of the two truths. Symbols and images are activated. It is open and ambiguous; there is no formula. A sense of endlessness and timelessness permeates the experience, defying definition. This is the place of mystery and no dogma.

Owning our common wealth will not occur until we let go of the psychological—the conversation—as the only means of achieving change. In discussion one often remains locked in battle between two truths and there is little movement. The psychological realm is saturated because Americans remain trapped in this middle position. People have mistakenly let go of the other two realms of learning: the concrete (because the facts are too painful), and the mythological realm of images and story which is not considered real. Serving the commons requires the talent of the dancer to help plant our feet on the ground and own the facts and the pain of the concrete world.

Lives in Paradox, Knowing the Opposites are
Secretly at One with Each Other

In the Commonwealth organization leaders must hold the tension of paradox. Instead of choosing ecology or commerce, one holds the tension inherent in bringing together the elements of ecology and commerce. The same tension has to be held with masculine energy which is instrumental and drives for separation and the feminine which strives for merging and connection. The same creative tension has to be held with two views of power. One view has power as finite; if I have it, you can't. In this view of power there is pie to be divided. On the other side of the tension, power is infinite and generative. In this view power is to be taken or owned, and the more I take the more there is in the world. Working with each paradox requires us to embrace Robert Johnson's notion of the mandorla or the space where the two opposites overlap. Keep both demands in focus by working in the mandorla, for this is the space from which the Commonwealth organization comes.

Rather than fight with tension, trying to choose one opposite over another, leaders must learn to work with the opposites. They must learn, as Marion Woodman counsels, "to stand in the tension of the opposites until a third thing emerges." We want it now, yet it comes only when it is ready.

Embraces Both Circle and Hierarchy in the Way Work is Organized and Completed

To achieve the noble ends of serving our common wealth, both circle and hierarchy must be used. One is not better than the other. Both are ways of making decisions and doing work, each with its own unique purposes and vitality. It is not *either/ or,* it is *both/and;* paradox is at play. The debate over circle or hierarchy is rooted in the age-old tension between self and other; between the rights of the individual and the good of the whole.

The dynamics of the workplace have become the central focus of organizations. The current mandate of "get flat or horizontal at all costs and use only teams to get work done" is flawed, dangerous, and contributes to much angst in the workplace. Further, the call to get flat at all costs contributes to a "bottoming out" because the business has not prepared the next level of leaders to take the business into the future. The single focus on flattening and teamwork deprives the next generation of leaders of the opportunity to think strategically and deepen the competence required to lead.

If only circles are used, the attention of leaders is kept at one level: the circle of equals. When hierarchies are praised and used for the distinguishing functions they must perform, then there will be progress on the workplace agenda. The leader will not only be able to look to the side (the circle) but up the hierarchy to the future as well. If you do not sanction hierarchy for the functions it must perform, it will eat up your attempts to change. Hierarchies foster acting and doing; thus they are instrumental in nature. A hierarchy formally allows for crisp decision making and profitability.

In the absence of hierarchy there is reduced empowerment. In part, empowerment comes from owning solo work, making decisions, and using your skills. With fixed accountability and authority, one is positioned to take responsibility. Once boundaries for a work position are set, they can be flexed, which occurs when one exceeds authority to get a product to market. This is taking the responsibility and owning power! If everything is shared and undistinguished, which is often the described character of the flat organization, where does an individual get to shine?

A lack of elegant hierarchy deprives the individual with an important source of self worth: the ability to influence events. Elegant hierarchy is different from the limited perception of hierarchy as being "everything top down," where all decisions are made at the top. It fosters the honing of individual talents. Elegant hierarchy distinguishes levels of work based on know-how required, the complexity of the work to be done, and the time horizon to be held in view. Finally, an elegant hierarchy allocates the accountability for decisions at each work level. Decisions are made at the authorized level without going to the top.

Yet, without the circle, there would be no striving for our common wealth or pulling beyond self to a higher social purpose. Circles provide the space for the collaboration among the people with the individual competencies required to complete complex projects of serving the common wealth. Such projects require each contributor's snapshot in order to see the whole picture. An individual strives for greater competency when he or she has a sense of ownership and control over a piece of the collaborative process. This contributes to the good of the whole project. Thus, individual power can merge into a group contribution. Herein lies the paradox.

Circles are expressive, with a focus on listening and being. Circles are used to make connections, build relationships and experience a sense of the whole. In a circle things go around and around; there is involvement, equality and a proper slowness. The circle opens the soul to the aesthetics of beauty and compassion. Circles come into play to achieve a sense of team and to achieve a sense of our mutual life in an era of deep angst.

Both circle and hierarchy have spirit and soul attributes.

Soul is not bad; it is just the other side of light. Both spirit and soul must interact for completion. On the shadow side, hierarchies can become over-controlling and strictly "top down." Too much control leads to paralysis at the top. Too much use of circles can be Kafkaesque and move everything to the lowest common denominator. Hierarchy and circle make organizations function. This is healthy, creative tension at its best.

The Outcomes of the Commonwealth Organization

Honors the Soul's Longing for Beauty

Beauty is an aesthetic response. Beauty is everywhere and is taken in through the five senses. We slow down to experience the pleasure of each nuance when we are arrested by beauty. The landscape of the workplace and the community requires radical renovation to create a place for beauty. They must become intimate and open to beauty. Natural light and the soul of buildings must seep into the workplace. Windows must open to let air in and allow the buildings to breathe. For example, North Western Mutual Insurance Company created a program called the "Power of Quiet in the Workplace." This created the necessary stillness to open its employees to being arrested by beauty in the workplace. When we take more pleasure, we have more beauty.

Creates a Sense of Place on the Landscape and Within the Community

Our communities require interdependence. The shadow we carry as a nation is seeping out in too many places. We can no longer stuff anything more in the gigantic shadow bag this country has created. We can no longer transcend by moving on to a better place. The rapidly rising "edge" cities are an ominous presence precisely because they turn their backs on our cities. Instead of entering the souls of our cities to revitalize them, developers have gone to fresh land to create cities that are closer to the suburbs. The cities represent problems and the suburbs a clean slate. Yet, it is the cities that hold the soul of the world to be released.

Experiences Work as Craft to Produce Intelligent Products

The Commonwealth organization provides a marketplace where enterprise and ecology interact to craft useful products that are sensitive to the natural environment. The work of

Michael Braungart, as described in Paul Hawken's declaration of sustainability, provides a new framework for manufacturing intelligent products. Braungart calls for three kinds of intelligent products: consumables, durables, and unsaleables.

Consumables can be eaten or turned to dirt. "The waste of a consumable has to be someone else's food." Consumables are designed to decompose and not just be recycled. As a consumer, consumables are the only product you could freely purchase.

Durables are things like cars and televisions. These products would never be sold, but rather would be licensed to you, the consumer, by the manufacturer, who always owns the product and must take it back when you are done with it. Durables are designed for disassembly, like the new BMWs.

Unsaleables are toxins, heavy metals, and chemicals. Unsaleables always belong to the original maker. When an unsaleable has no more use, it would be placed in a "secured parking lot" owned by a new kind of public utility where the product is stored in safe containers until it is benign. Moreover, the manufacturer pays rent for the storage.

Braungart and Hawken challenge us to radically alter the "how and what" of products we make and consume. A returnable BMW is only the beginning.

Integrates a Community of Work, Family and Diverse People

Today's workplace is loaded with messes. People are cut off from their families, the natural world, or they are out of work. The Commonwealth organization works in the marketplace and creates employment for those who want to work. It values family and work equally. The workspace offers the flexible landscaping of furniture and dividers so people can experience connectedness and move as a project evolves. Diversity in culture, history and thought are recognized and fostered. Workers learn how to learn and are supported in career choices. Flex- and part-time arrangements are the rule. Children and elders are acknowledged as assets to be nurtured with day care and elder care services provided on-site. In effect, the Commonwealth organization's workplace is surrounded by a worker opportunity zone where all of the social, educational, and human services are connected and located in, or just next door to, the workplace.

Commonwealth Financial Statement

5 SOURCES OF CAPITAL *	INVESTOR/ STAKEHOLDER	WHAT'S EXTRACTED- ACCOUNTABLE FOR**	5 BOTTOM LINES
human and intellectual capital	workers	know-how, brain use, soul	core competence
social capital	citizens	good will, energy of community	well-being of community
natural capital	nature	abundance, raw materials	sustainment
consumer capital	customer	buying power	strength of truthful franchise in marketplace
financial capital	shareholder	money	profit

*   Stock and flow of resources required to produce outputs from inputs.

** Acct: weight carried what your feet are held to the fire for.

Bolder Methods of Accounting and Measuring
A Commonwealth Financial Statement

The Commonwealth organization redefines the scope and nature of what it accounts for and to whom. It would issue a financial statement on the common wealth of the locality. This statement would declare the standards to which the organization would be held. There would be a narrative audit against the standards and objectives including the revelation of messes and violations. There would be truth and transparency in the narrative. It would account for five sources of capital to five stakeholders. It would issue a set of measurable indicators of well-being to report on business and common wealth results.

Be Accountable to Five Stakeholders
for the Use of Five Kinds of Capital

In granting the world its soul and in visualizing our role as stewards of well-being, capital is redefined. Capital is defined as the stock and flow of resources required to produce a product or deliver a service. For capital to do its work, it must flow and not be hoarded. Historically, business focused on financial capital and accounted to stockholders for its use. This produced the bottom line where all costs were either externalized—becoming someone else's problem—or minimized in order to produce maximum profit and a satisfactory shareholder return.

In contrast, the Commonwealth organization will issue, as part of the new financial statement, an integrated balance sheet of the commons that accounts for the use of five kinds of capital with five bottom lines:

- human and intellectual capital—the stock and use of a worker's brain and contributions
- social capital—the use of talent, energy, and good will of citizens and their communities
- natural capital—the stock and use of nature's abundance
- consumer capital—the stock and use of buying power in the marketplace
- financial capital—the stock and use of money

As a steward of the soul of the world with five kinds of capital to be accountable for, the Commonwealth organization has five stakeholders:

- consumers for the use of their buying power and choices
- workers for the use of their human and intellectual capital
- shareholders for the use of their financial capital
- citizens for the use of their social capital
- nature for the use of her abundance

The Commonwealth organization will report to all five stakeholders on change in the general welfare of humanity resulting from enterprise activity. No longer can the changes in the economic resources of shareholders be the sole measurement. The welfare of humanity becomes the well-being of the five stakeholders: consumers, workers, investors, citizens, and the natural world.

Go Public with an Integrated Set of Measures of the Business's Well-Being in Relationship to Its Context—the Commons

Measurement deals with the realm of the concrete. People pay attention to what is measured. Business yardsticks have to be expanded to account for the full use of human, ecological and social capital. Historically, business has viewed efficiency as the only yardstick.

Singling out efficiency has made it the ultimate and only cause. Thus, costs are externalized from the business and become the burden of someone else or the earth. In not honoring the material, or the idea and the purpose of the product, business has forsaken its duty to the earth, people and its social responsibility. The added friction of working with responsibility for the messes in the Commonwealth slows things down and allows soul to enter.

Measuring the well-being of the commons requires a business to properly treat the waste or, in environmentalist terms, close the manufacturing loop. For example, VeryFine, a maker of natural fruit juices in the US, has reengineered its manufacturing process to recycle 95% of the waste produced. VeryFine made the earth its customer. Yes, there is a cost, but the cost is now viewed as a valued contribution to the well-being of the earth, or an asset, and not an expense which reduced the traditional bottom line.

Distributes a Balance Sheet for the Well-Being of the Common Wealth

The "Well-Being of the Commons Balance Sheet" with five bottom lines becomes the tool for reporting on the general welfare of the five stakeholders and the use of the five sources of capital. A conventional, single bottom line balance sheet is a maximization of present value (profit + financial capital), while what is required is reporting on the maximization of future value of the common wealth to subsequent generations. This requires the Commonwealth organization to internalize costs and demonstrate how the internalization of costs adds value to the planet and the well-being of all.

1. *Intellectual accounting* is determining the value of the workers and their know-how to the business as human and intellectual assets.

2. *Social accounting* is determining the value of contributions including volunteering and education in the community as assets.

3. *Environmental accounting* is acknowledging the full cost of the use of resources in producing goods or services—including what it takes to reinstate the environment to wholeness.

   For example, BSO/Origin, located in the Netherlands, details in its annual report its impact on the natural world. A base line of livability is set in the community. BSO is after a net value extracted by subtracting the environmental expenditures from the cost of environmental impacts. BSO then calculates all of its direct and indirect environmental impacts and costs against the base line of livability. It goes upstream and downstream to assess its impact. As radical as this method is for our time it is still not yet complete.

4. *Consumer accounting* is determining the strength of a truthful franchise in the marketplace.

5. *Profit*....enough is known about how to account for this factor.

Lives in Integrity by Declaring Its Violations

The Commonwealth organization will own its violations by communicating to its five stakeholders the ethical issues in question and the lessons learned. This move to public transparency feeds the soul of the world.

Integrity requires living another paradox or creative tension. John Beebe, a Jungian, would say that "integrity is the play between the purity of a standard and the impurity of the action." Purity is derived from a code of conduct or an ethical standard—all driving toward a higher good. Impurity includes our shadow stuff, the screw-ups and the violations of the standard. You cannot live with integrity unless you experience the mess of impurity. You will not know what integrity is until you know what it is not.

The Commonwealth Organization Requires Radical Leaders

Shaping our common wealth requires diverse leadership images and tools. The leaders of Shorebank and the Rensselaerville Institute are social entrepreneurs using enterprise as a tool for social change. Such leaders take risks, innovate, and hold a high need for achievement. They maintain a results focus and a long-term view with a social purpose. These leaders have compassion and hold the tension of the paradox of the marketplace and the good of the whole. Social entrepreneurs will move enterprise to become, in the words of Hillman, "a cell in which revolution is prepared." The soul of the world requires a complete turn into the heart of business. In this way our ailing common wealth will be healed.

Part Five
Applying the Learnings

In this final segment, six original essays have been focused on application—applying the experiences, learnings, and desires generated from previous segments in this book.

Each of these authors offers pragmatic approaches to personal and organizational transformation in the workplace. Relating personal growth with company performance, becoming a transformative leader, and rekindling the soul of business, government, and the healthcare industry are topics covered in this section.

In the final chapter, an original writing by another best-selling author, the soul of business and how to care for it is directly addressed by Thomas Moore.

The editors hope that this segment will be the capstone for this collection, motivating the reader to apply the principles, the learnings, and the passion evoked by this book to everyday work life.

Marie Morgan serves as a leadership and management consultant to health care, business, and environmental organizations. Her company, Morgan Consulting Group, is based in Portland, Oregon. With a multidisciplinary doctorate in psychology, spirituality, and adult development, and a Masters in human values, she helps leaders create more purpose-focused organizations. She teaches collaboration skills to physicians and hospital management groups, conflict resolution skills to management teams, and group dialogue skills in a variety of settings. She speaks nationally on recovering the soul in health care and on creating workplaces with spirit. Her private practice also includes executive coaching and a year-long leadership course. Morgan is an ordained minister in the United Church of Christ, has finished one Portland Marathon, and aspires now to become proficient on her Nordic Track.

20

Letters to Andre: Becoming a Transformative Presence

Marie Morgan

Andre is a bright and capable professional who was given management responsibility for an international publication, the Greenpeace magazine, at a young age. When his publication was discontinued in a downsizing, he took the opportunity to redesign his career and has asked me to help design his year of intentional leadership development.

His goal is to become more proficient both as a manager and as a leader in the environmental movement. He has identified five areas of growth: intellectual (environment and social change); professional (including "presence" in public speaking); personal (courage, discipline, authenticity, spirituality); finance; and management (strategy, people, conflict, and projects).

One reason he chose to work with me on his development is that he sees his work and "life work" in a larger spiritual context. These letters are about "deepening soul" in his business and his life.

Month One

Dear Andre,

I am impressed with your strong commitment to increasing your effectiveness by taking this journey. You have many gifts to give the world as you seek both to make a living and to make a contribution. I notice you included spiritual growth on your study list—good choice! Over the years I have come to recognize this is the foundation for much of the world's greatest leadership. Gandhi has said that

We must *be* the changes we wish to see in the world.

Our work here concerns your becoming a *transforming presence*. How you understand yourself and your role, how you behave at every moment, the *presence* you bring to each interaction, will pivotally shape the outcomes of those interactions. Gandhi's profound challenge will stand as our guide.

When the organization where you were thriving "dematerialized" your position, you not only lost your job, but also, unavoidably, lost some of your sense of identity. Even though you consider yourself a flexible and adaptable person, you could not help but feel a need for stability. But you also feel a need to make a difference, to make some useful dent in the problems of the world, to make a contribution where you feel a sense of urgency. You also acknowledge that you need new skills *and* new insights, because who you were last year will not be sufficient for next year's challenges. To address these needs in the next three months we will talk about:

- Finding balance, and staying centered amidst conflict, through a personal spiritual practice.
- Defining reality through whole-system thinking, asking questions, and bridging polarities.
- Transforming groups through telling the truth and authentic dialogue.

Getting Personal, Getting Quiet

The foundation for becoming a transformative presence is staying *centered*—feeling balanced at all times, knowing who you are and what you are about. This used to be called "a personal matter" in workplace conversations, but the old compartments have dissolved. You *are* the person who goes to work. Andre, the proven route to a centered life is adopting some form of daily spiritual practice. Practice it faithfully for a year, and I guarantee it will change your life.

At the heart of each spiritual practice is an ability to stay in the silence until we come to find that it is no longer silent. For some people this means something as simple as a solitary run three times a week. Others find daily mind-clearing meditation calms and empowers the spirit like nothing else can. Focusing on ancient wisdom (scripture or other traditions), or on contemporary or ancient prayers, is more helpful to others. You may want to engage your body in the process. Yoga, tai chi, or a simple walking meditation may be your path. You will experience not only a mental shift, but also one that will transform your feelings.

I encourage you to consider equally the Western Judeo-Christian traditions and Eastern paths. Recently, being Christian has not been as "politically correct" as choosing an Eastern way. Andre, don't be so easily polarized by trends. There are jewels of great wisdom in every lasting tradition, though admittedly it takes some digging to get past old forms. The key is *regular practice*, and this is most likely on a path that suits your temperament.

Your spiritual practice will deepen and strengthen your spiritual and psychic "tap root." This tap root will anchor you when the gale force winds of change batter you. It will also help heal you of the "spiritual anorexia" rampant in our culture today. We simply must develop ways, each of us, for a deeper nourishment of the soul. Worthwhile and effective work requires it; our spirits insist on it.

Conflict, Compassion, and Ki

The most difficult time to stay centered, of course, is in the midst of conflict. But conflict is here to stay. Andre, you *can* learn to handle it with spirit and with soul. Today, many conflict resolution courses are based on either a win-by-intimidation model, or on finding common ground, a mediation/negotiation model. There is a more soul-nourishing path.

Aikido, a martial art based on compassion, was founded on the belief that conflict is based on misunderstanding, and that we should not punish an opponent for being ignorant. The physical moves are all designed to render the attack harmless without injuring either person.

In our year-long Formative Leadership course, we teach the Aiki approach because it resonates with our soul and spirit, whereas negotiation is based only on intellect. Ki involves your energy and presence. Aikido honors your opponent's energy and intent, while you stand balanced and relaxed at all times. When someone verbally attacks you, you stay centered. You can truly honor the fact that they have a concern, and that it is different from your own viewpoint. By sincerely acknowledging their position, you can stand side-by-side and cocreate a mutually helpful solution beyond the polarity of the original conflict. Your presence, Andre, the total of who you are in that moment, makes all the difference.

Your Assignment

1. Begin a regular spiritual practice. The first thirty days will be the most difficult. If you can establish a companion or a support group, getting started will be easier. After the thirty days, you'll find you miss it when you don't do it. Again, my promise: Do it for a year, and it will change your life.

2. Tom Crum's 1987 book, *The Magic of Conflict,* takes Aikido and adapts it to the verbal conflicts of the workplace. He walks you through an impressively creative and effective conflict-solving process. If you can, find an Aikido class near you and take introductory lessons as well—you do not need to pursue the full route of the martial artist. You will very soon experience the remarkable "full-body" sense of balance, and surprising inner power from a relaxed state of compassion.

Month Two

Dear Andre,

Last month we talked about you becoming personally centered. Today we turn to how you *think* about things, how you perceive reality. I'm talking about *discernment*—your ability to see patterns in the apparent chaos and recognize new patterns.

Whole-System Thinking: Setting the Stage for Compassion

Max DePree says the leader's first job is to define reality. Your job as a transforming presence is to define reality in its wholeness—nothing left out—which means you include soul and spirit. Peter Senge's *The Fifth Discipline* does an excellent job of teaching us to be whole-system thinkers (see your assignment below). Our purpose now is to open windows to spirit and soul for you, using a whole-systems perspective. Keen discernment is your goal.

A new director arrived at a major West Coast library. Her goal was to turn a hierarchical, "command and control" culture into a place that honored and served human beings. She sought to redefine the reality as whole, not divided. She talked about self-directed work teams, work redesign (reengineering), and going directly to the person who can help you solve your problem.

She announced an open door policy for her office.

One day a representative from the night custodial crew came into her office. The crew wanted to all work together, instead of each person being assigned a separate floor.

"I've been chosen by my crew..." the old man began his story. "We figure we can get more done. Right now we can't finish, and our supervisor won't let us change. He just tells us to skip the staff areas."

The director agreed to speak with the supervisor; she was impressed with the crew's initiative. She decided to meet the whole crew, which meant she had to come back down to the library at midnight. She found a multi-racial crew with varied backgrounds, including: The spokesperson, who had been a custodian all his life and had never finished high school; a young man recently released from a mental institution; a woman from a native tribe of the region, who acted very tough and had been released from the state women's prison six months before; a woman in her sixties who had worked as a house maid and custodian all her life; a Southeast Asian immigrant whose English was faltering, at best.

The director learned that the tough woman on parole had always taken time to wash the toys in the children's story room. It was not in her job description, she simply took responsibility to do what she thought was right. The team had come up with a plan to finish the entire building by the end of their shift in a way that allowed her to continue to wash the toys each night.

At the end of the year, at the first all-employees banquet, the director awarded the first annual Best Team Award. Andre, you can imagine the faces of the custodial crew when the director called them forward to accept the trophy. This director saw all her employees as one unit, one family. She treated them with dignity and compassion, and they responded in kind. By her absolute sincerity in the original invitation, and her perseverance, she changed the perceived reality at that library. She changed people's mental models. She sees in a whole-system way. She is a woman with soul. She is a transformative presence.

Asking, Not Telling

If one secret to being a transformative presence is treating people with respect and dignity, then we must acquire the courage to be colearners. As you well know, traditional management includes a lot of answer-giving and telling people what to do. Unfortunately, men have been programmed by our culture to act like they must always have answers. They fear deep inquiry because it brings up circumstances they had not anticipated where they might not have an answer ready...or worse, someone will mention a problem they do not want to hear about. Yet the breakthrough solutions lie in honest inquiry. Peter Senge emphasizes the importance of asking questions to check assumptions and understand mental models. Your modeling, your presence, can ease these fears and create a container of inquiry and learning.

Andre, you will find some penetrating and poignant examples in the life of Jesus that demonstrate the power of a few good questions. He was teaching once in a village when an angry group of men dragged a woman onto the scene and threw her at his feet. They shouted that she must be stoned to death, as was the custom for someone caught in adultery. He looked them in the eye and asked, "Who among you is without sin? Let him throw the first stone." It is said that the men quietly turned and slunk away, beginning with the oldest. He then turned to the still-terrified woman. "Where are your accusers?" "There are none," she answered. "Then go and sin no more," he replied.

I can imagine a far different outcome if he had tried to argue with the men. I cannot imagine a more effective way to help this woman feel the relief and forgiveness that would empower her to a new life than to help her recognize that no one in the village was in a position to accuse her any longer.

His questions called up the assumptions of the culture, requiring each person to fundamentally examine the values they were basing their actions upon. But his method also called into question the teacher/leader as authoritative decision maker. By asking carefully chosen questions, he put the responsibility for decision making back onto the people of the village, the ones most affected by the choices. His personal presence, his confidence and self-assurance, gave his unexpected approach a ring of authority and wisdom. People listened and responded because he was a transformative presence.

Bridging Polarities for Integral Leadership

Mike is the newly-hired president of a $90 million a year heavy equipment company. You might not expect to find a transformative presence in this setting, but Mike has been studying what he calls "integral leadership." To achieve the turnaround he sought, he had to redefine reality, one where he could be the coach and visionary leader and where everyone would be an important member of the team. The company culture was traditional and hierarchical. Employees were accustomed to bringing their problems to the previous president, who would listen briefly, then tell them what to do. Sales were down and a huge inventory threatened the company's financial health. In that culture the employees did not have to be either creative or responsible.

Mike was different. Two engine rebuild specialists showed up in his office in a raging fight, one accusing the other of sabotage because of some broken bolts. They expected him to decide who was right, and who was wrong. Mike listened carefully. He asked about the factual and safety issues. Then posed the question to both men, "Whose responsibility is it to be safe?" "All of us," was their unavoidable answer. His questions helped both men see that while one had been careless when he finished with the machine, the next man had not been diligent in check-off procedures before he began its use. Then Mike added, "I can't solve your personality clash. You'll have to do that for yourselves."

Andre, I'm going to arrange for you to spend some time "shadowing" Mike. You'll find that he creates bridges whenever the company presents "either/or" situations. He is a master at integrating differences so that people can solve problems together. He is able to act with soul because he actually sees this world as connected and connecting.

Your Assignment

1. Review *The Fifth Discipline* during the coming month. Look for ways you can ask new questions in your work because you are seeing it from a whole-system perspective.

2. Read *Necessary Wisdom* by Dr. Charles Johnston. He is Mike's mentor. Select the chapter that touches your life the most deeply (relationships? health care? the environment? conflict and peace?). See how many ways you can act in an integral way on that issue in the coming month.

Month Three

Dear Andre,

You have within you a marvelous power that you have only begun to tap. It is not *power over* any one or any thing, it is the power to bring more life to your relationships and the power to create more effective solutions in your work. You tap this power by telling the truth—with discernment, compassion, and sensitivity—but the truth nonetheless. One reason this is so powerful is that it is so rarely done. Most of the time we have an internal "editor" who prejudges the (presumed) acceptability of our words. Or worse, this editor skews what we see so that we cannot even recognize the truth in front of us.

Compassionate Truth

Bill, a manager with whom I work as an executive coach, tends to overexplain just about everything. And he oversells. His colleagues complain about this when he's not around. But nobody gives him the feedback he could learn from. One day in our session together, he tried to impress me with an extended paragraph on that week's activities. I leaned forward as he spoke, looked directly into his eyes, making the deepest heartfelt connection I could and, with a gentle smile, said, "Bill, I'm already impressed with your work. You're doing a fine job. You don't need to convince me." He looked startled, then he let out a deep sigh as his shoulders dropped, relaxed. All he could muster was, "Oh. Thank you." From that point on, he was much less verbal with me, and more gently confident. His coworkers started to notice that he was a bit more relaxed, more willing to let things flow, not needing to micro-manage everything around him. He was more fun to be around and easier to work with.

Patricia Sun offers an excellent rule of thumb: Always speak as if the other person can read your mind. I like to fuse this with deep compassion. I remind myself daily that most people are doing the best they can with what they have to work with. Even when people hurt us deeply, compassion allows us to forgive, recognizing that they too are afraid at some level, and are acting out of some sense of self-preservation.

I was called in to help a hospital's executive team work on several issues that had produced considerable misunderstanding. I could feel the tension in the air, so rather than trying to ignore it, I said, "I can feel how tense we all are about even trying to talk about this. I know from my interviews with you yesterday that you feel the newest member of the team (I named her) is the problem. But each of you knows enough about marriage to know that misunderstandings are never just one person's fault." Simultaneous sighs, weak smiles around the room.

One of the primary accusers ventured, "Yes, you're right Marie. I guess we've all contributed. How can we start to unravel this?" The tension was broken and we spent the morning sifting through the substantive problem areas from the fears, assumptions, and differing mental models. By noon they had reached agreements on new procedures that would not overburden the nursing staff, yet would still get the business office the information it needed. My willingness to name the core of the problem, bring the pain to the surface, and offer a new picture of reality where everyone could take responsibility, created a "container" where we could do constructive work together. In most organizations we are so used to a form of denial which I call "the emperor has no clothes," that speaking the radical, simple truth can bring almost instant results.

Personal Authenticity in Groups

Walter Brueggemann, an Old Testament scholar, maintains that the key element in the exodus of the Hebrew people out of slavery in Egypt was "the public processing of pain." He argues that only when we are able to articulate together our hurt and the injustice we feel, are we catapulted out of the suffering. When a hospital purchased three clinics in a small town, and the doctors all became employees of the hospital, I was called in to guide a meeting where the resentments and difficulties could be aired (and presumably solved). Because the clinics had competed against each other for many years, I did not underestimate the extent of the bad feelings. I first invited each doctor to recount his or her earliest inkling of going into medicine. We then set simple ground rules such as making "I" statements ("this is what's hard for me"), not blame statements ("you are making me..."). Then they each shared what was making the job most fulfilling and, in turn, what was making it most difficult for them to feel that fulfillment.

By the time they got to the difficulties, their common bond in a calling to heal had been established. As some expressed their feeling that the older doctors were refusing night calls and pushing more 2 a.m. work onto others, the younger doctors could allow themselves to hear the burnout-level stress from the oldest on the team. The older doctors, meanwhile, could hear the frustration from the emergency room doctors, who told about having a patient on the table while two doctors each in turn would tell them, "I'm not coming in. Call Dr. X back." Three hours later, they had worked out a more rational protocol that was only slightly different from what they had been doing all along. But everyone felt significantly better. They felt heard, and understood, and they were ready to move ahead. Because we had created a container for the "public processing of pain," they were able to begin collaborative team problem solving.

Creating Containers for Transformative Conversations

Andre, you already know from your national and international experience that today's problems are bigger than any one person can solve. Our only real solutions will come from more creative, collaborative groups. Typically, people's group skills are not nearly as sophisticated as their technology. Two colleagues and I have written some guidelines so our clients can bring authenticity and transformative solutions to group process. I'm enclosing these with this letter.

The essence of creating a transformative container, Andre, is building trust—trust in your own voice to add creatively to the dialogue (...where the talkers speak less, and the shy ones speak more); trust that others will also bring forth thoughts you would never come up with alone; trust that the group is wiser than anyone present. As you model these guidelines in your own groups, you will unfold the potential for creating truly generative conversations.

In a dialogue/think tank session in our Formative Leadership class, group members each took a turn being challenged on their most leading-edge leadership issues. A young engineer who was being groomed for senior management at an international steel company took his turn. Someone asked how he reconciled his words about care for the Earth with his company's manufacturing of logging clear-cut and strip mining equipment. Because of the safe container the group had created, he was able to lean out into uncomfortable, even "unthinkable," territory and talk about how he might raise questions of product and market redesign at his company—not when he became the boss, but in the coming year. Because the group was deeply committed to each member's success, members were able to help him uncover possibilities for conversations with superiors and his customers, based on the fact that neither his company nor their customers wanted to be put out of business by ecological pressures. Instead of polarizing the conversation into a we/they conflict of loggers and miners vs. environmentalists, he began to imagine a vision

Guidelines for Dialogue

Listen

- Listen, pause, consider.
  Take time to reflect, to let be.
  Slow down. Silence is good.
- Listen to your listening.
  Pay attention to how you are listening.
- Honor and respect others' viewpoints and concerns.
- Fully receive what others have said.

Inquire

- Listen for assumptions, what's behind the words,
  your own, and others.'
- Suspend your assumptions and certainties.
  Hold them out in front of you and then
  step back from them.
- Inquire about assumptions you hear.
  Ask from a place of curiosity and wondering.

Speak

- Speak from your exploring edge.
  Speak from a place of curiosity.
  (No speeches)
- Wait to speak until you are moved.
- Tell what's present for you here and now.
  Speak your truth in love.

© 1993 Marie Morgan and Peter & Trudy Johnson-Lenz.

where people who need resources from the earth could talk together with those who strive to preserve them. By everyone in the group practicing becoming a transformative presence together, they helped him stretch toward becoming this presence at work.

Your Assignment

1. For the next month, practice the "Guidelines for Dialogue" *just with yourself.* Don't introduce them to any of your

groups yet, just incorporate the disciplines listed here into your own practice. When you can embody it, you can begin to teach it. Remember Gandhi.

2. In the following month you can experiment with introducing the principles into one or more of your regularly scheduled meetings. Then let's talk about how it goes for you; debriefing is one of the best ways to learn what really happened and what you want to do next time. Remember, your presence is the most important teacher.

3. Meanwhile, if the occasion arises to experiment with the public processing of pain, remember:

    a. Invite the group to set its own guidelines first (no blaming, treat everyone with dignity, listen well, speak as you would want to be spoken to; they'll come up with a similar list). You may want to adapt a few points from the "Guidelines for Dialogue."

    b. When everyone has been heard, invite positive action. You'll be amazed at the creative energy in the room, once the air has been cleared.

Andre, this concludes the foundational phase of our work. Next month we launch our E-mail conversations as you begin integrating specific subjects into your daily work. If I were to summarize what we have done so far, I'd say it's all about love. Using the word has been overdone, but *doing* it hasn't. Being a transformative presence means loving people wherever you go. That assignment will continue for the remainder of your life.

Michael J. E. Frye, SB, MIES, FRAeS, is chief executive of B. Elliott plc., a British public company. He served as executive chairman of Rotaflex plc. and Concord Lighting. He serves as non-executive director of Thorn Lighting Group (TLG plc.) since 1993, and served as chairman of the RSA (the Royal Society for the encouragement of Arts, Manufactures & Commerce) from 1991-93; he now serves as a vice-president and on the Council.

Frye is a member of the CBI National Manufacturing Council, a deputy chairman and director of London First, and is also chairman of West London Leadership (WELL), West London Training & Enterprise Council and Business Link London. He is also Honorary Fellow of the RCA (Royal College of Art) and fellow of the Royal Aeronautical Society (FRAeS). He graduated from MIT in management and mechanical engineering.

21

Toward One Heartbeat: Enhancing Organizational Performance and Personal Growth

Michael Frye

The Roots of Change

As the overall consciousness of humankind evolves there is a continuing need to throw off the yoke of out-dated approaches, systems, and practices. At the same time there is an important and ongoing need to maintain a suitable regard for standards. This means standards both in their own right (as regulators of human activity), and also in relationship to the way they protect the dignity of humankind, its beliefs and spiritual values.

The need to progress is not abstract or absolute. It fuels, and is fueled by, new discoveries in every field of human activity. This creates a level of turbulence within society as the various effects of change are felt. The extent of the new discoveries, the scope of change and rate of that change—all these things are directly interrelated.

In this changing process, science has often led the way. It has effectively challenged the past. When we review the extent of that scientific change in history, we begin to appreciate the rate at which change will increase and accelerate. In this century the new discoveries in science have been vast. So vast that we experience difficulty in the way we try to accommodate those changes, and their consequent effects on our lives. It is a difficulty that will continue to be experienced well into the next century. We will see changes such as moving from linear, mechanical, and mechanistic physics, to nuclear, molecular, and sub-atomic physics; from simple cause and effect, to complex interdependent three- (and more) dimensional and abstract models; and from communications by word of mouth and by writing, to instantaneous communications by telephone, satellite, television, information technology, and interactive multi-media.

This scenario of radical change raises important questions from leadership, management, system, and organizational perspectives. The key question is this: How can we most appropriately engage in, and effectively facilitate, this process of change within our own selected organization without trampling on the individual and his or her personal development, values, and beliefs?

Perhaps that way of asking the question does not take the issue far enough in a positive way. Perhaps this is an area where the problem, the opportunity, and the solution should all be set within an approach which provides the possibility of doing more than simply shielding an individual from change. Perhaps the context should rather be one of enhancing the scope and reach of an individual's personal development, values, and beliefs, while at the same time moving towards the optimum performance of the organization.

To do that would be to tackle issues of social change and business growth within a genuinely ethical framework. In this approach, ethics would not simply refer to the conscience of an organization, but rather to its raison d'être.

The Organization and the Individual

We must begin by focusing on some of the *preliminary* ethical issues in dealing with both individuals and organizations. Before we can go much further in exploring the interrelationship of *organization* and *individual*, however, we need to have a basic understanding of why that relationship is important.

An organization is like a person. Although you cannot take the analogy too far, it is one that provides several useful insights. Just as an individual has a consciousness, so too does an organization. Just as an individual goes through phases of development, so too does an organization. One major difference, of course, is that an organization can recreate itself.

The anthropomorphic characteristics of an organization are helpful in working towards a solution that respects equally the needs of an organization and of the individual. If we can accept this as a way of approaching the issues, then we ought also to be able to look at an organization from an existential point of view.

We must understand that an organization, like an individual, is both what it is *now*, and also what it has the potential to *become*. To acknowledge that, however, is simply to beg the next question. From what is that potential *derived?* From where does it come and what should we be trying to do with this collection of people?

If we are to explore these questions in an open and positive way, we must first try to *eliminate the bias of many current perspectives* on this and related issues. We must explore the role that *perception* plays in the way we approach the subject.

Perception as the Determining Factor

What does it mean to eliminate the bias of many current perspectives? It means, first of all, taking a critical look at the way things currently are. We live in a world which is dominated by physical things. We also live in a world characterized by the exclusive validity of logical thinking. That bias towards logical thinking is to the detriment of the other ways in which we relate to our world: ways which are essentially intuitive, creative, and, I would argue, ethical.

If we are to eliminate that bias, we have to look first at attitude and perception—the power that they have, and the influence they exert on our lives. At one level perception determines action. Changes in perception can create changes in action or, at the very least, the *opportunities* for creating changes in action.

As an illustration of this we can look at money and the various ways in which it is perceived. Different people have perceived money in different ways at different times. In the New Testament one of the words used for a unit of money is "talent." The story in Matthew's Gospel (Chapter 25, verse 14) has played its part in extending the meaning of the word. We think of a latent talent as something to be developed and multiplied.

Money can also be represented, or perceived, as a latent asset, in that it can be exchanged for selected physical goods. Or it can be seen as energy—latent energy that will drive an activity. This raises questions as to how our individual perception of money influences our behavior at different times, and what perception will best influence how we operate with money.

The purpose here is not necessarily to ask people to change their perceptions of money, but to provide them with an opportunity to perceive money in a new or additional way—that is, from a new vantage point. It is then clearly up to the individual whether he or she chooses to behave differently or not.

I will take four examples using money to illustrate the point. When we see money as an asset, the tendency is to own it, defend it, or protect it. When we see money as power, the tendency is to use it for purposes of control. When we see money as talent, the tendency is to release the expression of that talent. Whereas seeing money as energy encourages the releasing of the flow to make something happen. The overriding question must be, which perception is most appropriate, useful, or constructive when an issue or choice is addressed at any one point in time?

Changes in perception lead to changes in attitude. Changes in attitude lead to changes in the agenda. Changes in perception also potentially lead to changes in behavior. If you accept this, then it is clear that everything is dependent on how individuals *perceive* what is going on around them.

In the case outlined above, money is a symbol for several attitudes. It is also, however, the litmus test for how an organization sets its priorities, and how it sets the balance between the different kinds of perception, and therefore the different potential actions.

Relating Perception to Feedback

Perception has its own difficulties. How do we as individuals see, understand, interpret and communicate a set of ideas or a string of concepts when the delivery system is suspect—suspect because it is itself derived from old thinking, old concepts, and old constructs? To use an analogy, how can we as individuals accurately understand, interpret, and communicate what we see through the lens of a camera when the subject, the lens, the seeing eye, our perceptions, and the constructs of our mind translating the picture into words, are all changing simultaneously and are also interdependent and interrelated?

The critical question is always going to be "Who exactly is

doing the perceiving?" If you think of a soccer game, there are likely to be many different perceptions of how a team is playing. There will be the perceptions of the players themselves, the coach, the referee, the spectators, the people who see the highlights on television that evening, and those who read the very different reports of the sportswriters in the newspapers the following day.

All those perceivers will claim to have a valid interpretation of the way the team played. Ultimately, however, the most powerful view of what the issues were *on the ground* will be the one that comes from the players. In exactly the same way, the most powerful view of an organization's operations will come from those whose task it is to carry out the operations.

If this is the case, then a critical part of organizational planning and management will be that part of the communication loop called "feedback." When we look at the concept of feedback in its psychological context, then we can see that it can be treated in four different ways.

First, there is *truth,* when the feedback is an accurate reflection of what has happened.

Second, there is *rationalization* or *generalization,* when the experience is subject to excuses or rendered in such a way that it fits in with expected patterns.

Third, there is *distortion,* when what happened is changed beyond immediate recognition.

Last, there is *denial,* when it is denied that the original experience took place at all. Individual and organizational impotence increases the further you move away from *truth* towards *denial.* Once *denial* occurs, there is little or no hope of positive or remedial action.

The main point to stress here is that these aspects of feedback are found within organizations, and that when they combine with the biases referred to earlier, they produce an environment within which the *avoidance* of important issues becomes the norm.

If we wish to address these issues, we have to begin with the individual. There are, I believe, two primary elements of an individual's life. The first is the natural instinct for lifelong development. The second is the urge to use *natural* talents, and to develop *new* ones. This is compatible with what Maslow refers to as self-actualization in his hierarchy of human needs, where self-actualization is the process of searching for fulfillment, beyond the basic needs of warmth, food, shelter, etc. Once again, these anthropomorphic characteristics can be seen in the life of an organization.

The acceptance of this thinking, however, leads to the perhaps inevitable conclusion that the way forward lies in lining up these two basic goals of the individual with the stated goals of the organization in which those individuals live and work.

Such an objective would leave the management of the organization with the task of working out how best to optimize the potential of every individual. The challenge would therefore be to achieve the optimal performance of the *organization*, whilst at the same time offering the *individuals* the opportunity to express talents and to be in an environment where lifelong learning is a shared goal.

Leadership towards Independence

If you accept this as the goal, then you take an important step in the direction of *leadership towards independence.* One of the keys to making this work in an organization is by effectively reversing the flow of ideas. This involves changing a *forced* flow of ideas into a *natural* flow. What does this mean?

Let us assume that, simplistically, a typical corporation has three levels of personnel—corporate, management, and operations. At the corporate level, directors direct the work of management, who manage the work of operations—the shop-floor workers.

Over time, barriers (typically around territorial issues and turf battles) build up between these areas, and these barriers inhibit communications and the flow of ideas. At the corporate level, the directors talk more to each other than they do to the management. The same kind of insularity is characteristic of the other two sectors. In the end the barriers between them are little less than brick walls, with the only flow of ideas being a *forced* one—from the corporate level *down* through management to operations.

The solution to the problems brought about by this situation is achieved by removing the barriers and allowing each sector to take on some of the role of the sector immediately above it. In this way the Operators become managers of the work that is being done. The Managers become facilitators and coaches of the operation and the operators. The Corporate executives are freed to spend much more of their time on the development of strategy, whilst retaining the freedom to intervene in the process as and when blockages occur. This change in the process shifts the organization away from a regime of a *forced* flow of ideas to a state where it enjoys a *natural* flow of ideas.

Change is facilitated to a large extent, at least by the application of the principles of Total Quality Management (TQM), and by the implementation of Kaizen (continuous improvement) in line with psychoanalyst and writer Wilfred R. Bion's concept of sophisticated groups. Many organizations that claim such methods, however, fall short of implementing them fully. It is easy to distinguish those companies that live TQM and Kaizen from those that talk it.

The changes brought about by such a shift of priorities is, after all, a fundamental one. The unwritten contract between the individual and the organization changes. The individual moves from thinking, "I'm here at work to do this job," to thinking, "My job here is to improve the work of the company." In turn the company's offer includes regular training for the individual, with both operating in a context of continuous improvement.

This means that more is being invested in the future of the organization. It also means that the individual feels himself or herself to be in a situation where the organization is facilitating personal development and increased responsibility. The ultimate corporate-wide goal should be to devolve responsibility to those who perform the task.

If we assume that, in corporation X, there are 15 corporate directors and executives, 150 managers, and 1600 operators, then it is clear that no matter how enlightened those are at the top, a forced flow of ideas entails the ideas of the few being passed on to the many.

If the adoption of a natural flow of ideas brings about a ten percent improvement in efficiency and commitment all round, then not only do you gain a ten percent improvement in the organization as a whole, but you achieve it in the operators as well as in the managers. Simple arithmetic shows that a ten percent gain in that group provides a better total return. Understanding the leverage of the different sectors in this way makes it easy to see that the task of management must be to release the efficiency where the greatest numbers and potential are. In addition, this shift provides the organization with 1600 new and free minds, which is a very important factor in producing the natural drive of ideas.

Towards a New Ethics

As the roles change, then, the company becomes a learning organization. It becomes an organization that recognizes that people are their most important asset. It also acts on that recognition, thereby releasing the potential of those people for the good of all. If, as assumed earlier, any organization is at one level simply a collection of people, then the synchronization between individual and organizational goals will be at the heart of what we might call a corporation's "soul." In simple terms, the argument is that unless you put spirit into the people, there will be none in the organization. The starting point must always, therefore, be the people.

Although the roles of the various sectors and individuals may shift within the organization, the ultimate goal must always be for the company to work with one heartbeat. That means everyone moving towards the goal of continuously improving the organization, whilst the organization itself offers training and lifelong development opportunities to release the potential of its individuals.

There is a consequent and virtually simultaneous change in the role of, and the attitude toward, knowledge in the organization. The shift has to be away from an organization where knowledge is pushed into individuals, to an organization which is always learning, where pertinent knowledge is sought through every conceivable source.

There are, of course, practical issues that need to be addressed as soon as the principles are accepted. First, once plans are made there needs to be in place a system of measures so that performance, relative success, and failure can be measured against the shared goals.

Second, communication must be central and ongoing— particularly regular communication with the work force on a face-to-face basis. Once the benefits of this approach are evident, then it is essential to apply the principles in practice. The organization must train its people, allow them to contribute, develop in ways that benefit the organization, and devolve responsibility to those who perform the task.

The barriers to change should not, however, be underestimated. As P. Ranganath Nayak has said, "If the top is committed deeply to maintaining the status quo, then there's no hope." The whole process has to be top-down. It will not work without the commitment and enthusiasm of those who lead organizations and who set the agenda for their development. Words are never enough. We do not want leaders who espouse enlightened philosophies whilst continuing entrenched practices. All too often we see new structures which are marked by old behaviors.

People at the top of organizations usually do not want to change. When they consider ethics in the context of their organizations, they may recognize its importance. They may even recognize that at the center of ethics are principles of human behavior. On the whole, however, they want to deal with the issues by simply adding ethical concerns to the existing business agenda and structures. Their consequent preoccupation with matters of conscience, governance, and other forms of policing runs the risk of detracting from the solution. It is a preoccupation that focuses excessively on certain outputs, and avoids focusing on the essential inputs and real values. They may not fully appreciate that ethics in the context of corporations implies a basic shift in the way organizations operate and develop. This can only be done by addressing the key asset within a business—the individuals.

That means shifting the perception of our main asset so that we see it as energy and talent. Once we perceive people in those terms, then we will surely want to find ways of releasing that energy and expressing that talent. When that happens the organization is alive and growing because its people are alive and growing. The facilitation of that growth is what leadership should be about. It is certainly what ethical behavior is all about.

Principles and Benefits

Ethical behavior is not simply a virtuous ambition. It is the means to a more productive and responsible society. It is not simply an objective based on reason. It is a goal that should be fired with passion. That is because it is far from being only a peripheral and optional issue. It is, and must be seen as, central to human growth, progress, and sustainability.

There are three basic principles which drive this passion and anchor ethics into the world of practical action and responsibility. The principles are: first, the passion for developing people's talents in a context of continuous improvement. This must underpin everything we do. We can never be satisfied with systems and structures that provide less than the full expression of the potential of all our people.

Second, we must always plan and act for the good of "customers" by satisfying their needs. The word "customer" is used in the broadest sense here, so that we begin to think of everything we do (as TQM and Kaizen theory suggests) in terms of the "customer," internal and external, the one who is the recipient of whatever it is we say and do. We must ensure that the recipient is always a beneficiary, and that value is always added at every possible interface of individual and organizational action.

Third, we must focus with passionate intensity on the way we handle all available resources. That means our own individual resources. It also means the resources of the organization or corporation, including the money that moves through such an organization. At one level the increasing velocity of money through an organization is not only the sign of an enhanced performance and a healthy cash flow (an improving and sustainable one), it is also an indication of the use of that money in releasing, through investment, latent skills and potential. At another level, however, the responsible stewardship of resources means the wider role that we all play in the continuing sustainability of our environment and the world as a whole.

Without the passion that underpins these principles, we run the risk of providing no more than the dry bones of an argument. An argument that may win the minds of those who have the ability to effect change, but not one which will win the hearts of everyone who has a role to play in making it happen. When we succeed in creating corporations working with one heartbeat and dedicated to these three principles, we will have put the soul back into business. We will enhance organizational performance while at the same time respecting individual values and creating greater opportunities for personal growth. In this way we will optimize organizational performance while at the same time adhering to collective and individual values and creating greater opportunities for personal growth.

Evangeline Caridas has a comprehensive and highly successful background in management consulting, training, and sales. A native of Houston, Texas, she holds a Bachelor's degree in retailing, merchandising, and consumer sciences from the University of Houston, and a Master of Arts degree in organizational development from Loyola University of Chicago. She is a senior manager with the Performance Improvement Group of Ernst & Young Management Consultants in Houston, Texas.

Among her career achievements, she ranked first among the Xerox Corporation's nationally rated major account representatives in 1985 and was among the top ten percent of that company's national sales rankings for nine consecutive years.

Her graduate study involved measuring employee productivity and its link to participation in the workplace for a division of a major insurance company. Her study represents a groundbreaking first application of the concepts of flow in American industry.

22

Creating Optimal Performance in the Workplace

Evangeline Caridas

> To laugh often and much; to win the respect of
> intelligent people and the affection of children; to
> earn the appreciation of honest critics and en-
> dure the betrayal of false friends; to appreciate
> beauty, to find the best in others; to leave the
> world a bit better; whether a healthy child, a
> garden patch, or a redeemed social condition;
> to know even one life has breathed easier be-
> cause you've lived. This is to have succeeded.
> — Ralph Waldo Emerson

We have a moral and ethical obligation to integrate our concern for profitability and the bottom line with our knowledge of how to create workplaces that enhance the total person. Productivity, profitability, an organization's long-term viability, and employee health and well-being are interrelated. These issues must be the focus of both organizational study and organizational change.

Healthy companies are the product of healthy people, and healthy people require much more than a paycheck. Yet American business has continually failed to recognize that people bring their entire beings to the workplace—not only their knowledge and skills, but also their hopes, dreams, fears, foibles, and faith—indeed, they very souls. In spite of frenetic and expensive corporate efforts to re-engineer, incorporate total quality management, or otherwise increase effectiveness, positive, sustained change remains negligible. In the workplace, people have the opportunity to experience wholeness. Instead of wholeness, however, they often experience illness and disintegration of spirit.

Expressing our spiritual nature through our work is possible when we engage the whole person. We are spiritual, emotional, mental, and physical beings. When we fail to factor this totality into our daily work, we neglect our essential nature. Our emotional nature, for example, allows us to express ourselves freely—this is where our passion lives. When we are tuned into our emotions, important information becomes available regarding what works and what does not work in our lives. In most organizations, emotional expression is frowned upon, except among a privileged few at the top. Is it a wonder that in many corporations the energy level is flat? Emotions are the gateway to creativity. If we are to unleash creativity in people, they must be free to express themselves. Blocked emotions do more than stifle creativity—they also cause illness.

We can do better—for the well-being of people is fundamental not only to profitable businesses but also to the well-being of society in its entirety. Our challenge, therefore, is to create environments where people can do their best, for when we use human assets fully, we unleash an enormous store of talent in our organizations. As Leon Warshaw noted in his book, *Managing Stress,* "Work serves to produce goods and services; it also performs essential psychological functions. It operates as a great stabilizing, integrating, ego-satisfying central influence in the pattern of each person's life. If the job fails to fulfill these needs of the personality, it is problematic whether men can find adequate substitutes to provide a sense of significance and achievement, purpose and justification for their lives."

Several years ago I conducted a study with two departments of a major insurance company based in Chicago that integrated numerous elements of the work experience typically addressed separately: ergonomics (biotechnology) and the healthy workplace, the quality movement as applied in one company, and the design of workplace tasks. I used the integrative concepts of "flow" and the "active job" to measure the impact of employee participation and empowerment on productivity.

During this year-long project, I experienced these concepts

as more than theory. Becoming more integrated and complex myself as I struggled to overcome barriers to the project and bring it to fruition, I worked for extended periods of time at my own peak of optimal performance, an experience best defined as an epiphany.

Apart from personal growth, I became totally committed to the belief, along with others in organizational studies, that integrating individual and business agendas will further the objectives of the larger society. While the financial objectives of companies must be met in order to ensure continued productivity and employment, the workplace must also evolve into a place of personal actualization if workers are to attain true well-being.

The High Cost of Stress

By diminishing the quality of work life, stress takes a heavy toll on American productivity and the American worker. Profits decrease as healthcare costs attributable to job-related stress increase. According to the National Science Foundation, the US economy currently loses an estimated $150 billion every year because of job stress. Workers compensation, designed to pay only for disability and death claims, now covers stress-related illness also, and job stress-related claims are continuing to rise.

Robert Karasek of the University of Massachusetts has conducted more than 40 studies of health and work in seven countries, examining turnover, sabotage, absenteeism, and the cost of providing manpower to replace stress-impaired workers. In his book, *Healthy Work,* co-authored with Tores Theorell, Karasek estimates that the preventable cost of lost effectiveness equals close to five percent of the wage bill, a cost that could be prevented by work redesign strategies, They also estimate that a reduction of up to 16 percent of direct healthcare costs is feasible—a savings of $80 billion in this country alone. Job stress is not inevitable. Its causes can be found in the traditional models of work organization, and the solution lies in the transformation of the workplace.

The traditional organization is based upon the century-old ideas of Adam Smith, who believed that fragmenting work would increase productivity. The ostensible advantages were greater depth of skill, leading to higher output; less labor wasted by shifting between different tasks; and fewer machines for each person to master. Over time, the switch from physical to mental work and the use of broad-based computer interfaces have clearly weakened the last two advantages.

Smith's failure to envision the downsides of task fragmentation has earned him considerable criticism, for the downsides include not only stress resulting from repetitive work, but also the huge costs of employing managers to coordinate many divided activities.

Fundamental to our understanding of the relationship between job-related stress and productivity is the reality that negative changes in body chemistry (endocrine stress reactions) triggered by the performance of their jobs parallel the poor work satisfaction, high absenteeism, and high frequency of health complaints of people doing repetitive work. According to Karasek and Theorell, the solutions to the productivity problems of the traditional workplace are the same as the solutions that enhance employee health.

Stress has a significant physiological impact upon the heart rate and pulse. As Gareth Green and Frank Baker point out in *Work, Health and Productivity,* "These strains are important because of their long-term effects; coronary artery disease and hypertension are the ultimate outcomes of uncontrolled heart rate and blood pressure." In *Healthy Work,* Karasek and Theorell emphasize that too much stress actually destroys heart muscle. Clinical studies of emotional reactions to job pressures often overlook the fact that the release of cortical hormones during long periods of stress causes physical damage to the heart. For many, work is literally the most heartbreaking element of their lives.

In modern Western business the focus is on productivity, quality is a secondary issue, and well-being is the least important. As Frank Heckman points out, these three should not be considered separately—they are interrelated. "When this system is well balanced," he states, "the outcome is sustained growth. Clearly, in most businesses today, the paradigm through which economic growth is viewed does not find its roots in well-being."

Approaches to Workplace Transformation

Because progressive organizations recognize that learning is the key to success in the new business environment, timing is right for using what we know about effective learning to transform the workplace. Both learning and the resultant emotional satisfaction help determine high levels of performance in mental work. Furthermore, effective learning occurs in situations challenging enough to be interesting, but not so demanding that they exceed the worker's capabilities.

Karasek cited a 1971 study in which people repeatedly confronted with stressful situations where they had no control over the outcome simply stopped tackling problems. Sixty percent of those interviewed agreed that "since we have no control, why should we try?" Even when workers begin their careers with significant skills, these skills may be lost on the job through learning in reverse: learned helplessness, or passivity. Behavior patterns are molded by the job, and poor motivation to work may actually be learned in poorly designed work situations. Comments like "It's not my job," or warnings against rocking the boat are heard where taking initiative and using extra skills and judgment may lead to penalties.

The synthesis and application of three conceptual models set forth by pioneers in the fields of learning theory, industrial health, and organizational development can help fuel current efforts to redesign the American workplace, as they incorporate the human element for optimal performance. The three models— the concept of flow, the concept of the active job, and the concept of participative democracy—have numerous commonalities.

The Concept of Flow

Dr. Mihalyi Csikszentmihalyi, former chairman of the psychology department at the University of Chicago, conducted a groundbreaking study on the nature of optimal experience, or what he calls *flow,* which demonstrates that people have the ability to find happiness and meaning in their daily work. His research indicates that people experience flow at work more than any other time. Csikszentmihalyi states, "The best moments usually occur when a person's body or mind is stretched to its limits in a voluntary effort to accomplish something difficult and worthwhile."

The key element of an optimal experience is that it is an end in itself. In his work, Csikszentmihalyi has found that every flow activity provided a sense of discovery, pushing the person to higher levels of performance. Flow actually transforms the self by making it more complex. According to Csikszentmihalyi, the more enjoyable a job is, the higher the probability that people will want to engage in it. Jobs that resemble a game with variety, flexible challenges, attainable goals, and immediate feedback are the most enjoyable.

Csikszentmihalyi believes that flow theory could have a powerful effect in the business world by providing a blueprint for becoming more conducive to optimal performance. In *The Evolving Self* he discusses flow's characteristics, noting that any job could be changed to make it more enjoyable by redesigning it to incorporate these factors:

- Clear and challenging, yet attainable, goals. A distinctly defined objective; immediate feedback: one knows instantly how well one is doing.
- Opportunities for acting decisively are relatively high; they are matched by one's perceived ability to act; personal skills are well-suited to given challenges.
- Enjoyment.
- Action and awareness merge.
- Work as an end in itself. Concentration on the task at hand; irrelevant stimuli disappear from consciousness; worries are temporarily suspended.
- Excitement: a sense of power and strength.
- Increased concentration and focus; loss of self-consciousness; moving beyond one's own ego, a sense of growth and of being part of some greater entity.
- Emergence of a stronger, more complex self.
- An altered sense of time, which usually seems to pass faster.
- Performing the act or task for its own sake because it is valuable to the individual.

Csikszentmihalyi notes that truly creative individuals are measured, in part, by their ability to handle the pressures of conventional wisdom and their own instincts as they act in ways that may enhance the freedom and happiness of other people. To avoid unquestioning acceptance of inherited, historical, or cultural convention requires belief in freedom and self-determination. One is unlikely to take risks and work for the common good unless he or she believes that the risk is balanced by the promise of making a difference. The primary cause that shaped the lives of St. Francis of Assisi, Gandhi, or Socrates was a belief that their actions mattered and that they had a responsibility to change the world around them.

The Concept of the Active Job

In the past the individual was held responsible for staying well, but work design creates the environment within which people exercise this responsibility. This issue creates a dilemma between focusing solely on productivity versus building an organization for the good of all stakeholders. Karasek and Theorell describe a four-part model for examining the degree of activity or passivity inherent in various jobs, along with levels of stress associated with work, that can assist in designing healthier workplaces:

Active jobs are those in which the high pressure to perform is coupled with high decision latitude (control) in a socially supportive work environment. They define high decision latitude as a combination of skill, discretion, and decision. These jobs allow people to make the most of their skills at work by making their own decisions about pace, materials, control of time, relations to others, and planning. Critical to a sense of control is the appropriate matching of a person's skills to the skills required by a specific job. This matching is essential to optimal performance. Executives, physicians, and engineers are examples of people holding active jobs. A supportive work environment encourages social contacts that allow new learning (augmented by technology) and collaboration.

Passive jobs, in contrast, make low demands on skills and mental processes, but they are usually accompanied by few possibilities to learn or make decisions. Examples include positions held by billing clerks, janitors, and key punchers.

Low strain jobs, as categorized by Karasek and Theorell, may be characterized by low demands and a high level of control, or they may be the self-paced occupations held by tenured professors, repairmen, and successful artists.

High strain jobs, on the other hand, require a heavy pressure to perform with little control. Assembly line workers, waiters, nurses aides, and telephone operators are examples. People with high strain jobs show dramatic increases in physical illness and more symptoms of psychiatric distress. In addition, when Karasek and Theorell consider risk factors such as age, race, education, and even smoking, they find that employees on the bottom of the organizational chart fall in the top ten percent of the workforce population suffering from illness.

The concepts of "flow" and "the active job" are complementary to widely utilized work design principles of participation and self-managed work teams. These two concepts of work design define more fully the psychosocial context in which issues depleting health and economic growth can be resolved. Combined with the concept of participative democracy as applied in business, the possibility for authentic transformation of the work environment increases.

The Concept of Participative Democracy

In spite of slogans of participatory decision making, most management decisions still follow old models. Few major structural or philosophical changes have occurred in American companies. Among the Fortune 1000, only slightly more than one percent have majority self-management programs in place. In fact, corporate financial goals are still broadly accepted as the ultimate criteria of the success of humanistic job redesign efforts. Likewise, passive jobs pervade in spite of organizational efforts to change.

Fred and Merrelyn Emery, Australian social scientists and recognized pioneers in organizational development, and authors of *Participative Design for Participative Democracy,* have concluded after twenty-four years of testing applications in the field that the participative, self-managed work environments are the key to high performance and even the survival of organizations. They believe that the reason for the failure of bureaucratic traditional organizations to yield sustained high performance is that their structure promotes internal competition rather than collaboration. In competitive situations, shared information or open communication cannot work to the employee's advantage. One person's gain is another's loss—if you win, I lose.

The Emerys emphasize that when command and control are located one level above the work, we look to established authority for all the answers. The resulting inability to provide quick responses and the flexibility required by today's fast, turbulent business climate creates a competitive disadvantage. Only the organization that harnesses the full capability of its employees will win the highly competitive war of productivity. In this context, the bureaucratic structure of the majority of western organizations is clearly ineffectual.

Several processes to create participative work environments have been developed by the Emerys and successfully applied in various parts of the globe, yielding increased productivity, company profits, and employee satisfaction. Their work is based upon Design Principle One and Design Principle Two, two contrasting principles of organizational design. Design Principle One, the bureaucratic model, is characterized by redundant parts. With structural redundancy, when one part of the organization fails, another takes over. This model requires narrow skills and replaceable people whose work is controlled and coordinated by supervisors one step above the work. Design Principle Two, the democratic model, by contrast, is characterized by redundant functions, each performing multiple tasks and helping ensure greater success to one area or to the entire system. Each person can perform many functions and contribute to a broader variety of job requirements. People use a wide variety of technical and social skills in the democratic model. Self-managing work groups take responsibility for the control and coordination of their own work. According to the Emerys, this type of organizational system demonstrates faster responses to internal and external demands. In addition, in the democratic model organizations inevitably create learning environments because the employees need a variety of skills.

People have six requirements for optimal performance, according to the Emerys:

- Adequate elbow room and adequate control in order to organize their work.
- The chance of learning continuously on the job. Learning is possible when people can set goals that are challenging and obtain feedback so that actions can be corrected.
- An optimal level of variety, to avoid fatigue and boredom, and work in a personally satisfying rhythm.
- Work conditions that include help and respect from co-workers, where collaboration is in their mutual best interest.
- A perception of the social benefit of one's work, which occurs when people see the entire product of their work and understand its value.
- A desirable future in the form of a career path that allows for both personal growth and skill development.

Evaluating Employee Improvement Initiatives

The administrative operations group of a major national insurance company wanted to evaluate the employee empowerment initiatives that formed an integral part of the company's approach to quality. They asked me to conduct a study to measure the results of the company's change process, and I seized the opportunity to utilize two existing instruments related to flow and the active job as a test of the applicability of the concepts of Karasek, Theorell, and Csikszentmihalyi to the business organization. My colleague and friend, Frank Heckman, agreed to collaborate with me, seeing it as a major opportunity to work in an area profoundly important to him as an established organizational development consultant to major corporations.

The study was designed to reveal the link between well-being, organizational design principles, and organizational performance. The study focused on these questions:

1. Do the jobs within the two groups measured come close to being "active jobs"?

2. How do decision latitude (control) and psychological demand (workload) correlate to health?

3. What is the frequency of work-related flow in each group? How is that specifically related to the kind of work they do?

The study compared a high performance group (a group that was more creative and autonomous, making decisions on how to improve their work) with a traditional group (a group where decisions were made one level up). While both groups were quite productive, their approaches to work demonstrated considerable contrast.

Analysis of the survey results showed a high level of control perceived by members of the more traditional group. This group was in the "Low Strain" quadrant of the Karasek and Theorell Demand/Control Model. Employees in this quadrant have fairly high levels of control, with moderate workload demands, accompanied by reasonable decision authority and skill utilization. Although the traditional group surveyed did not fall into the ideal "Active Job" quadrant, we observed that many positive changes were being made by this empowered group of people. Careful analysis would be needed before increasing psychological demand or work load, the requirements for movement into the active job quadrant.

By contrast, the more progressive department scored in the "Active Job" quadrant, an indicator that employees were able to maintain the critical balance between control and the psychological demands regarding workload, pace, time to complete work, and similar measures placed on each individual. Our study also examined correlations between control and workload demand relative to health by measuring psychosomatic strain and sleeping problems. While both groups scored very low, making health risks a matter of low-level concern, the more traditional group reported less psychosomatic strain than did the progressive group. Results of the Flow Survey showed that the experience of flow was high in both groups. Overall, the two groups experienced above average degrees of flow at work, and the frequency of such experience was high.

The vice president for administrative operations was pleased with the results of the study; he observed that it added validity to the work of the ergonomics committee. The link between well-being and empowerment was clear. Many initiatives already in progress, such as quality teams and increased employee participation, complemented the study on well-being. A more systemic change process was now possible. The recommended next steps included analyzing employee health claims and examining individual and organizational risk factors. Organizational issues might be examined more closely, looking beyond obvious organizational problems and related personal behaviors to the match between employee characteristics and the organizational nature of the workplace itself.

This work became a personal journey of self-discovery for me. I worked for long periods in a state of flow, a process exemplifying the quintessential active job. Theory and ego were left behind as I struggled to gain acceptance of these theories in the workplace, a cause to which I was passionately committed.

The Promise of the Optimally Performing Workplace

A high performing workplace and the associated profitability require—and feed into—the healthy individual worker, the nurturing family structure, the sound educational system, the safe environment, the more wholesome community, and an enhanced society. These outcomes depend upon active learning, the basis of a participative work environment. A workplace of this kind provides the wholeness and true health in which people deserve to live and work.

Alex N. Pattakos, PhD, is president of Creative Learning Technologies, Inc., an Idaho-based consulting firm. He is also president of Renaissance Business Associates, an international, nonprofit association committed to enhancing integrity and elevating the human spirit at work. A political scientist by academic training, he has taught at the university level, conducted research and published on a wide range of public policy and management issues, and consulted with all levels of government, nonprofit entities, and businesses.

He has also served as director of a multidisciplinary university public affairs institute and a graduate degree program in public administration. Pattakos is a former member of the National Council of the American Society for Public Administration and was an evaluator/faculty associate for the Innovations in State and Local Government Program at Harvard's John F. Kennedy School of Government.

23

Searching for the Soul in Government

Alex N. Pattakos

The nation that destroys its soul destroys itself.
—Franklin D. Roosevelt

The November 1994 elections did not speak well for public trust and confidence in government in the United States. Indeed, Americans in large numbers seem not only to distrust but also resent their government.

"They have become convinced that government, especially the federal government, is wasteful, oppressive, and insensitive, and people have come to doubt that public officials act in the public interest or in accordance with commonly held values." This statement did not come on the heels of the 1994 election. Instead, it was part of the opening chapter to a book entitled, *Managing the Public's Business,* published in 1981, following the election of Ronald Reagan as president. The book's author, Laurence E. Lynn, a professor of public policy at the John F. Kennedy School of Government at Harvard University, was a former Assistant Secretary in both the US Department of Health, Education, and Welfare, and the Department of the Interior.

The state of affairs that had brought about this collapse of popular confidence in government in 1980 had been referred to as a "crisis of competence," and Professor Lynn's book was focused on improving the capacity of government executives to practice their craft more effectively. Importantly, he did not propose that good public management was simply a matter of applying the latest techniques of business administration to government. Instead, he distinguished the role of the government executive from that performed by managers in the business sector and offered a framework for improving governmental competence.

Managing the public's business has never been as important as it is today. Political realignments, increasing global competitiveness and interdependencies, and emerging developments in technologies, all contribute to the need to carefully examine the public's return on investment in governmental affairs. Indeed, the very nature of the *public's business,* by definition, establishes it as the "biggest business" in the public marketplace, even in those countries that are still viewed as undeveloped or underdeveloped.

Public perceptions about government, however, are not determined by executive competency alone. In the United States, for instance, the 1994 election may be a signal of a transformation in American politics and governance on a much broader scale than that associated with "reinventing government." Introduced conceptually in 1992 by David Osborne and Ted Gaebler in their book by the same name, the reinventing government charge at the federal level was given to Vice President Al Gore who, in September 1993, released the report of a six-month study entitled, "From Red Tape to Results: Creating a Government That Works Better and Costs Less." It is important to point out that this National Performance Review "focused primarily on *how* government should work, not on *what* it should do."

Taking their lead from the business/corporate community's restructuring and "reengineering" initiatives of the past decade, governments were struggling to do the same thing. Governmental competency again was being called into question—much like that described by Professor Lynn in 1980. And again, efforts to tinker at the margins of governmental operations were proposed as practical solutions to the dilemmas of doing business in the public arena. Unfortunately, these remedies are destined to fall short of their mark since they treat only the symptoms, not the root causes, of the public ills that continue to plague the nation. Our nation, as well as so many others around the globe, suffers not so much from a "crisis of competence" but a "crisis of spirit" when it comes to their public affairs. It is the *essence* of government, at its most fundamental level, that is at risk, not the capacity of public officials to discharge their responsibilities effectively and efficiently. This essay contends that only by reconnecting with its "soul" can *good government* be exposed and the challenges of guarding the *public's* interest be accommodated with integrity and dignity.

To be sure, this will require a different paradigm than that which currently guides the public sector. For one, it will require that we collectively raise our consciousness and, as Marvin Weisbord has proposed through the use of future search conferences, "discover common ground" about the purpose and meaning of government. In the same vein, activist Jim Wallis, the founding editor of *Sojourners* magazine, has argued that *"we can find common ground only by moving to higher ground.* Constituency-based politics, with its factional interests, will not lead us to this higher ground. Politics has been reduced to the selfish struggle for power among competing interests and groups, instead of a process of searching for the common good" [emphasis added]. Professor Amitai Etzioni, a former White House adviser and principal architect of the Communitarian Movement, also underscores the need for a new paradigm to guide our collective, *public* actions. Writing in *The Responsive Community,* he calls for a paradigm "that recognizes that societies are composites and are not cut from one principle, and that the main element of this composite is a tensed relationship between the common good and individual rights."

Finding *the* point of balance between the common good and individual rights is no simple matter, especially when one recognizes that there is no such point—at least not one that is fixed in space and time. As British author Charles Handy has pointed out, we live in an "age of paradox" and finding the balance will require a sincere commitment to continuous learning, a high tolerance for ambiguity, a reliance on three key senses (continuity, connection, and direction), and a capacity grounded in the theory of "multiple intelligences." Taken together, these attributes portend to provide a foundation for maintaining an identity of *self* in the midst of all the paradoxes and chaos of our times.

The conditions for living in an age of paradox certainly seem to apply to the governmental sector where the lack of order and clear-cut policy direction are commonplace. Sorting out the contemporary role and purpose of government appears to be more of a straightforward undertaking than Professor Handy may admit, in light of the various proposals from conservative quarters to shrink the public sector in favor of private enterprise. Indeed, Thomas Paine, a proponent of the American Revolution, once observed that "Society in every state is a blessing, but Government, even in its best state, is but a necessary evil; in its worst state, an intolerable one." More recently, political commentator Rush Limbaugh offered the following proposition about governmental intervention:

> It is axiomatic that the more intrusive govern-
> ment becomes, the fewer individual freedoms
> the people will have. Freedom should be the goal
> we strive for, not forced equality brought about
> by government redistribution.

> —Rush Limbaugh
> *See I Told You So*

To be sure, not everyone would agree that the relationship between government and individual freedom, both in terms of its direction and intensity, can be characterized so simply. What *is* clear is that government, however defined, tends to elicit deeply-seated value propositions about the boundaries between the public and private spheres of human existence. It is precisely this passionate desire for demarcation that sets the stage for understanding the spiritual side of public affairs and, more explicitly, points to the seat of the soul of government as a living entity in its own right.

Spirituality and the State

It is important to acknowledge that references in this essay to the notions of "soul" and "spirituality" should not be confused with their institutional counterparts, i.e., church and religion. As we shall see, soul and spirit are used (almost interchangeably) to express a concept that is intangible yet holistic, integrative, systemic, developmental, and cross-cultural in its connotation. In other words, it is both boundary-*less* and boundary-*spanning* at the same time. The institutions of church and religion, especially those denominations that are "fundamentalist" in their orientation, on the other hand, are basically boundary-*setters*.

In this regard, the Fundamentalism Project of the American Academy of Arts and Sciences studied fourteen separate fundamentalist-like movements in seven religious traditions and five continents over a twenty-five year period. The Project tested the hypothesis that there were "family resemblances" among disparate movements of religiously inspired reaction to aspects of the global processes of modernization and secularization in the twentieth century. In *Fundamentalisms and the State,* it is reported that religious fundamentalism has manifested itself as a strategy, or set of strategies, "by which beleaguered believers attempt to preserve their distinctive identity as a people or group. Feeling this identity to be at risk in the contemporary era, they fortify it by a selective retrieval of doctrines, beliefs, and practices from a sacred past." Moreover, the Project's principal investigators summarized that,

> Such an endeavor often requires charismatic and authoritarian leadership, depends upon a disciplined inner core of adherents, and promotes a rigorous sociomoral code for all followers. *Boundaries are set, the enemy identified, converts sought, and institutions created and sustained in pursuit of a comprehensive reconstruction of society* [emphasis added].

Fundamentalism, in this context, is viewed as the struggle to assert or reassert the norms, values, and beliefs of "traditional religion" in the public order. These norms, values, and beliefs establish the framework within which public officials may govern and societal development may occur. The fact that the basis for this framework, according to the fundamentalists, is derived from a divinely revealed or "otherwise absolute source of knowledge," contributes to the dogmatic, exclusivist, and oftentimes confrontational mode associated with fundamentalist positions. In turn, this serves to convince some observers, according to the directors of the Fundamentalism Project, that "fundamentalism is essentially antidemocratic, anti-accommodationist, and antipluralist and that it violates, as a matter of principle, the standards of human rights which are defended, if not always perfectly upheld, by Western democracies."

In contrast, it is interesting to note that the "religious motive" did not appeal to the ancient Greeks, who originated political thought and are credited with establishing the principles upon which Western democracies rely. Sir Ernest Barker, an expert on Greek political philosophy, has revealed that Greek city-states—self-governing communities comprised of free citizens—each developed a political "consciousness" that was directly connected to ethics and spirituality but not religion. He described this phenomenon in the following way: "Each [city-state] was aware of itself as a rounded whole, possessed of moral life, created and sustained by itself; and it expressed this sense in the conception of the 'self-sufficingness' of each political unit."

Government, in the words of the philosopher Aristotle, "...is more than a legal structure, more than an arrangement of offices; it is a manner of life, a moral spirit."

The Essence of Governance and Government

"It's close enough for government work." "Creativity in government is an oxymoron." Unflattering statements like these do little to engender public confidence in government or public officials. Indeed, my own personal experience with preparing students for public service careers in the United States suggests that many "aspiring" public servants view government service as a "last resort," something to pursue in case one is unable to land a preferred job in the private sector. Not only does this make it difficult to recruit the best talent into government (professional associations like the American Society for Public Administration dedicate considerable resources to confront this ongoing challenge) but it also tends to corroborate the public's suspicions à la Thomas Paine that government is at best a necessary evil. Bureaucratic encounters, sluggish and seemingly ineffective congressional and legislative processes, and televised judicial productions only serve to add to citizen disillusionment with governmental policies and institutions.

To be sure, "government" manifests itself in many different ways and therefore conjures up a wide variety of images in the minds of its observers. In the United States, for example, jurisdictional boundaries alone account for some 80,000 "governments," running everything from local schools and water supply systems to the Defense Department. Moreover, the pervasiveness of the governmental sector is compounded by the intricate web of federal-state-local relations that exists in this country, as well as a plethora of public policies that sometimes touch even the most intimate aspects of human existence, each formulated to guard the "public's interests."

The objective of governmental action presumably is the formation and implementation of policies which reflect and promote the public interest (i.e., the common good). Political scientist David Easton, drawing on a systems approach to understanding government and politics, defines public policy as the "allocation of *values* for a society" [emphasis added]. Easton's conception strikes at the very heart of the governance function for it helps to explain the wide variation that exists in governmental structures, processes, and outcomes among the various political entities that "govern" this planet. Government, in this sense, is a reflection of preferred values, aggregated in some way so as to advance the interests of an identifiable "public."

More fundamentally, these value propositions are determined by the *collective* identity that best represents the public jurisdiction (i.e., nation, state, community, etc.) pursuing its common purpose (that is, in addition to the pursuit of constituent self-interests). To the extent that government is viewed as the physical manifestation of a collectivity of living beings provides reason to believe that it possesses qualities of human systems of its own. Hence, it is no accident that the name "body politic" has been used frequently throughout recorded history when referring to government and its proper place in society.

Along similar lines, Pope Pius XI, who reigned from 1922 to 1939, formulated the principle of subsidiarity as it applied to government. He condemned Communism, Nazism, and Fascism and contended that government "should, by its very nature, provide help [subsidium] to members of the body social; it should never absorb or destroy them." Professor David Hollenbach, who served as a principal consultant to the National Conference of Catholic Bishops, moreover, has observed that the Greek city-state may not be achievable in a nation as large, diverse, and complex as the United States, "but there needs to be a conscious acknowledgment of and commitment to moral interdependence, based on the principle of subsidiarity." Although he stresses the importance of subsidiarity on a local community level, which supports directly the notion of communitarian values, he also underscores the need for a more universal form of subsidiarity at a national level. Daniel Doherty and Amitai Etzioni, two leaders of communitarian thinking, on the other hand, have reported that "76% of Americans believe that our society is experiencing 'moral decay.'" By this it is meant that Americans: (1) are abandoning moral standards (i.e., values); and/or (2) are not living up to the moral implications of a commitment to such values. In *The Responsive Community* journal, they cite the following statistics, among others, as empirical evidence of this "commitment gap":

- Whereas some 94% of Americans say that voting is an important obligation, only 55% of eligible voters voted in 1992, and only 39% in 1994.
- Whereas 92% say that jury duty is an important obligation, only 50% show up at court when called to serve (1994 data).
- Whereas 92% believe that "keeping fully informed about news and public affairs" is an important criterion, only 52% read a newspaper daily (1994 data).

One is forced to wonder whatever happened to the sense of civic duty that once formed the backbone of this great nation. Has the search for common meaning and purpose been unduly sacrificed to the whims of private interest? Or, have citizens simply lost their feelings of political efficacy, that is, their ability to make a difference? You know, "Why vote, it won't matter anyway?"

This "commitment gap" would have been unheard of in the city-states of ancient Greece. To the Greeks, according to Barker, "The good of the individual is the same as the good of the society; his virtue is the same as that of the state; there is no discrepancy between individual and social morality....It is the science of the whole duty of man—of man in his environment, and in the fullness of his actions and relations" that enabled the state to attain the true moral spirit. Because the individual clearly felt himself to be an influence in the life of the whole—which we referred to above as a sense of political efficacy—he did not find the need to assert personal rights against the whole. Put differently, this person was secure in his social value (i.e., his connection to the bigger picture) and therefore did not suffer from low self-esteem. Hence, says Sir Barker, "...starting from an ethical point of view, and from the conception of the State as a *moral association*, Greek thought always postulated a solidarity which is foreign to most modern thinking" [emphasis added]. Rather than seeing the state (i.e., government) as being a natural stimulus to achieving the moral life, modern thinking instead casts the state in the role of preventer and guarantor—its primary mission is to prevent infringement upon and guarantee *individual* rights. Citizen responsibility for and to the state as a symbol of the "common good" receives by default less attention from this perspective.

Greek political thought, on the other hand, began and ended with the *whole,* as described so eloquently in the following passage from Sir Barker's work:

The State is an organic growth—but man cooperated in the growth, and man can modify its character; man is inevitably knit to man, and to the whole society in which he lives—but it is for the achieving of his own "independence" that he becomes dependent on others....A contractual conception degrades the State into a business partnership (*societas*), whose members are linked by a purely voluntary tie of self-interest. The organic view, on the contrary, substitutes a vital for a voluntary tie. Members of one whole, the citizens are members one of another: as every limb seems to ache when one limb is pained, so the poverty and degradation of one class must impoverish the life of the rest; and the education and assistance of the weaker members is thus inculcated upon the stronger; as the very condition of their own welfare. The conception of a common weal and a vital union supersedes that of self-interest and a casual nexus.

To effect reform in Greek society, both Plato and Aristotle ultimately resorted to "spiritual means" as the preferred course of action. It was their view that in order "to heal disunion and division of spirit, one must employ a common education, which will put all men on the same spiritual level, and initiate them into the same spiritual community." It is then, and only then, muses Sir Barker, that a truly integrated community can be established out of discord.

The Roots of a "Common Education"

It is the concept and process of *dialogue* that are linked most closely to the notion of a "common education" to build the spiritual community envisioned above. The word dialogue actually comes from two Greek words—*dia,* meaning "through," and *logos,* most frequently but only roughly translated as "the meaning." Upon closer examination, the various translations of the word *logos,* a common Greek word, reveal that it has deep *spiritual* roots. In fact, the concept of *logos* can be found in most of the great works describing the history of Christianity, as well as throughout the literature on religion and Western philosophy. In this regard, one of the first references to *logos* as "spirit" came from the Greek philosopher, Heraclitus, around 500 BC. The *logos* of Heraclitus has been interpreted in various ways, as the "logical," as "meaning," and as "reason;" but, as the German philosopher Martin Heidegger has pointed out, "What can logic...do if we never begin to pay heed to the *logos* and follow its initial unfolding?" To Heraclitus, this "initial unfolding" viewed the *logos* as responsible for the harmonic order of the universe, as a cosmic law which declared that "One is All and Everything is One."

The doctrine of the *logos* was the linchpin of the religious thinking by the Jewish philosopher, Philo of Alexandria, who, while not always consistent in his use of the term, clearly established it as belonging only to the "spiritual" realm. Indeed, Philo sometimes suggested that the *logos* is the "highest idea of God that human beings can attain...higher than a way of thinking, more precious than anything that is merely thought." For Philo, the *logos* was Divine, it was the *source of energy* from which the human soul became manifest. Consistent with the logocentric character of Philo's thought, "it is through the Logos and the Logos alone that man is capable of participating in the Divine." Moreover, Philo's confidence in the human mind rests on the self-assurance that the human intellect is ultimately related to the divine Logos, "...being an imprint, or fragment or effulgence of that blessed nature, or as he occasionally puts it, being a *portion of the divine ether*" [emphasis added]. To Philo, the origins of *logos* as "spirit" were clearly well-documented in the writings of the early Greek philosophers and the theologians of his era. This kind of interpretation of *logos* received attention most recently in Karen Armstrong's bestseller, *A History of God*, in which she notes that St. John had made it clear that Jesus was the *Logos* and, moreover, that the *Logos* was God.

Interpreting *logos* in this way, that is, viewing it as a manifestation of spirit or soul, carries with it significant implications, both conceptual and practical. Dialogue, as a concept, takes on a new and deeper meaning when it is perceived as a group's accessing a "larger pool of common spirit" through a distinctly spiritual connection between the members. This suggests more than "collective thinking," although dialogue certainly is a determinant of such a holistic process. Spirit flowing through the participants in dialogue leads to collective thinking which, in turn, facilitates a common understanding thereby resulting in "common education," or to use today's jargon, collective learning. Furthermore, true dialogue enables individuals to acknowledge that they each are part of a greater whole, that they naturally resonate with others within this whole, and that the whole is, indeed, greater than the sum of its various parts.

Rediscovering Good Government

Because its roots are concerned primarily with relationships or connections—between spirits, ideas, people—on such a fundamental level, dialogue provides a solid base upon which the notion of "community" can be built. Sociologist Ferdinand Tönnies, in his classic work *Gemeinschaft and Gesellschaft,* which first appeared in 1887, examined the nature of "relations between human wills" and determined that this relationship could be conceived of either as being "real and organic life"—the essential characteristics of the *Gemeinschaft* (community); or as imaginary and mechanical structure—this is the concept of *Gesellschaft* (society). Tönnies' conception of community is probably not far removed from the characteristics that would be used today to describe an ideal community—shared purpose and values, common sense of identity, openness and trust, feeling of belonging, caring, and so forth.

Community does not imply that dissimilarities between members are denied or circumvented so that consensus can be reached. In the language of dialogue, the development of "shared understanding" means that the group has reached an appreciation, understanding, and acceptance of individuals' assumptions or mental models. It does not mean that everyone *shares* the same mental models. Conceptually, this fits nicely the essence of *logos,* which purports to bring order to a chaotic universe. Another Greek philosopher, Pythagoras, who applied the concept of *logos* to mathematics (i.e., as a ratio, *logos* was an essential mathematical connection between numbers), was guided by the desire to bring order and structure to the universe. Ideally, it is through dialogue that the elusive point of "balance" between individual freedom and social responsibility will become manifest. (This is basically what Jim Wallis has proposed recently as the "new political morality.") It is important to underscore that dialogue, as conceptualized in this essay, is more process than product. As such, it requires a heightened tolerance for ambiguity and a predisposition towards learning (and unlearning) during the continuous unfolding of shared understandings.

Achieving this kind of "collective consciousness" so that personal preferences can be aggregated to advance the public interest or common good, which essentially is the heart of politics, is admittedly no simple matter. The purpose and role of government, public officials, and "private" citizens under this scenario, including the relationships between them, are fundamental to success (however it may be defined). In short, "good government" is not about partisanship but about partnership. Good government, moreover, is not simply a "movement" to reform bureaucratic institutions, eliminate "politics" from public service, or operate government as a business. On the contrary, the essence of "good government" is less tangible and perhaps more metaphysical in nature.

Connie McLaughlin and Gordon Davidson, in their 1994 book, *Spiritual Politics: Changing the World From the Inside Out,* do an excellent job of applying new paradigm thinking, and specifically, ancient spiritual wisdom, to contemporary political affairs. The parallels to our earlier discussion about *logos* are striking when they expound in great detail upon the cosmic forces behind human affairs. They envision a form of "evolutionary governance" based on whole-systems thinking and an enlightened consciousness that will help to create a new planetary order. Moreover, they see public service in a new light—"to make the work of public service an inspiring calling that will draw our best people to serve our society." In this connection, they propose the following guiding principles for public life:

1. Upholding the Highest Good

2. Resolving Conflict for the Good of All

3. Furthering Cooperation for Mutual Benefit

4. Sustainability for Future Generations

5. Co-creative Relationship with the Natural World

6. Upholding Human Rights

7. Supporting Sharing and Personal Initiative

8. Honesty and Personal Responsibility

9. Being an Example of Service

10. Serving the Whole and Not Oneself

The faithful application of these principles not only would help to transform the "aura" of governance in society but also would contribute positively to the public's confidence in government policies and operations. Robert Denhardt, a national advocate for reforming and transforming the public service along similar lines, also calls for a revolution in public management in which the "pursuit of significance" will guide, if not drive, governance to a higher ground. And it is here where we become really conscious of (and connected to) the "soul" in government.

Mark Leavitt, MD, PhD, a veteran of ten years of medical practice, is the founder and president of MedicaLogic, Inc. in Beaverton, Oregon. His company's purpose is to help doctors and nurses to focus on healing again by supplying electronic medical records that ease the burden of healthcare paperwork. He is a nationally prominent speaker on this topic. He is a nationally prominent speaker on this topic.

Marie Morgan, MA/V, DMin, serves as a consultant to healthcare professionals, teaching leadership and collaboration skills to physicians and healthcare administrators. With a masters in human values and a doctorate in psychology, spirituality, and adult development, she speaks nationally on the challenges of keeping healing and wellness as the primary focus. Morgan is an ordained minister in the United Church of Christ. Her company, Morgan Consulting Group, is located in Portland, Oregon.

24

Recovering the Soul of Health Care

Mark Leavitt and Marie Morgan

The Scene

Two friends, a physician and a minister, meet for a cup of espresso after a Saturday hike. The physician is troubled by the changes going on in health care, and he asks if his theologian-colleague might serve as a sounding board.

The Predicament

Marie (the theologian): What is it about the changes that worries you, Mark?

Mark (the physician): Well, Marie, you've often used the concept of "inner voices" to represent the various experiences and biases that affect our behavior. Lately, with all the turmoil affecting health care, I find far too many inner voices intruding on the patient-physician relationship, possibly threatening the healing process itself. Let me give you an example:

Olivia was a bright, talented art teacher in her late thirties. After several years of providing her primary care—check-ups, pap smears, the occasional bout of flu—I found a small mole on her neck that proved, on biopsy, to be a malignant melanoma. Although the surgeon to which I referred her removed it without difficulty at the time, two years later the cancer returned and spread to several locations within her body. She still felt fine, but my "textbook medical knowledge" told me she had less than six months left in her life.

I had to tell Olivia the sad news, but I sensed that the manner in which she was told, and the interpretation she placed on her condition, could have a most profound impact on her life. I recalled Dr. Larry Dossey's book, *Meaning and Medicine,* where he explains how the *meaning* of an illness to a patient may be of far greater importance in determining their course than all of the treatments prescribed.

I became aware of a multitude of those "inner voices" you've talked about. It was as if time stood still.

Marie: Yes, sometimes the voices are like verbatim tapes of important things other people have said, sometimes they represent our cumulative learning, and other times they can represent archetypal voices of society. Of course this is also how we experience our conscience getting through to us, as well as our vital access to the Larger Wisdom, however we understand that. What particular "voices" have you been hearing as a doctor?

Mark: The first voice comes from medical training. I'll call it the "Professor of Medicine." The Professor expounds pertinent scientific knowledge, such as the expected survival and the course of the disease. From the same textbook comes cool but reasonable-sounding advice about how to deal with the patient: speak in a gentle, but professional manner, and fully inform them about their diagnosis and prognosis.

Marie: That sounds a little impersonal, Mark, but of course I understand how caregivers sometimes have to distance themselves emotionally in order to cope with what they see every day. And I do appreciate the objectivity this can bring. Tell me about the other voices.

Mark: The next voice might be called the "Malpractice Lawyer." It's a nagging, worrying voice that wonders whether you may have made a mistake anytime during the course of treatment.

Marie: I'm beginning to see how wearing this could be on your spirit, but go on.

Mark: At this point the next voice I hear is that of my nurse pointing out that, because of spending so much time with Olivia, I have a waiting room full of angry patients

Marie: (Smiling) Why don't we stick to the *inner* voices?

Mark: Sorry, I just had to share that, in case *you* end up someday waiting an hour for a doctor, no doubt for a similarly valid reason.

Marie: I'm glad your sense of humor is intact. But seriously, I do know that large delivery systems are putting more pressure on doctors to see a certain number of patients per day, as a measure of "productivity." I never seem to hear the system designers mention the *quality* of the personal encounters, only the numbers.

Mark: There are some other voices that were not present during my interaction with Olivia, but that intrude more and more these days. One is what we might call the "Voice of Health Care Economics," and another is new, called the "Voice of Micromanagement."

In the past, it was considered unseemly to acknowledge the Voice of Health Care Economics; we insisted that it had no influence on patient care decisions. But lately, this voice has gained a megaphone, because some reimbursement systems put the doctor "at risk" for all the health care expenses of the patient.

Marie: I've heard this is increasing dramatically. How does it take shape?

Mark: When a physician is "at risk financially" in some reimbursement systems, she may receive a fixed monthly payment for each patient, and be responsible for all of their medical needs. If the patient develops a serious illness requiring surgery, the primary care physician may literally have to write a check for thousands of dollars to the specialist performing the service. Do you think that's an appropriate voice to be speaking while your doctor makes decisions about your care and treatment?

Marie: That's frightening. An unintended consequence of cost-control efforts, I suppose. What about the Voice of Micromanagement?

Mark: It isn't so much a voice as a jabbering. It's bureaucracy, regulation, and hassles. It's like a seasoned surgeon having to dial 1-800-MAY-I-CUT to get permission for surgery, to talk to a recent high school graduate reading out of an instruction manual. It's bad for the soul.

Marie: Yes, I was beginning to wonder what toll all this was taking on your soul. You started out by expressing your concern that the healing process itself may be threatened. My training as a theologian and as a counselor, and my own spiritual practice over the years, has taught me more about the human soul and spirit than it has about medicine. But I think I do understand something about healing. Fortunately we have come to acknowledge recently that mind–body–spirit distinctions are artificial, and that our mechanistic worldview may be less helpful than we thought.

Mark: I'm glad you mentioned that. Just when we're starting to appreciate the importance of the mind–body connection, which Bill Moyers describes so provocatively in *Healing and the Mind,* the health care delivery system is changing in ways that may actually reduce the spectrum of choices available to healers and to patients.

Marie: Fewer choices? How so?

Mark: There is a movement afoot to standardize the process of health care, using something called "critical paths." There are definite benefits, such as assuring that every patient gets the proper preparation before surgery. But I'm worried that this concept can also be carried too far.

Marie: Even without clinical training I can intuitively see that there are tremendous differences between people and how they cope with illness. Has that appreciation really been lost?

Mark: I worry that it may be at risk. Even if the critical paths aren't fully enforced, the notion that the inherent individuality of patients is something to be suppressed could have a dangerous effect. It's like treating patients as if they were Toyotas, and nurses and doctors as assembly line workers. The more identical Toyotas are, the higher the quality, but for human beings the converse is true: their value lies in their individuality. It's ironic that just as other industries are moving away from hierarchical, centralized-control models toward more local autonomy and front-line worker responsibility and initiative, health care seems to be moving toward a "General Motors in 1970" paradigm.

Marie: Mark, the system is losing sight of its purpose! What are we trying to create here? If we can't see the central purpose of our endeavor, a system that doesn't truly serve our needs will take on a life of its own. And we blindly continue working for it.

In a 1994 *Harvard Business Review* article, Christopher Bartlett and Suamantra Ghoshal suggest that "purpose is the embodiment of an organization's recognition that its relationships with its diverse stakeholders are interdependent....Purpose is the...company's moral response to its broadly defined responsibilities, not an amoral plan for...commercial opportunity."

A commentator from a decidedly different sphere, Jim Wallis, in *The Soul of Politics,* speaks of "...an illness of spirit which has spread across the land...." It's not surprising that health care has caught this contagious illness from the surrounding society. This business we call healing and wellness has been affected by our culture's profit-worship, infatuation with technology, and the misguided conviction that bigger is always better. My fear is that health care will be one of the last industries to take Bartlett and Ghoshal's counsel to heart.

Somewhere we seem to have lost sight of the fact that *people* are the whole point of health care. Not the delivery systems, not the technology. Not the business, not the profit. Not the cost-effectiveness, not the egos. Not the government, not the hospital. Not the specialist, not the HMO. Not even universal access, *per se*. The purpose of health care is *healing and wellness* and *doing what is life-giving for every human being.*

Mark: We've gone pretty far astray, haven't we?

Bridging the Gaps

Marie: Yes, we have taken compartmentalization, and denial I might add, to new heights. Your experience with Olivia, however, suggests to me that we may be able to bridge the gap. What voices did you end up listening to?

Mark: As I said, time stood still while all these voices were weighing in with their opinions. But something inspired me to be patient and hear them out, and finally a "still, small voice" urged me to focus only on that which would help Olivia cope—and even thrive—within the boundaries of her new reality. After I had gently told her the news, I remember Olivia saying that for years she had dreamed of resigning her teaching position, to travel to Italy, and then to spend all her time painting, but that her limited savings would be depleted in six months. And then she asked for my advice.

Although I can't remember making a conscious choice to do so, I know that my wisest voice responded—overriding the professor, the lawyer, and the rest of the chattering—as I offered her my counsel that, perhaps, on a spiritual level, her disease might represent an event, or a message, meant to free her to pursue her artistic dreams. Olivia appeared at peace, and it was clear she then made her decision quickly.

Marie: What happened to her?

Mark: She followed her dream, and quickly became an acclaimed artist on the local scene. I attended one of her showings, and the love and admiration she received from the community was obviously more life-giving that any chemotherapeutic agent could have been. She died with little pain six months later, after thanking me many times for providing the support and guidance that helped her to reach fulfillment before her life ended.

Marie: It sounds like you were able to keep the most soulful values at the forefront. But, did the fact that she died feel like a failure of health care?

Mark: A failure? Not at all. If it did, we would have to say that every death is a failure of health care, and that no one should ever die. Unfortunately, sometimes we act as if we believe that absurd statement. That's why an inordinate portion of our health care resources are consumed by expensive, but often futile, attempts at treatment in the final weeks of life.

Marie: Quantity without regard to quality? Or is that too simple a way to characterize it?

Mark: Well, let me sketch some graphs on this napkin for you.

Mark: These graphs I've sketched represent quality of life,

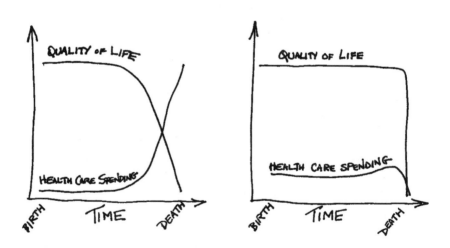

and health resources expended, over time, from birth to death. The left graph represents the present, *de facto*, approach. We spend very little keeping people healthy. We don't vaccinate all of our children, and not all pregnant women get prenatal care. But after the patient gets sick, we pour resources into "fixing them."

When we do this near the end of life, we end up extending the number of days spent in a terminal state, maintaining "life" by artificial means.

Marie: And what does the second graph represent?

Mark: A more purposeful approach. We should expend resources on wellness, so that more people would enjoy good health throughout life. Then, at the point when death is inevitable, we should focus on comfort and care of the soul, not on high priced, high technology means to artificially extend life.

Marie: In Olivia's case, you were able to make a soulful choice, though I doubt you were aware of it at the time. I'm curious...where did that wise voice of yours come from? Where did you learn it?

Mark: It's a natural voice that speaks only when we feel free to act as healers. The challenge is to prevent the other voices, the pressures, from drowning it out.

Marie: I'm reminded of 16th Century history, when scientists were trying to define a different reality than the church's worldview. Clearly it was a needed correction at the time, but the polarization between spirit and "pure" objectivity has outlived its usefulness. I also find it amusing that cultures all over the world have had their shamans, their gifted healers, yet we in our Western European tradition assume there would be no such healers amongst us. I find it quite plausible that our physicians, nurses, and, yes, other "alternative" practitioners, might also be endowed with healing instincts, healing gifts. I know many health care providers who feel a very deep sense of calling but rarely talk about it. Physicians and other mainstream caregivers are not currently free—or encouraged—to deal with people in wise, holistic ways.

Mark: Well, as I said, I made a purposeful but not fully conscious choice that day with Olivia. I'm wondering how we can protect this delicate, perhaps even "sacred" dimension of the healing relationship, in the face of all these pressures and changes. We probably need to start with a better understanding of what soul has to do with healing.

Reconnecting Soul and Healing

Marie: Ask anyone what is truly most important to them— especially if they have faced a difficult illness in the family—and they usually answer, "my health." If health is dearest to everyone's soul, I would say health care is the most soulful of endeavors.

Soul is that hard-to-define but easy-to-recognize quality at the heart of what it means to be human. I would contend that *health care is unhealthy without the component of soul.*

I'll admit I'm not an expert on science, but I love to read, and I am repeatedly awed by the miracles and mysteries of life. At the cellular level, the way the body *heals itself*—given half a chance—is quite remarkable. The way the patient's own belief system contributes to the body's healing capability reflects the extraordinary relationship between mind, body, soul and spirit. Scientists are discovering what community healers have known for centuries, that mutual support, love, and connection to one's immediate community can also affect not only healing from illness, but also motivation to prevent sickness and preserve health.

The business of health and healing is inescapably *integral:* it is about body and mind, soul and spirit, all connected. The soul in health care—a lot of the "magic" of the whole process—is in the people and relationships, just as much as it is in the treatments, the drugs, the surgeries, the brilliant technologies.

Mark: What can be done to pull things back into perspective?

A New Mental Model: Integral Thinking

Marie: If we are going to have any hope of altering the course, we as a culture will have to change our whole way of thinking. Without that kind of revolution, mere incremental changes will have little effect because those "voices" you describe represent very powerful forces.

Our "mental models" determine what we can conceive of and therefore also our expectations and solutions; only here lies the source of lasting change. As you know, for four centuries our Western minds have been trained to see the world mechanistically; we assume reality can be controlled if we can measure it, and we believe this all can be done in fully rational and linear ways. This view exiles soul. Your sketch of the competing voices demonstrates how our mechanistic, compartmentalized assumptions have set us up for answers that minimize soul and erode health and healing.

Mark: You mentioned the concept of an integral approach a moment ago. What do you mean by integral thinking? Could you give me an example of what that might look like?

Marie: Yes, lets start at the systemic level first, and then we can talk about the personal level. Integral thinking means we see everyone involved as interconnected and part of the best solutions.

In our community—which differs from other cities only in the details—we have had divisive and compartmentalized thinking. We've seen severe competition for market share between our major hospital groups. We have debates over whether to establish a second heart transplant center in the city. We have HMOs jockeying for market share among the larger employers, and we have hospital–HMO entities trying to squeeze one another out by cornering the market for managed care contracts. The physicians polarize into groups, destroying historic collegiality and communication.

Integral thinking on the part of all the stakeholders, including the consumer, might look like this: representatives from all these groups come together, in the same room—or many different forums perhaps—to talk and to learn from one another.

We would talk about where our common interests lie. How are we "all in this together?" Do we not all want a healthy community? Don't we all acknowledge the need for the poorest among us to receive basic care, and equitably cover those costs? Does any one really want to lay off or overwork nurses? Who would want to run up costs by duplicating services? What primary care physician wants responsibility for unusual medical conditions not within her or his control? Mark, you know better than I how long this list of common concerns could get. By making the assumption that we are all interconnected, we surface different questions than does an "us versus them" approach.

Integral thinking means we seek to uncover unspoken assumptions. I see heated debates in the press—accusations about others' motives. This is always a dangerous venture, for who can guess what is in another's heart without honest and direct inquiry? I sometimes wonder if people assume that market share, for example, is the only principle that can drive a system today. Every assumption needs to be held up to the light, in a spirit of inquiry and in a genuine desire to learn together.

Mark: Sounds like a fascinating experiment. Has anything like this been tried?

An Experiment in Dialogue

Marie: Yes. In Grand Junction, Colorado, facilitators from the MIT Dialogue Project—an outgrowth of Peter Senge's work—were invited in to help promote conversations between three hospitals in that city, plus other interested parties. Hospital competition was so sharp that before the dialogue meetings began, the chief executives of those three institutions had never had a conversation together. The initial dialogue sessions included the hospital senior executive teams, a state legislator, heads of area major employers, and senior management of the local HMO. They came together to explore sources of underlying fragmentation and create an ongoing forum where they might reach shared understanding about more integrated health care delivery for the Western Slope region.

Slowly, common ground was uncovered by practicing the basic ground rules of dialogue, including listening with respect, inquiring into assumptions, and seeking to learn from one another rather than giving speeches. Unlike most meetings, these sessions explored the meanings embedded in the conflicts and polarities, holding the tension so the participants could learn, rather than trying to cool the tension and negotiate a quick result. Over more than a year they explored competing models for what a new integrated system might look like.

While they were still meeting, two major national insurance carriers approached the local HMO with serious offers to buy it. Because the local participants had a common experience, developed from meeting in a "container" of growing trust, they were able to resist these acquisition attempts. As we speak, the local HMO has created an open space, a moratorium on purchase, to give time to develop a local alternative, specifically an integrated physician–hospital organization with insurance coverage. Remarkably, there are now approximately 20 entities, including small rural hospitals and clinics, that have been able to come into the process and, with a minimum of coaching, enter into the dialogue process skillfully. As growing trust and skilled communication replaces automatic assumptions about inevitable competition, they may be able to create a cost-effective, community-based regional system.

Mark: It sounds like some fundamental human values and behaviors can make or break this approach.

Marie: Yes. And it's important to remember that there is no one model or "right" answer. What is important is that creative, healing alternatives can be developed. What we find with the example I've sketched is that:

- Disparate stakeholders can come together in a spirit of respect, inquiry, and collaboration;
- Refined tools of communication and creativity can be learned to bring out the best from everyone present; and,
- Participants can develop the capacity to be "large enough" to accept the possibility that others with whom they find they disagree also have legitimate concerns, and that the answers to be found are larger than any one viewpoint at the table.

Mark: This is where the personal responsibility comes in, isn't it?

Marie: Yes. In the dialogue process it is essential that each participant takes responsibility to practice the guidelines. All of us who work in health care, for example, will have to learn new collaboration skills. But as Keshaven Nair says in *A Higher Standard of Leadership: Lessons from the Life of Gandhi,* "It is at the individual level that we must commit to principled actions and service." At the systemic level, the soul of health care will only be restored to the degree that each individual takes responsibility to embody soul personally. When people take more responsibility for keeping themselves healthy, honoring what research has shown us about the causes of heart disease, cancer, or osteoporosis, the system as a whole can be more life-giving. When people take responsibility to design systems to be life-giving and healing to employees, health care will have more soul.

Mark: I believe that physicians also need to take more leadership in reshaping the system. With a clearer vision of what is possible and some effective methods, more doctors can take on collaborative leadership roles.

Marie: There is also a place for a lot more citizen involvement, consumer responsibility, in health care. Companies, concerned about benefit packages, speak for their workers to some extent, but usually it's from a cost perspective, not from the standpoint of personal healing relationships.

I have an image of a great uprising of physicians, consumers, nurses, and others—all the people who care most deeply about patient care and about keeping people healthy. I see us objecting vociferously to the way things are going, objecting to these systems that have taken on a life of their own, and then calling into being hundreds of local and regional, and eventually national dialogues to see how we can create constructive alternatives.

Mark: You sound like a preacher. But, then again, you are!

Marie: We cannot afford to go forward without compassion and a spirit of healing at the center of the vision. We cannot afford to go forward giving lip service to "health care" and "health maintenance" while the vast majority of attention and resources are focused on sick-care. We cannot afford to go forward building bigger and more dehumanizing systems as if soul did not matter. Until we learn to listen with respect and speak with a willingness to learn, we will keep creating soul-starved institutions and systems. With compassion at the center of each person's spirit, we have hope of creating life-giving health care systems.

Thomas Moore is the author of the best-selling books *Care of the Soul* and *Soul Mates*. For seventeen years he had a private practice of psychotherapy, and before that he taught religion and psychology at several universities. He has been a leading spokesperson for "archetypal psychology," an approach developed by his colleague and friend James Hillman.

Among his other books are *Dark Eros, The Planets Within,* and, most recently, *Meditations: On the Monk Who Dwells in Daily Life,* Moore also publishes audio tapes and writes music in the electronic studio he has built in his home in western Massachusetts.

25

Caring for the Soul in Business

Thomas Moore

"Care of the soul" is an ancient phrase used for many centuries to describe the work of the priest as his mere presence in a community guided people through illness, marriage, birth, death, crisis, and other rites of passage. In those earlier times, people recognized that something deep in us and at the core of our identity, the soul, requires constant tending with ritual, story, and the kind of guidance that is not mere problem solving.

I have borrowed this phrase, applying it to modern life as a way of re-orienting our perspective on emotional issues and matters of meaning. In our devotion to the external physical world, we have largely forgotten the soul. Even modern psychology has focused so often on behavior and mechanical means for normalizing life that it, too—a field that has the Greek word for soul in its very name—has largely neglected the soul. We suffer this neglect in the many symptoms that afflict not only individuals but also organizations and institutions. Even business, an area of life unlikely to be considered in relation to soul, shows painful signs of its neglect.

In a field of activity as externally directed as business, it's tempting to divide experience into things and people. Things become the concern of the business person, and people are consigned to the psychologist or personnel specialist. Or, as customers, they may also be treated as things. Even some recent writings on the soul in business assume that the soul is an aspect of the person and not of the business. But centuries of writing about the soul suggests that business itself has a soul or suffers the lack of it. So, as we consider the soul in business we could look into every aspect of business life—money, goods, management, architecture, society, manufacturing, and the work-place—and ask if the soul is being cared for.

One key idea in caring for the soul is that like the body, the soul needs nourishment. As the most vital essence of our being, it gives us, as the ancients would say, our vitality. So, it has to be fed. It thrives on the particular things that keep it vibrant, and if it is deprived of those things, it shows clear signs of neglect and undernourishment. The easiest and most direct way for a business person to restore soul to the workplace would be to consider those needs carefully and simply address them with constant care and attention.

This idea of care and nourishment goes against the modern habit of taking a heroic stance in the face of all challenges: solving tough problems, thoroughly understanding what is going wrong, and making grand designs that assure health and success. Care of the soul is more subtle, though no less demanding. Although I don't intend any sentimentality when I use the word "care," and although I'm aware that such "care" often requires courage and vision, in most matters I do advocate a deepening of perspective instead of heroic problem solving.

In the face of problems and failure, we tend to quickly judge, blame, and analyze. But care of the soul demands that we withhold such judgments, being open to whatever the soul is presenting. It asks us to be wise, not clever, in our response. Such wisdom can only arise from depth of insight. Care also means constant attention rather than simply reacting to emergencies. Rather than a set of strategies, it amounts to a particular posture in life, one that values wisdom and depth of vision.

Feeding the Soul in Business

Intimacy

One of the primary needs of the soul is intimacy. Something else in us enjoys the excitement of working in a wide-ranging, fast-paced world, while the soul searches out sources of close-ness. This intimacy may be found in close connections to fellow workers, to the products of the business, or to customers. It may also be felt in long-standing relationships between a business and its community—the town, city, or region with which it's identified. Intimacy may take many forms, and exploring that variety offers an exciting and creative way to bring soul to business.

For two thousand years and more, for example, literature on the soul returns again and again to the theme of friendship. Friendship seems a simple element in everyday life, but its simplicity and obviousness are deceptive. To the soul it's a necessity. If it is neglected or interfered with, one might expect to see emotional problems or lowering of morale. If a company is devoted to a cold vision of productivity, it may overlook the need for friendship and actually discourage employees from talking to each other and becoming close.

A company could make a radical turn toward soul simply by recognizing the need at all levels of an organization for something as simple as friendship. Attention to architecture, furnishings, schedules, and rules, seeing how each of these either contributes to or stands in the way of friendship, could make a significant shift in the morale and effectiveness of a company. Care of the soul doesn't usually ask for changes on a grand scale. Small adjustments, based on clear perception of soul needs, go a long way toward restoring soul in the workplace.

We can cultivate intimacy not only with people, but with things too. Knowing how a thing works and how it's put together is not the same as knowing it firsthand, close up, and intimately. We often value knowledge that is distant and abstract. Yet, most business people realize that classroom learning is not the same as learning out in the field. That realization could extend to all aspects of a business.

Maybe if employees knew the history of a business, the story of its founders and developers, they would feel more attachment. If workers in one department, area, or level knew the persons, conditions, and activities of other areas, the business itself might hold together better, through the glue of friendship and acquaintance. I once consulted in a business where people from one area of the company would spend a few days in departments that ordinarily they would never see. Workers told me how important it was for them to make these connections and feel closer to the enterprise as a whole, to say nothing of making further personal attachments.

I once visited an extraordinary elementary school in the Southwest. When I arrived, a young girl in fourth grade became my guide and took me from room to room, introducing me to all the teachers and staff. I thought to myself, how different it was for me in grade school. I never knew the names of teachers in grades other than my own, and certainly never felt acquainted with the staff. Never would I have felt comfortable leading a visitor around my school, introducing him to authorities. Yet, this school could serve as a model for all kinds of businesses, showing how we could diminish the class distinctions that severely limit humane friendship and acquaintance in the workplace.

The language of advertising is another area in which soul could be introduced. Usually crisp, direct, and full of energy, it tends to be more spirited than soulful. An alternative style might invite people to a closer connection with the business or the product. The soul prefers stories to straight presentation of facts, and so stories, however brief, could draw the public more intimately to a product or business. It also thrives on full-bodied images rather than on the abstract symbolic pictograms so many businesses use.

The soullessness of our age is sometimes manifested in our devotion to facts and information. When I read material on a package of food or a flyer describing a product, I'm usually told the facts, whereas a story would stimulate my imagination and offer an opportunity for some degree of relationship. If I were packaging food, I'd minimize the chemical information and instead tell stories of the company or of the raising and harvesting of the food, or maybe of the family who started the company and its values. Or, why couldn't we invite real writers to publish short pieces of fiction or poetry on the packaging of products?

I've worked with many small businesses who have consulted me about the way they present themselves publicly. Often I've noticed how businesses which are dedicated to strong social values and to individuals will unthinkingly advertise themselves with geometric or symbolic designs. The soul is drawn more to images that are organic and reflect life's complexity and fullness. Abstractions satisfy the mind, not the soul.

Another specific intimacy need of the soul is family. From the very beginning, a human being needs the comfort, belonging, closeness, protection, and identity of a family. That need never goes away, but it does change over time, becoming more subtle and less literal. Although most of us move away from our childhood home early in our lives, the need for family doesn't go away. The soul craves strong experiences of family every day of our lives. When a business describes itself as a family, I take that image seriously, knowing that the spirit of family, incorporated in a business in a variety of ways, provides for an essential need of the soul.

If a business truly wishes to have soul, it would have to generate a genuine sense of family among its employees, and even with the public. This sense of family may extend into a feeling of neighborhood and community. A town may feel that a business is part of its family, taking pride in the relationship. Or, when that business decides it must uproot and relocate, the town may feel betrayal or profound loss.

Not long ago, I listened to a radio interview with a CEO who was moving his company to a new city after it had been central to the life of the town for forty years. The interviewer asked the man if he had considered the devastating impact the move would have on the town. The man answered in typical tough terms saying that he had to look only at the interests of the business and its shareholders. I felt the CEO was avoiding the truly difficult question about the relationship between a business and its community—the soul question.

As business people, we can say that we want soul in our work, but to get it we may have to do more than experiment with a few good ideas here and there. We may have to reconsider some basic attitudes, such as our narrow focus on self-interest. Soul is always both individual and communal, and the interesting challenge in soul work is to find a way to embrace the paradox of strong self-interest and community. Of course, sometimes companies have to relocate, but if in their decision making they avoid the soul issue of community, their move may be soulless and filled with difficulties. This particular CEO might have gained something important for his business in the move if, instead of denying its relevance, he had confronted the community issues involved.

Relocating, though painful and disruptive, can be a time of significant maturing for a company, provided it doesn't run away from the complex issues and emotions of community, family, and personal loss that are entailed in such a move. Soul is usually fostered more in times of intense struggle than in periods of relative ease. But in order to get that potential soulfulness, we have to enter the complexities with courage and openness. The only alternative is self-protective avoidance.

This executive's lack of community sensitivity betrays another serious problem that stands in the way of soul in business—narcissism. Narcissism is rooted in an anxiety about self—a fear that one is not being recognized or taken care of. Like all attitudes born of anxiety, it shows all the marks of neurotic behavior, in particular an excessive, obsessive, largely unsatisfied attempt to keep one's self visible and cared for. The tragedy of narcissism is that, since it is symptomatic and filled with anxiety, it never achieves the desired result. It only grows more anxious and feels less and less satisfied.

Neurotically insisting on one's own interests is a sure way to prevent their satisfaction. The narcissistic attitude ignores the paradoxical fact that individuality and self-interest are only fulfilled in community. Splitting one's own concerns from the needs of community may seem simplistically to be the way to protect oneself, but that point of view is an illusion. It only divides oneself from the very community that has the power to give the person or the business the satisfactions it craves.

In their advertising, promotion, and many other modes of expression, businesses often seem to believe that they have to sell themselves extravagantly in order to keep up with the competition. But for the soul of the business, it may be important to distinguish between strong self-expression and narcissism. In an individual, a company, or even a building or product, narcissism can be perceived by its excessive, hollow, and dishonest insistence on self-interest. Yet, it's possible to be confident, grounded, and strong in one's self-assertion without operating from anxiety.

A narcissistic attitude corrodes intimacy, whether among individuals or in public life. I would think that a business could benefit in many ways by transforming its narcissism into confidence and its braggadocio into honest expression of its nature and services. I'm not suggesting self-effacement—there's little danger of that in today's world anyway—but rather including sophisticated awareness of narcissism in a business's various attempts to show itself to the world and to provide products and services that make a real contribution to the community.

Creative Work

Engaging in creative work is another way to nourish the soul, and business is one of the most creative acts a person can engage in. Every day in business, products are being imagined, designed, and produced. Lives and careers are made and lost; companies are born, die, and are reborn. Money is an object of vast creative handling, and business relationships demand the utmost in personal character and imagination. A person entering business is stepping into an infinite potential for creative work. Then why does business so often feel uncreative?

Misconceptions about creativity keep it at a distance from many people, especially those in business. We tend to think of creativity as extraordinary self-expression, the work of the artist who is frequently inspired and who comes up with unceasing novel ideas and productions. But creativity could be imagined in less spirited terms.

C.G. Jung said that creativity is an instinct, a drive, or impulse common to everyone, as much a part of instinctual life as sex and hunger. Imagine that we all have a need for creativity based deep in the marrow of our existence—a deep activity of the soul. Imagine that a CEO of a company and its lowest entry-level employee both have an equal need to be creative. Again, creativity doesn't require astonishing feats of invention; it may be felt in an ordinary morning's financial decision or in a well-organized stockroom. It does ask for a measure of recognition and esteem.

Renaissance theologians described creativity as a participation in the ongoing creation of the world. From that point of view, our daily creative work could be a way in which we ordinary mortals approach divinity. The Renaissance idea of the dignity of the human being comes from our capacity to be creative, and to continually generate life and to make things. This creativity is manifested not only in art, but in everything we do, including homemaking and business. But note the Renaissance coupling of creativity and dignity. One is necessarily related to the other, and both are essential nutrients of the soul.

Invoking soul in business doesn't demand new techniques and strategies nearly as much as a re-imagining of business and work. People in business could find deep soul pleasure in the exercise of their own creativity. But in order to do so, they would have to be supported in their capacity to work in their own ways. The image of the creative person as an exceptional artist keeps the satisfactions of creativity away from the average worker. We feel average because we imagine ourselves that way, and we are imagined uncreative simply because we aren't a Michelangelo.

Business needs to appreciate creativity as a less exceptional, more ordinary activity in which we are each "making the world," participating in creation. How different this image is from the one so common in an industrial culture in which the worker is a cog in a great machine. Soul could be invited into business through a simple change in imagination—from the mechanical view of work and worker to Jung's view of creativity as a fundamental drive manifested in anything that we do.

Of course, we can find ourselves in uncreative work in an uncreative company. If we are treated as parts in a machine, we will sense no soul in our work, and naturally we won't feel creative. Traditional writings on the soul always say that the soul makes us human. If we aren't feeling human in our work, if we feel like robots, then we have lost our souls in this important part of life.

In spite of the tendency to think of it sentimentally, creativity has its many shadow elements that sometimes make creative life and work extraordinarily difficult. Initial inspirations and final satisfactions are mere moments in any creative endeavor, which usually requires long hours, days, and months of hard work. Getting to work every day, whether or not you feel inspired, is an important part of the creative life.

Creativity also challenges us to make changes when the spirit moves, when we feel stagnant in what we're doing, or when we feel an inner urgency to move in a new direction. Creative making of the world applies not only to products and businesses, but to our own careers as well. Some people seem to believe that the truly creative person moves in a straight line up the ladder of success, but biographies of people who have made obvious contributions demonstrate a different approach. Their lives are often marked by radical shifts in direction, by failures in important projects, and by periods of loss and rejection. The creative life embraces a wide range of experiences, both good and bad. So we might be prepared, as we invite soul into business, for considerable upheaval, loss, and disappointment, as well as satisfaction.

A creative company doesn't have to win all the time. One trouble with fanatical attempts to succeed at all costs and at all times is the tendency to be completely undone by failure, by taking failure literally as an absolute death rather than as part of the creative life. Creativity is not a constant march of progress. In fact, one sign of a creative business is its capacity to deal with failure, especially to have enough imagination and vision so as to know the role of failure in every creative endeavor.

Nature and Beauty

Just as the soul needs family, friendship, and creativity, it also needs nature in some form. Again, people vary in the ways and degrees in which nature satisfies them. Some crave frequent trips deep into the woods, while others are content with a single plant in a window overlooking a busy city street. The Jungian analyst James Hillman points out that there is no need to take nature literally. A landscape painting may give the imagination an important means of contemplating nature. Years ago I gave a lecture on lawns and billiard tables, noting that both give us an image of the "field" on which life plays itself out. The rules and pockets in billiards were once seen as representative of the obstacles that always interfere with the smooth running of life, while the green felt table is equivalent to the village green or even the front lawn, itself an image of the world stage on which we live out our lives.

No matter where a business is located or how busy the day's schedule, everyone from top to bottom of the roster of employees needs a daily chance to contemplate nature. Some businesses recognize this need and give attention to landscaping or to interior design. But often we go about our business focused on productivity, with little regard for needs of the soul that appear to be irrelevant to the business at hand. We may fail to notice connections between a purely mechanical working environment and problems of morale or personal and family difficulties. We may treat tardiness and absenteeism as a moral issue rather than as a reflection of the soullessness of the job and its environs.

We all need vacations—not just to take time away from work but to have the opportunity to refresh ourselves in nature. Automobiles clog highways out of our major cities on Friday evenings and especially at the beginning of holidays—a sign of the importance of nature. Somehow each person finds a way to have both nature and culture, city and country, in life, even if "country" amounts to little more than a week-end escape from the city or some time in a park within walking distance.

Nature offers many things: relief from a mechanical world, meditation on one's cosmology, exposure to different rhythms of time, fresh air and growing things, space and the absence of crowds, contact with animals, and memories of a simpler life.

These things may seem minor in comparison to the making of culture. Yet each has enormous importance for the soul. Nature also provides us with what may be the most important source of soul nutrition in all of life—beauty.

Modern culture is so focused on survival and success in life that we undervalue those things that are not so closely related to our ambitions and heroic activity. To the individual intent on creating a business empire of major or minor proportions, beauty may seem unessential. Yet to the soul the contemplation of beauty is a sine qua non; it can't get along without it. To the soul, beauty is one of the most satisfying gifts of living on this earth. In the modern world, when we think of the soul at all we speak of emotions and relationships. We borrow ideas of well-being from the body. We're concerned about emotional health and minimal conflict. But to the soul the healthy life isn't nearly sufficient. It thrives on a measure of conflict. It comes to life in moments of passionate feeling and reaction. For its positive satisfaction, it requires the beautiful, not necessarily the healthy.

The soul-oriented business will take beauty into serious consideration in its architecture, furnishings, advertising, and use of language, both in relation to its employees and to the public. Beauty doesn't require extraordinary expense, but it does demand sensitivity and attention. Most of all, it asks us to depart from the purely pragmatic agendas that often preoccupy businesses. As a writer, I get business letters that torture the language—"As per your recent missive, pleased be advised...." In our age of easy computer graphics, it is also becoming increasingly rare to find the presence of an artist's hand in advertising, logos, reports, and other presentations of image.

Oddly, we have many artists and writers in need of work. Yet we put our energy into devising new computer programs for graphics and design, rather than inviting these imaginative and skilled people to bring soul to our productions. Good tools, such as computers and software, obviously have their place, but they don't carry much soul. They come with spirited fantasies of speed and efficiency rather than beauty and craft.

The soul is sensitive to color, texture, and sound. Yet often our ever-building society operates as though these qualities were unimportant in a busy life dedicated to schedules of production. These qualities may not increase the tempo of manufacturing and accounting. In fact, they may even slow the speed somewhat, but they feed the soul which goes hungry in their absence.

Marsilio Ficino, writing in late fifteenth-century Florence, a city that was effectively able to blend business and art backed by a philosophy of soul, noted that whether we like it or not, we are filled with the spirit evoked by the materials, shapes, and images around us. Live in a thoroughly plastic world, and we become plastic people. Have a little wood, stone, textile, and color in our work lives, and we become colorful, interesting people.

Beauty is arresting, it invites us to stop and look. But in a world on the move, pausing to behold the beautiful may appear as an obstacle to progress. The soul needs moments of arrest and pause. Business has "busy" in its very name. It isn't easy for goal-directed business people to appreciate the need for stopping and pausing in order to let the world gain entrance with its sensuality. The word we associate most closely with beauty—aesthetics—means to feel or sense. The whole point in beauty is to stop, look, and be open to the incursion of the physical world. The soulful business may have to discover artful ways of stopping, ways that don't come across as mere obstacles to work, and then let the beautiful do its job of nourishing the soul.

Spirituality

According to ancient traditions, the soul needs a spiritual life of some kind or else it lacks something essential to it. Just how to provide spirituality in business is a difficult challenge for a number of reasons. The main difficulty is that in our time, as in many periods in the past, we are going through a serious transition in our awareness of what religion and the life of the spirit are all about.

Encountering unfamiliar traditions and beliefs has always been a challenge, but it is a special problem in our day when education is widespread, experimentation in values and styles is common, and information about other cultures pours in by the minute. Perhaps in reaction to all of these factors, some people gather together in mutual defense and insist that their way is the only acceptable one.

Some business people try to include a spiritual element by framing their business around their beliefs. Occasionally I will make a purchase, and then I'm handed a pamphlet on the religious beliefs of the store's owners. I feel uneasy then because, as much as I appreciate the presence of spiritual conviction in what is usually a secular environment, I don't want to be proselytized just because I happen to be doing business in a place.

Many would like to keep business and religion separate, but in that case we find little basis for ethics and little vision beyond the profit margin. Spirituality provides a ground for an ethical way of life, and it gives a vision of human activity that transcends the pragmatic. Spirituality can also foster a sensitivity to communal aspects of daily life, and thereby counter the tendency in business toward narcissistic self-interest.

Perhaps we need a fresh way of imagining the spiritual life, one that is not so closely tied to belief and institution, and yet is solid and authentic. I can imagine a society in which spiritual values are a visible and influential part of public life and, at the same time, individuals practice their own particular beliefs privately or in dedicated communities. These days some people like to distinguish between spirituality and religion, the latter interpreted as an institution or tradition. Perhaps because I have an academic degree in religion and find so much of value in the world's religious traditions, I prefer to keep the word religion, while expanding and deepening it beyond the connotation of institution.

For me, religion is an attitude that colors all of life, bestowing on all our thoughts and actions a deep appreciation and reverence for the sacred. This spirit of religion may or may not be fostered by institutional religion and beliefs, and there may be an infinite number of paths to that profoundly important attitude. Without getting caught in the tangles of beliefs and loyalties, business could be deeply enriched by such an attitude.

This spirit of the sacred need not flow directly from the personal convictions of the people involved in a business, but may first come from the work itself. Our very words "merchandise" and "commerce" come from a Latin word *"merx"* which is closely related to the god Mercurius, patron in ancient Roman culture of business and commerce. Every time we use the word "commercial," we are invoking the name of a spirit or divinity. Apparently we have forgotten what our ancestors knew long ago: that even so worldly an enterprise as business has its ethics, its beliefs, and its ultimate context and relevance.

The Romans also honored the goddess Ceres, from whom our word "cereal" derives, the patroness of managing goods and services. Ceres was the daughter of Ops, from whom we get "opulent." As goddess of growing grains, she also gives us our words "increase" and "concrete," suggesting respectively growth, which is such a prominent image in business, and the real world of particulars, which is what business imagines as its concern.

To us, "business spirituality" may sound like an oxymoron, but if the ancient insight that business has its own divine patronage is difficult for us to comprehend, it only shows us how far we have moved away from religion. Business has profound meaning and relevance to us as individuals and as a society, more profound than a secular mind might be capable of imagining. Hints that this is true are to be found in the impact economics has on us. When business is faring well, the whole society prospers in every area of endeavor. When we go through an economic depression, we are truly depressed in soul. Money, business, and goods carry with them our thoughts, images, and feelings about life itself, about its bounty and its value, its delicate balances and its promises, its deep holes and its peak experiences.

Business is also the experience of community *par excellence*. In business we interact with each other, struggle and collaborate, love and hate. In business we make identities and careers, and also crush them and lose them. We see today how close business and government come to each other, to the point that one wonders if we are not ruled more by business than by government. Kings used to be divinely anointed. These days it seems that some business leaders consider themselves among the nobility, and sometimes even seek out symbolic anointing through association with the clergy. This is a subtle indication of the profound role business plays in the lives of us all.

The relationship between business and community, whether local or global, is so serious as to touch upon ultimate values. The business person who seeks only to exploit that relationship for personal gain fails to perceive the theological roots of business, the fact that business is deeply involved in matters of ultimate meaning. Ethics in business is not a tangential concern, but speaks to the very heart of business life.

Sometimes when I speak to business people about the soul in their work, they ask anxiously about profit, the bottom line. My response is that there is a whole world, an underworld, beneath the so-called bottom line. If we make profit the ultimate concern of our work, then the soul has no recourse but to appear in negative ways—as low morale, symptoms among workers, conflict with society, and even poor quality of products.

Placing profit as the ultimate bottom line appears to me as a defense. It shows many signs of anxious self-protection and perhaps an excuse for greed and excessive power. Defensiveness and obsessiveness in any area of life are not only signs of neurosis, they are also an invitation to deepen the very matter at hand. I have no intention of speaking moralistically against profit-making, but the presence of greed or obsessive attention to profit that excludes other important values indicates that we are not getting the satisfactions we're searching for. It could be that wealth and profit are more satisfying when they aren't identified wholly with money, but rather when money has a convivial relationship to other values like community, peace, care for nature, just distribution of resources, and other deep values.

I use the word "convivial" carefully and somewhat technically. "*Convivium*," meaning "living together," was a special term used frequently by Renaissance authors from whom I get many of my thoughts about soul. People can live convivially when they enjoy each other's company while appreciating their differences. A convivial relationship among people, things, or ideas is one in which variety and difference are valued. Indeed the richness of experience comes not from trying to achieve dominance of one over the other, or even from attempting some kind of intellectual amalgamation of differences, but rather simply from allowing them to exist together. In this sense, profit can have a convivial relationship with responsiveness to community, attention to workers and the workplace, impact of the business on nature, and many other factors.

In a convivial setting, profit making can be enriched, not threatened, by nature, workers, and community setting. Philanthropy, an important and central activity of the convivial business, can be a positive, honest, pleasurable aspect of business life. Convivial philanthropy is quite different from the cynical kind in which community involvement is only feigned, or is limited artificially by narcissistic concerns of the business. Philanthropy, which means "love of human beings," could include care and attention that goes beyond money, including sincere involvement in all aspects of community.

How can business become more spiritual? The avenues to spirit are not all arcane and anachronistic. Business could constantly educate itself in values, for example. That does not mean adhering to certain absolute values, but rather sustaining discussion aimed at deepening values that can be held with intelligence and sophistication. Education itself is a path toward spirituality. Business could make real contributions to the education of its leaders, its employees, and its communities as a way of nurturing the spiritual life. Honest social concern and community involvement would be both signs of a spiritual posture and a way of fostering spirituality.

It would not be out of order to consult spiritual leaders of the present or the past for wisdom in living a spiritual life. The excellent texts of Chinese wisdom alone offer extraordinary guidance in this direction. One has to remember that it's possible to consult a spiritual leader without becoming a member of his or her organization. You don't have to become a follower in order to benefit from a person's or a tradition's wisdom. Some of our best spiritual leaders are to be found in seemingly unsophisticated places: in Tibet, traditional Africa, deep Australia, native America, remote areas of South America, and in many, many other places.

Business could encourage and provide occasion for contemplation and meditation. In medieval and Renaissance Europe every castle had a chapel. Every business, large and small, could have a room set aside or a meditation area, and a few moments of time allotted for contemplation. It's impossible to have a spiritual life without a modicum of silent reflection.

The spiritual life I am describing is not a matter of belief or adherence to doctrine. It's concerned with a spirituality that could act as ground for belief and religious practice, but it also stands by itself. We can nourish our spirituality without even coming close to differences in belief. It is this basic ground in the spirit that could make a significant contribution to the soul life of a business.

I know from speaking with many business people that they often sense a hunger for meaning, substance, and depth. They may or may not believe that this hunger can be satisfied in their work. Often they look outside their work for the experiences and values that they find lacking there. I would like to suggest that work itself, no matter how deeply mired in money and profit making, can be tapped for its own inherent spirituality. This, in fact, is the kind of spirituality that can benefit our communities, and not just the business people themselves.

How can an ordinary person cultivate this brand of spirituality? Read the *Tao Te Ching*, Sufi poems, native American prayers, ancient Jewish tales, Zen stories, and the parables of Jesus. They are filled with pointers toward a spiritual life that can be cultivated in business. Read our own poets and philosophers like Ralph Waldo Emerson, Henry Thoreau, and especially Wallace

Stevens, who lived the life of a successful insurance executive while becoming one of America's most important poets.

Incorporate moments for contemplation into the work day, perhaps using spiritual sources or the arts as a focus. Nothing satisfies the soul's need for spirit more than silence—just a few moments, best when associated with even a small beautiful object or space. Contemplation need not be the extraordinary kind, but maybe just a simple opportunity to become absorbed in a painting, a garden, a good piece of music, or a carefully made fountain or pond. In a world so driven to "busyness," any encouragement toward simple and brief contemplation offers an excellent way to care for the soul.

The soul-oriented business does not set up unnecessary and artificial oppositions between beauty and efficiency, profit and responsiveness to community, or spirituality and worldliness. It doesn't confuse caring for the soul with the personal growth of individuals. It finds limits to the desire for power and wealth not by looking for some outside moralistic super-ego, but in the conviviality of many desires, goals, and values. It appreciates values of soul like beauty, nature, intimacy, and creativity for their own sake, not only by the measure of financial profit. It doesn't imagine care of the soul narcissistically, but with pleasure and struggle works out its communal relationships among workers and society.

Soul gives a business a strong identity and makes it capable of firm and lasting relationships. It inspires trust, and attracts a public from its own integrity rather than by means of exploitive advertising. It also relieves anxiety, so much a part of much business life.

I don't mean to suggest that soul is a panacea or to describe it sentimentally as a thoroughly peaceable way of life. Yet, I do suspect that loss of soul is responsible for much of the distress and destruction one finds in business. Slow and gradual cultivation of soul might well give a business positive qualities it never knew it needed or wanted. It's in the nature of a more spirited approach to mark out clear goals and strategies. It's more in the style of the soul to cultivate the values I've sketched here and then watch for unexpected developments.

Conclusion

A Final Editors' Note

"Rediscovering" the soul in business means to reclaim what was once an essential part of being human. Soulful work is the quintessential human experience, embodying the spirit, the pathos, the successes and the losses associated with productive labor. Rediscovering the soul does not mean adding a new spin to the traditional management approach—using it as a tool to get workers to be more productive. It does mean providing a hospitable environment for the complete human experience, so that people can have a reunion with those parts of themselves that have been disenfranchised as a result of scientific management and the command and control style of the past generations.

This book is not intended to provide yet another management model, nor to serve as fodder for the gossip mill of "what's hot and what's not." It is intended to be a wake-up call to industry and to the complete human being who invests a significant part of his/her energy in the community of the workplace.

This book can be interpreted as a collection of ideas to consider and possibly implement in changing the "form" of what is done in business. It is the hope of the editors and the publisher that it also inspires a shift in consciousness—toward an integrated state of mind, body, heart, and soul—in a complete human being who goes to work everyday rejoicing in the soulful experience of meaningful endeavor.

We have presented this broad range of writings to provide a larger perspective as well as specific applications, from the personal point-of-view to the organizational, from narratives to metaphor, and from conceptual theory to anecdotal stories. All of these writings and approaches came together through a creative process to create a potpourri of richness for the visionary business reader.

It has been an incredible adventure for us as editors, starting when we first met in the Fall of 1993. The work of compiling this collection has been a labor of love for us both.

—Bill DeFoore and John Renesch
co-editors
Summer 1995

Recommended Reading
and Resources

Armstrong, Karen. *A History of God.* New York: Ballantine, 1993.

Arrien, Angeles. *The Four Fold Way: Walking The Paths of the Warrior, Teacher, Healer, and Visionary.* San Francisco: Harper/Collins Publishers, 1993.

Autry, James A. *Love and Profit.* New York: Avon, 1991.

Autry James, A. *Life and Work.* New York: William Morrow and Company, 1994.

Axelrod, Dick. "Using the Conference Model for Work Redesign," *Journal for Quality and Participation.* December, 1993.

Barrentine, Pat. *When The Canary Stops Singing: Women's Perspectives for Transforming Business.* San Francisco: Berrett-Koehler Publishers, 1993.

Barker, Sir Ernest. *The Political Thought of Plato and Aristotle.* New York: Dover Publications, 1959.

Barnard, Chester. *Organization Management: Selected Papers.* Boston, Massachusetts: Harvard University Press, 1948.

Bartlett, Christopher A. and Sumantra Ghoshal. "Changing the Role of Top Management: Beyond Strategy to Purpose," *Harvard Business Review.* November/December, 1994.

Bethel, Shelia Murray. *Making a Difference: Twelve Qualities That Make You a Leader.* New York: Berkeley, 1990.

Block, Peter. *Stewardship.* San Francisco: Berrett-Koehler Publishers, 1993.

Bly, Robert. *A Little Book on the Human Shadow.* New York: Harper and Row Publishers, 1988.

Borei, Jeanne. "Chaos to Community: One Company's Journey to Transformation," Barrentine, Pat. (ed.) *When The Canary Stops Singing: Women's Perspectives for Transforming Business.* San Francisco: Berrett-Koehler Publishers, 1993.

Borges, Jorge Luis. *Seven Nights.* New York: New Directions, 1984.

Brueggemann, Walter. "Transformed Redescription of Personal Identity," (audio cassette), Institute of Faith Development, Emory University, Atlanta, 1981.

Campbell, Joseph. *The Farther Reaches of Outerspace.* New York: Alfred Van Der Marck Editions,1986.

Campbell, Joseph. *The Power of Myth.* New York: Bantam Doubleday Dell Publishing Group, Inc., 1988.

"CEO Follows Founder's Lead With Courage and Vision," *The New Leaders,* San Francisco: New Leaders Press, Nov./Dec., 1993.

Chappell, Tom. The *Soul of a Business: Managing for Profit and the Common Good.* New York: Bantam Books, 1993.

Chawla, Sarita and John Renesch (eds.). *Learning Organizations: Developing Cultures for Tomorrow's Workplace.* Portland, OR: Productivity Press, 1995.

Cleveland, Harlan. "The Age of People Power," *Futurist.* Jan/Feb., 1992.

Cooper, Cary L. and Roy Payne. Causes, Coping and Consequences of *Stress and Work*. New York: John Wiley and Sons, 1989.

Covey, Stephen R. *Principle-Centered Leadership*. New York: Simon & Schuster, 1992.

Cox, Harvey. "Business in a New Age," Letters to the Editor, *Harvard Business Review*. May, 1994.

Csikszentmihalyi, Mihalyi. *The Evolving Self*. New York: Harper Collins Publishers, Inc. 1993.

Denhardt, Robert B. *The Pursuit of Significance: Strategies for Managerial Success in Public Organizations*. Belmont, CA: Wadsworth Publishing Company, 1993.

DePree, Max. *Leadership Is An Art*. New York: Doubleday, 1989.

De Tocqueville, Alexis. *Democracy in America*. New York, NY: Alfred A. Knopf Inc., 1994.

Dickens, Charles. *A Christmas Carol*. Cutchogue, NY: Buccaneer Books, Inc., 1983.

Dossey, Larry, M.D. *Meaning and Medicine: Lessons From a Doctor's Tales of Breakthrough and Healing*. New York: Bantam Books, 1991.

Drucker, Peter. *Management: Tasks, Responsibilities and Practices*. New York: Harper and Row Publishers, 1972.

Eck, Diana and Jain Devaki, eds. *Speaking of Faith: Global Perspectives on Women, Religion and Social Change*. Philadelphia: New Society Publishers, 1987.

Eisler, Riane. *The Chalice and the Blade: Our History, Our Future*. San Francisco: Harper and Row, 1988.

Elias, Nabil. "Human Resource Measurement and Socio-Psychological Variables," A paper presented at the American Accounting Association annual meeting, 1972.

Ellis, Marc H. and Otto Maduro, eds. *The Future of Liberation Theology: Essays in Honor of Gustavo Gutierrez*. Maryknoll: Orbis Books, 1989.

Emery, Merrelyn. *Participative Design for Participative Democracy*. Centre for Continuing Education: Australian National University. 1993.

Etzioni, Amitai. *The Spirit of Community*. New York: Simon & Schuster, 1994.

Fabella, Virginia and Sun Ai Lee Par, eds. *We Dare To Dream: Doing Theology as Asian Women*. Maryknoll: Orbis Books, 1990.

"First Lady Campaigns for End of Spiritual Vacuum," *The New Leaders*, San Francisco: New Leaders Press, July/Aug. 1993.

Fisher, Roger and William Ury. *Getting to Yes*. New York: Penguin Press, 1981.

Fox, Matthew. *The Reinvention of Work*. San Francisco: Harper Collins Publishers, 1994.

Fox, Steve. *Toxic Work*. Philadelphia: The Temple Press, 1991.

Fuller, R. Buckminster. *Operations Manual for Spaceship Earth*. New York: E.P. Dutton, 1963.

Green, Gareth and Frank Baker. *Work, Health, and Productivity*. New

York: Oxford University Press, 1991.

Godfrey, Joline. *Our Wildest Dreams: Women Entrepreneurs Making Money, Having Fun, Doing Good.* New York: Harper Business, 1992.

Gozdz, Kazimierz (ed.). *Community Building: Renewing Spirit and Learning in Business.* San Francisco: New Leaders Press, 1995.

Haessly, Jacqueline. *Learning to Live Together.* San Jose, CA: Resource Publications, 1989.

Haessly, Jacqueline. "Quest for Quality with a Difference: Values for a Global Marketplace," in Barrentine, Pat, (ed.) *When The Canary Stops Singing: Women's Perspectives for Transforming Business.* San Francisco: Berrett-Koehler Publishers, Inc. 1993.

Handy, Charles. *The Age of Paradox.* Cambridge, MA: Harvard Business School Press, 1994.

Handy, Charles. "What Is a Company For?" Michael Shanks Memorial Lecture. RSA, December 5, 1990.

Hanson, Peter G., M.D. *The Joy of Stress.* Canada: Hanson Stress Management Organization, 1985.

Harman, Willis and Hormann, John. *Creative Work: The Constructive Role of Business in a Transforming Society.* Indianapolis, IN: Knowledge Systems, 1990.

Hawken, Paul. *Ecology of Commerce.* New York: Harper Collins Publishers, 1993.

Heckman, Frank. "Well-Being: How to Cut Your Healthcare Bill in Half, Raise Your Productivity and Improve Your Quality." September, 1992.

Hellriegel, Don, John W. Slocum, Jr., and Richard W. Woodman. *Organizational Behavior.* New York: West Publishing, 1992.

Henri, Robert. *The Art of Spirit.* New York: Harper Collins Publishers, Inc., 1984.

Hillman, James. *Re-visioning Psychology.* New York: Harper and Row, 1975.

Hillman, James. *We Have Had 100 Years of Therapy and the World is Getting Worse.* New York: Harper Collins Press, 1992.

Hoffmeister, Sallie. "Offbeat California Agency Flourishes by Uncovering the Soul of its Clients Brands," *The New York Times.* August 2, 1994.

Isaacs, William. "Dialogue: The Power of Collective Thinking," *The Systems Thinker.* 1993, Vol. 4, No. 3.

Isasi-Diaz, Ada Maria. "A Hispanic Garden in a Foreign Land" in Russell, Letty, Kwok Pui Lan, et al, (eds.), *Inheriting Our Mother's Gardens: Feminist Theology in Third World Perspectives.* Philadelphia: The Westminster Press, 1988.

"Is Herb Kelleher America's Best CEO?" *Fortune Magazine.* May 2, 1994.

Johnson, Robert. *Owning Your Shadow: Understanding the Dark Side of the Psyche.* New York: Harper Collins, 1991.

Johnson-Lenz, Peter and Trudy. *Organizational and Societal Learning: Groupware for a Small Planet.* Lake Oswego, OR: Institute for Awakening Technology, 1994.

Johnston, Charles M. *Necessary Wisdom: Meeting the Challenge of a New cultural Maturity.* Seattle: ICD Press/Celestial Arts, 1991.

Karasek, Robert and Tores Theorell. *Healthy Work.* New York: Basic Books, 1990.

Keen, Sam. *Hymns to an Unknown God.* New York: Bantam Books, 1994.

Ketchum, Lyman D. and Eric Trist. *All Teams Are Not Created Equal.* Newbury Park, CA: Sage Publications, 1992.

Krohe, James Jr. "Musical Chairs," *Across the Board.* May, 1993.

Legge, Gordon. "Religion, Faith and Values," *Calgary Herald.* May 21, 1994.

Levey, Joel and Michelle Levey. *Quality of Mind: Tools for Self Mastery & Enhanced Performance:* Boston: Wisdom Publication, 1991.

Levey, Joel and Michelle Levey. *The Focused Mind State* (audio tape). Chicago: Nightingale Conant, 1993.

Levey, Joel and Michelle Levey. "Wisdom at work: An Inquiry Into the Dimensions of Higher Order Learning." In Sarita Chawla and John Renesch (eds.) *Learning Organizations: Developing Cultures for Tomorrow's Workplace.* Portland, OR: Productivity Press, 1995.

Limbaugh, Rush. *See I Told You So.* New York: Pocket Books, 1994.

Lulic, Margaret A. *Who We Could Be at Work.* Minneapolis: Blue Edge Publishing, 1994.

Lynn, Laurence E. *Managing the Public's Business: The Job of the Government Executive.* New York: Basic Books, 1981.

Machiavelli, Niccolo. *The Prince.* Palm Springs, CA: ETC Publications, 1988.

Marty, Martin E. and R. Scott Appleby, eds. *Fundamentalisms and the State.* Chicago: University of Chicago Press, 1993.

Maslow, A.H. "A Theory of Human Motivation." *Psychology Review.* 1943, Vol. 50.

McCreary, Lew. "Civilizing Cyberspace," *CIO.* March 1, 1994.

McLaughlin, Corinne and Gordon Davidson. *Spiritual Politics: Changing the World From the Inside Out.* New York: Ballantine Books, 1994.

Moore, Thomas. *Care of the Soul: A Guide for Cultivating Depth and Sacredness in Everyday Life.* New York: Harper Collins Publishers, 1992.

Morgan, Marie. "Spiritual Qualities of Leadership in Business," *World Business Academy Perspectives.* 1993, Vol. 7, No. 4.

Mottinger, Betty A. *Power, Poverty and the Role of Women,* UMI Dissertation Services, 1991.

Moyers, Bill. *Healing and The Mind.* New York: Doubleday, 1993.

Nair, Keshavan. *A Higher Standard of Leadership: Lessons from the Life of Gandhi.* San Francisco: Berrett-Koehler, 1994.

"Norman Lear Calls For Leap of Faith—to Enter Dialogue About 'The God Thing,'" *The New Leaders,* San Francisco: New Leaders Press, May/June, 1993.

O'Neil, John R. *The Paradox of Success.* New York: G.P. Putnam, 1994.

Osborne, David and Ted Gaebler. *Reinventing Government: How the Entrepreneurial Spirit is Transforming the Public Sector.* Reading, MA: Addison-Wesley Publishing Company, 1992.

Ostrander, Sheila and Lynn Shroeder. *Super Learning.* New York: Dell Publishing Company, 1980.

Peters, Thomas J. and Robert Waterman, Jr. *In Search of Excellence.* New York: Warner Books, 1984.

Ray, Michael and Alan Rinzler (eds.) *The New Paradigm in Business.* New York: Tarcher/Perigee, 1993.

Ray, Michael and John Renesch (eds.). *The New Entrepreneurs.* San Francisco: New Leaders Press, 1994.

Rehm, Robert. (unpublished manuscript) "Participate Design: An Interpretation of the Work of Fred and Merrelyn Emery."

Renesch, John (ed.). *Leadership in a New Era.* San Francisco: New Leaders Press, 1994.

Renesch, John (ed.) *New Traditions in Business: Spirit & Leadership in the 21st Century.* San Francisco: Berrett-Koehler, 1993.

Renesch, John. "Where is Spartacus When We Need Him?" *The New Leaders.* San Francisco: New Leaders Press, Mar./Apr. 1995.

Responsive Community, The. The George Washington University, Washington, D.C.

Roddick, Anita. *Body and Soul.* New York: Crown Publishers, Inc., 1991.

Rose, Frank. "A New Age for Business?" *Fortune.* October 8, 1990.

Russell, Letty, Kwok Pui Lan et al. (eds.). *Inheriting Our Mother's Gardens: Feminist Theology in Third World Perspectives.* Philadelphia: The Westminster Press, 1988.

Sardello, Robert. *Facing the World with Soul.* New York: Lindisfarne Press, 1992.

Schor, Juliet B. *The Overworked American: The Unexpected Decline of Leisure.* New York: Basic Books, 1993.

Schumacher, E.F. *Small is Beautiful.* New York: Harper & Row Publishers, Inc., 1973.

Schumpeter, Joseph A. *The Economics and Sociology of Capitalism.* Princeton, NJ: Princeton University Press, 1991.

Senge, Peter. *The Fifth Discipline.* New York: Doubleday/Currency, 1990.

Spencer, Sabina. "Seven Keys to Conscious Leadership," in Pat Barrentine (ed.), *When The Canary Stops Singing: Women's Perspectives for Transforming Business.* San Francisco: Berrett-Koehler, 1993.

"Spirit in the Workplace: A Movement of the Verge of Taking Off," *At Work: Stories of Tomorrow's Workplace.* San Francisco: Berrett-Koehler, September/October 1993.

Stack, Jack. *Great Game of Business.* New York: Doubleday Currency, 1992.

Stafford, William. *The Darkness Around Us is Deep: Selected Poems by Robert Bly.* New York: Harper Perennial, 1993.

Steindl-Rast, David. *A Listening Heart: The Art of Contemplative Living.* New York: Crossroad, 1984.

Stone, Donald E. *Management Accounting and Sustainable Development.* Research Report, University of Massachussetts School of Management. Amherst, MA. June 1993.

Sun, Patricia. "Authentic Action" (audio cassette). San Francisco: New Dimensions Radio, 1990.

Thompson, Curt. "Preparation is Key to Successful Change," *HR Focus.* April 1994.

"Tom Peters Digs in on Spirituality and Business Issue." *The New Leaders.* San Francisco: New Leaders Press, Sept./Oct. 1994.

Tönnies, Ferdinand. *Community and Society.* New York: Harper & Row, 1957.

Ulrich, David N. and Harry P. Dunne, Jr. *To Love and Work.* New York: Brunner/Mazel Publishers, 1986.

Wahlberg, Rachel Conrad. *Jesus According To A Woman.* New York: Paulist Press, 1975.

Wallis, Jim. *The Soul of Politics.* New York: The New Press/Orbis Books, 1994.

Weisbord, Marvin R. et al. *Discovering Common Ground.* San Francisco: Berrett-Koehler, 1992.

Wheatley, Meg. *Leadership and the New Science.* San Francisco: Berrett-Koehler, 1992.

Whyte, David. *The Heart Aroused: Poetry and the Preservation of the Soul in Corporate America.* New York: Currency/Doubleday, 1994

Woodman, Marion. *Holding the Tension of the Opposites* (audio cassette). Sound True Recordings, CO. 1991.

Zukav, Gary. *Seat of the Soul.* New York: Simon & Schuster, 1989.

Associations

Business for Social Responsibility
1030 - 15th Street N.W., #1010
Washington, D.C. 20005
202/842-5400

Renaissance Business Associates
Box 197
Boise, ID 83701
208/345-4234

World Business Academy
P.O. Box 21470
Washington, D.C. 20009
202/822-4022

Periodicals

At Work: Stories of Tomorrow's Workplace
(bimonthly newsletter)
Berrett-Koehler Publishers, Inc.
155 Montgomery St.
San Francisco, CA 94104-4109
800/929-2929

Business Ethics
(bimonthly magazine)
Mavis Publications
52 S. 10th Street #10
Minneapolis, MN 55403-2001
612/962-4700

The New Leaders:
The Business Newsletter for Transformative Leadership
(bimonthly newsletter)
New Leaders Press
1668 Lombard Street
San Francisco, CA 94123
800/928-LEAD

World Business Academy Perspectives
(quarterly journal)
Berrett-Koehler Publishers, Inc.
155 Montgomery St.
San Francisco, CA 94104-4109
800/929-2929

How to Contact Authors and Editors

RICHARD BIEDERSTEDT
104 Oakbrook Drive
Lewisville, TX 75057
214-918-6770

MICHELLE BLESKAN
442 Mount Curve Blvd.
Saint Paul, MN 55105
612-698-4909

COLLEEN BURKE
10 Chestnut St. #2302
Exeter, NH, 03833
603-778-8563

EVALGELINE CARIDAS
3223 Albans Road
Houston, TX 77005
713-984-1874
713-668-6697

BILL DeFOORE
4201 Wingren, #201
Irving, TX 75062
214-791-0144

DOROTHY FISCHER
4201 Wingren, #201
Irving, TX, 75062
214-647-9696

MATTHEW FOX
Holy Names College
3500 Mountain Blvd.
Oakland, CA 94619
510-436-1206

MICHAEL FRYE
B. Elliott plc
Elliott House Victoria Rd.
London, U.K. NW10 6NY
44-181-961-7333

ELAINE GAGNÉ
11030 Thomas Rd.
Colorado Springs, CO 80908
719-495-9616

JACQUELINE HAESSLY
Peacemaking Associates
2437 N. Grant Blvd.
Milwaukee, WI, 53210
414-445-9736

CHARLES HANDY
73 Putney Hill
London, U.K. SW15 3NT

LOIS HOGAN
74 Main St.
West Newbury, MA 01985
508-363-2000

RON & SUSAN KERTZNER
780 Poplar Ave
Boulder, CO 80304
303-415-9347

ROBERT LEAVER
Organizational Futures
One Allens Ave.
Providence, RI 02903
401-351-7110

MARK LEAVITT
15400 NW Greenbriar Pkwy #400
Beaverton, OR 97006
503-531-7000

JOEL LEVEY
5536 Woodlawn Ave. N.
Seattle, WA 98103
206-632-3551

THOMAS MOORE
c/o Harper Collins Publishers
10 E. 53rd St.
New York, NY 10022
212-207-7000

MARIE MORGAN
3138 SW Fairview Blvd.
Portland, OR 97201
503-228-6860

ALEX PATTAKOS
Creative Learning Technologies
P. O. Box 418
Boise, ID 83701
208-345-4235

KATHLEEN REDMOND
Cardinal Concepts
65 E. India Row, #39 F
Boston, MA 02110
617-723-6101

JOHN RENESCH
Sterling and Stone
1668 Lombard St.
San Francisco, CA 94123
415-928-1473

JULI ANN REYNOLDS
26 Constellation Wharf
Charlestown, MA 02129
617-345-0200

MAGALY d. RODRIGUEZ
Rapid Change Technologies Inc.
542 S. Snelling Ave. #104
Saint Paul, MN 55116
612-698-4284

JAYME ROLLS
1436 - 20th St. #2
Santa Monica, CA 90404
310-315-9780

BARBARA SHIPKA
P. O. Box 50005
Minneapolis, MN 55405
612-374-4488

PETER B. VAILL
The George Washington Univ.
403 Monroe Hall
Washington, DC 20052
202-994-7597

MARK YOUNGBLOOD
1208 Serenade Lane
Richardson, TX 75081
214-437-6527

GARY ZUKAV
P. O. Box 1333
Mount Shasta, CA 96067

Index

Additional copies of

REDISCOVERING THE SOUL OF BUSINESS

can be purchased from the organizations listed below:

CALIFORNIA
Rolls & Company, Santa Monica — 310-315-9780

COLORADO
Elaine Gagné, Colorado Springs — 719-495-9616
Ron & Susan Kertzner, Boulder — 303-415-9347

IDAHO
Creative Learning Technologies, Boise — 208-345-4235

MASSACHUSETTS
Cardinal Concepts, Boston — 617-723-6101
Lois Hogan, Consultant, West Newbury — 508-363-2000
Juli Ann Reynolds, Charlestown — 617-345-0200

MINNESOTA
Creative Breakthroughs, Inc., Saint Paul — 612-698-4284
Partnership for Transformation, Saint Paul — 612-698-4909
Barbara Shipka, Consultant, Minneapolis — 612-374-4488

NEW HAMPSHIRE
Colleen Burke, Exeter — 603-778-8563

OREGON
TWIGGS Fulfillment Center, Newberg — 800-713-9935

RHODE ISLAND
Organizational Futures, Providence — 401-351-7110

TEXAS
Evangeline Caridas, Houston — 713-984-1874; 713-668-6697
Dorothy Fischer, Irving — 214-647-9696
Quay Alliance, Inc., Richardson — 214-783-2070
Transformational Business Solutions, Lewisville — 214-221-7468

WASHINGTON
InnerWork Technologies, Inc., Seattle — 206-632-3551

WASHINGTON, DC
Peter B. Vaill, Washington, DC — 202-994-7597

WISCONSIN
Peacemaking Associates, Milwaukee — 414-445-9736

UNITED KINGDOM
B. Elliott plc, London — 44-181-961-7333

OTHER BUSINESS ANTHOLOGIES
developed by New Leaders Press

Community Building: Renewing Spirit & Learning in Business
Authors include John Gardner, George Land and Beth Jarman, Jordan
Paul, M. Scott Peck, Michael Ray, Marvin Weisbord, and over twenty
others; edited by Kazimierz Gozdz.
Hardcover; New Leaders Press; $37.75 (U.S.); call 1.800.928.LEAD.

**Learning Organizations: Developing Cultures for Tomorrow's
Workplace**. Authors include Peter Senge and Fred Kofman, Charles
Handy, Rosabeth Moss Kanter, and over thirty other authors; edited by
Sarita Chawla and John Renesch.
Hardcover; Productivity Press; $35.00 (U.S.); call 1.800.394.6868.

**Leadership in a New Era: Visionary Approaches to the Biggest Crisis
of our Time.** Authors include James Autry, Carol Sanford, Barbara
Hauser, Ann Morrison, Ed Oakley, Kate Steichen, Barbara Shipka, Tina
Rasmussen, Larry Spears, Elemer Magaziner, Susan Campbell, Robert
Rabbin, Margaret Wheatley, John Adams, Martha Spice, Carol McCall,
Max DePree, Perry Pascarella, and Stewart Emery (interview with
Norman Lear); edited by John Renesch.
Hardcover; New Leaders Press; $34.50 (U.S.); call 1.800.928.LEAD.

The New Entrepreneurs: Business Visionaries for the 21st Century.
Authors include Anita Roddick, Peggy Pepper, Betsy Burton, Greg
Steltenpohl, Ron Kovach, Jeff Sholl, Jacqueline Haessly, David P.
Jasper, Richard B. Brooke, Sharon Gadberry, John H. Stearns, Cheryl
Alexander, Marjorie Kelly, Chris Manning, Paul Hwoschinsky, William
B. Sechrest, Nicholas P. LiVolsi, Bill Veltrop; edited by Michael Ray and
John Renesch.
Hardcover; New Leaders Press; $29.95 (U.S.); call 1.800.928.LEAD.

**New Traditions in Business: Spirit & Leadership in the 21st Cen-
tury.** Authors include Willis Harman, Michael Ray, Herman Maynard,
Jim Channon, William Miller, Peter Senge, Terry Mollner, Robert Rosen,
Juanita Brown, Cynthia Barnum, David Gaster, Charles Kiefer, Carol
Sanford, John Thompson, and Ken Blanchard; edited by John Renesch.
Paperback; Berrett-Koehler Publishing; $17.95 (U.S.); call 1.800.929.2929.

**When the Canary Stops Singing: Women's Perspectives on Trans-
forming Business.** Author's include Riane Eisler, Carol Frenier, Kathleen
Keating, Marie Kerpan, Barbara Shipka, Kim McMillen, Jacqueline
Haessly, Jan Nickerson, Anne L. Rarich, Jeanne Borei, Hope Xaviermineo,
Cheryl Harrison, Mitani D'Antien, Barbara Fittipaldi, and Sabina Spen-
cer; edited by Pat Barrentine.
Hardcover; Berrett-Koehler Publishers; $24.95 (U.S.); call 1.800.929.2929.